Alice 3 in Action

Computing Through Animation

Joel Adams

Calvin College

CENGAGE
Learning

Australia • Brazil • Japan • Korea • Mexico • Singapore • Spain • United Kingdom • United States

CENGAGE
Learning·

Alice 3 in Action: Computing Through Animation, 2e
Joel Adams

Product Director: Kathleen McMahon

Senior Product Manager: Jim Gish

Senior Content Developer: Alyssa Pratt

Development Editor: Kent Williams

Product Assistant: Gillian Daniels

Senior Content Project Manager:
Cathie DiMassa

Art Director: Cheryl Pearl, GEX

Production Management, and Composition:
Integra Software Services Pvt. Ltd.

Cover Designer: GEX Publishing Services

Cover image credit: ©Morphart Creation/
Shutterstock

For product information and technology assistance, contact us at
Cengage Learning Customer & Sales Support, 1-800-354-9706

For permission to use material from this text or product, submit all requests online at **www.cengage.com/permissions**
Further permissions questions can be emailed to
permissionrequest@cengage.com

Library of Congress Control Number: 2013957889

ISBN-13: 978-1-133-58922-8

ISBN-10: 1-133-58922-7

Cengage Learning
20 Channel Center Street
Boston, MA 02210
USA

Cengage Learning is a leading provider of customized learning solutions with office locations around the globe, including Singapore, the United Kingdom, Australia, Mexico, Brazil, and Japan. Locate your local office at **www.cengage.com/global.**

Cengage Learning products are represented in Canada by Nelson Education, Ltd.

Purchase any of our products at your local college store or at our preferred online store **www.cengagebrain.com.**

Printed at CLDPC, USA, 10-16

Brief Contents

Contents

Preface

I wrote this book to address some of the problems in today's introductory computer programming (CS1) courses. To put it bluntly, most CS1 books are boring. They simply fail to capture the imaginations of most of today's students. No matter how often I suggest it, many of my students don't bother to "read the book." Now, these students aren't blameless, but it isn't entirely their fault. Many CS1 books present computer programming in a dull, abstract, mind-numbing way that's great if you're trying to fall asleep but not so good if you want to learn how to program a computer.

This is a tragedy, because in today's world writing software is one of the best opportunities to exercise creativity. Traditional engineers and scientists are limited in their professions by the physical laws that govern our world. But software engineers are mainly limited by their imaginations—if they can imagine something, they can usually make it happen within the virtual world of the computer screen. The best games and apps are the ones that combine creativity with technical excellence.

Unfortunately, acquiring that technical excellence takes time and effort. Many students who enroll in CS1 drop out, at least in part, because the subject matter fails to motivate them to invest that time and effort. CS1 courses are the starting point for software engineers; every student who drops out of CS1 is one less potential software engineer, and from social networks to stock exchanges, smartphones to smart cars, our daily lives increasingly depend on software. Those of us who are CS1 instructors need to do everything we can to attract and retain students in CS1. This book is an attempt to address these problems.

Why Alice?

At the 2003 ACM SIGCSE conference, I saw the late Randy Pausch of Carnegie Mellon University demonstrate 3D animation software he called *Alice* (actually, Alice 2.0). Using Alice, he built a sophisticated 3D animation (like *Shrek* or *Toy Story*, but much simpler) in just a few minutes. To do so, he used the traditional computer programming tools: variables, if statements, loops, subprograms, and so on. But his Alice software offered some startling advantages over traditional programming, including the following:

- *The appeal of 3D graphics*—It is difficult to overstate the visual appeal of 3D animations, especially to today's visually oriented students. When your program works, you feel euphoric! But even when you make a mistake (a logic error), the results are often comical, producing laughter instead of despair.

- *The Alice IDE*—Alice includes a drag-and-drop integrated development environment (IDE) that eliminates syntax errors. This IDE eliminates all of the following: missing semicolons, curly braces, and quotation marks; misspelled keywords or identifiers; and other syntax problems that bedevil CS1 students.

- *Object-based programming*—Alice includes a huge library of off-the-shelf 3D objects and a variety of predefined methods. Alice makes it easy to build 3D worlds from these objects. Those objects can then be animated using object-oriented programming.

By using 3D animation to motivate students, eliminating syntax errors, and turning logic errors into comedy, Alice transforms the CS1 experience from frustration to excitement. In short, Alice makes it *fun* to learn about programming!

As I watched Professor Pausch's demonstration, it became apparent to me that Alice could help solve many of the problems afflicting CS1 courses. If instructors would use Alice to initially *introduce* each programming topic, Alice's engaging environment would help motivate students to master that topic. Then, with that mastery to build upon, the instructor could *review* that topic in a traditional programming language like Java or C++, reinforcing its importance.

What's New in Alice 3

Before his untimely death in 2008, Randy Pausch announced that the Alice team was working on a new version of Alice: Alice 3. Since Randy's passing, his Alice teammates (Wanda Dann, Dennis Cosgrove, Dave Culyba, and others) have worked hard to bring his vision to fruition. Some of the features of this new version of Alice include:

- *The Sims 3D models*—Electronic Arts has supported the Alice project by donating 3D models from its popular *Sims* games to the Alice project. These models are incorporated into Alice 3, providing a rich set of characters and props for building 3D animations. Thank you, Electronic Arts!

- *Object-orientation*—Where the previous version of Alice was object-*based*, Alice 3 is fully object-*oriented*, meaning it incorporates modern software development concepts, such as classes, class hierarchies, and inheritance. As a result, Alice 3 is a much better way to introduce students to object-oriented programming than Alice 2.

- *Java*—Alice 3 has been completely rewritten in the Java programming language, and the Alice system has been accordingly updated. In fact, when you write an Alice 3 program, the Alice system is actually creating a Java program beneath the surface, and when you run your Alice 3 program, it is running on the Java virtual machine. This makes it easier for students to transition from Alice 3 to Java than from Alice 2.

For all of these reasons, Alice 3 is an excellent way to introduce students to the wonderful world of modern software development. This book shows you how.

Why This Book?

Despite what I said at the beginning of this preface, many instructors are content with the textbooks they use in their CS1 courses. In order for such instructors to use Alice, someone needed to write a concise Alice book to supplement their CS1 texts. I decided to

write a "short and sweet" book that would present just what you need to know to use Alice well and to learn the ideas behind object-oriented programming. This book is the result.

The previous edition of this book came out of a Fall 2004 sabbatical at Carnegie Mellon, working as a member of the Alice team and helping them find errors in Alice. That time was invaluable, as it helped me understand Alice's strengths and weaknesses, and decide which Alice features to include in that book.

This new Alice 3 edition extends this same approach that made the previous edition so successful. The book leads the reader through the thought processes and methodology of designing object-oriented software. By doing so, the book leverages Alice's two greatest strengths: visual appeal and freedom from syntax errors. Alice's elimination of syntax errors is especially important for novice programmers, as it frees them to master the concepts that underlie computational thinking without getting bogged down in syntax.

All the examples in this book were written and tested for correctness using the most recently available version of Alice 3 at the time of publication (version 3.1.85.0).

Pedagogical Features

To help students master the concepts of programming with objects, this book uses a number of pedagogical features, including the following:

- *A Running Example*—The book includes numerous stand-alone examples; it also presents a running example whose development spans all six chapters. This example shows students how to develop a complete multi-scene animation project, which helps them see how the concepts covered in different chapters relate to one another.

- *Integrated Software Design*—Beginning in Chapter 1 and continuing throughout, this book emphasizes software *design*. Each chapter shows how that chapter's concepts fit into the overall software design methodology. Students following this methodology can never say, "I don't know where to start."

- *Movie Metaphors*—Movies are pervasive in our culture. Since Alice programs are similar to movies, this book uses the language of movies to introduce software design ideas. Using this approach, the book builds a conceptual bridge from a student's existing experiences with movies to the new ideas of software design.

- *Detailed Diagrams*—This book contains roughly 300 color screen captures. Many of these demonstrate the exact drag-and-drop steps needed to use Alice 3 effectively.

- *Engaging Alice Examples*—Using Alice's rich library of 3D objects, this book includes examples that keep students engaged as they learn about programming. Here are a few examples:

  - People doing an aerobic workout

  - Three ogres facing off against a wizard

  - A pig singing "Old MacDonald Had a Farm"

  - A line of penguins jumping into a pool of water

  - A dragon flapping its wings and flying

- ■ A girl walking in a spiral to follow a treasure map
  - ■ and many more!
- *Alice Tips*—This book includes numerous notes and sections that provide important tips and techniques that help students use Alice 3 efficiently and effectively.
- *Chapter Summaries*—The final section of each chapter includes a bulleted list of the key concepts covered in that chapter, plus a separate list of that chapter's key vocabulary terms.
- *Programming Projects*—Each chapter concludes with 10–12 projects of varying levels of difficulty.

Using This Book

This book is intended as a supplemental text for CS1 courses, but it can be used by anyone wishing to learn about object-oriented programming. Its six chapters introduce the central concepts of object-oriented programming in Alice, as follows:

1. Getting started with Alice: using objects and methods
2. Building Alice methods: using abstraction to hide details
3. Variables, parameters, and functions: computing and storing data for later use
4. Control structures: controlling flow via Alice's `if`, `while`, and `for` statements
5. Data structures: using and processing Alice's arrays
6. Events: handling mouse and keyboard input in Alice

You may use these six chapters in a variety of ways, including:

- *The Spiral Approach*—Spend 4-6 weeks introducing all the programming concepts using Alice (the first spiral). Then spend the remainder of the semester revisiting those same concepts in Java or a different language (the second spiral). In this approach, the concepts are covered in two distinct "batches": an Alice batch followed by a Java batch.
- *The Interleaved Approach*—For each concept (for example, parameters), introduce that concept using Alice. After the students have that hands-on experience with that concept in Alice, immediately revisit that same concept in Java or a different language. In this approach, the concepts are covered sequentially, with the Alice and Java coverage interleaved.

If an instructor does not normally cover event-driven programming in CS1, that material may be omitted. However, most students find this material to be *very* engaging, as it lets them start building games! If an instructor wants to cover events, they may be introduced at any point after Chapter 3.

As students work through the examples in this book, they should save their work regularly. We will begin some examples in one chapter and add to those examples in another chapter, so students should save at the end of each example. Each example should be saved with a unique and descriptive name so that it can be easily located later.

Appendices and Cover Material

The appendices provide resources and material supplementing what is covered in the chapters. Appendix A presents an exhaustive list of Alice's standard methods and functions, including detailed behavioral descriptions.

Appendix B provides a "supplemental chapter" on recursion, beginning with visual examples that help students understand what happens during recursion.

Appendix C provides an overview of Alice 3's class hierarchy, showing the relationships between the classes and which methods each class defines.

The inside covers contain two useful Alice "Quick Reference" pages. Inside the front cover is a list of the standard procedural messages that can be sent to most Alice objects. Inside the back cover is a list of the standard function messages that can be sent to most Alice objects. This arrangement lets a student quickly identify the particular method he or she needs.

Web Materials

Copies of the example programs from this book are available online, at

- CengageBrain.com (search for the book via ISBN)
- The author's Alice Web site (*alice.calvin.edu*)

A feedback link and errata list are also available at the author's Web site. If you find a mistake, or want to point out a feature that works especially well, please use that feedback link. Some of the improvements in this edition of the book are the result of such feedback.

The Alice 3 software can be freely downloaded from *alice.org*.

Instructor Resources

The following supplemental materials are available when this book is used in a classroom setting. All instructor teaching tools, outlined below, are available at sso.cengage.com to instructors who have adopted this text.

Electronic Instructor's Manual. The Instructor's Manual that accompanies this textbook includes:

- Additional instructional material to assist in class preparation, including suggestions for lecture topics

Cengage Learning Testing Powered by Cognero is a flexible, online system that allows you to:

- author, edit, and manage test bank content from multiple Cengage Learning solutions
- create multiple test versions in an instant
- deliver tests from your LMS, your classroom or wherever you want

PowerPoint Presentations. This book comes with Microsoft PowerPoint slides for each chapter. These are included as a teaching aid for classroom presentations, either to make available to students on the network for chapter review, or to be printed for classroom distribution. Instructors can add their own slides for additional topics that they introduce to the class.

Solution Files. The solution files for all programming exercises are available.

Acknowledgments

A book cannot be developed without the help and support of many people. My heartfelt thanks go to Wanda Dann of Carnegie Mellon University for leading the Alice team and bringing Alice 3 to fruition. I would also like to thank the Alice team, especially Dennis Cosgrove and Dave Culyba, who patiently answered many questions about Alice 3.

The following people served as reviewers, whose careful reading of early drafts and constructive criticism helped make this book what it is. My thanks to Mary Anne Egan, Siena College; Jenneth Honeycutt, Fayetteville Technical Community College; Paul Mullins, Slippery Rock University; and Nina Peterson, Lewis-Clark State College.

A number of people at Cengage Learning also played important roles. My thanks to Alyssa Pratt, Senior Content Developer, and Jim Gish, Senior Product Manager, for helping me produce the book. I am also thankful to Kent Williams for his careful guidance through the production process, as well as Serge Palladino and Chris Scriver, who checked and rechecked each chapter and program for quality assurance. I am also grateful to John Bosco, of Green Pen Quality Assurance, for his contributions to the previous edition. This book would not be what it is without the careful attention to detail of all of these people.

I would also like to thank the staff at Integra Software Services, especially Gordon Matchado, who smoothly guided the production process.

A special "thank you" goes to Calvin College and its Department of Computer Science, whose support made this book possible.

I also wish to thank my wife Barbara, and my sons Roy and Ian, for their patience, understanding, and support over many months of writing. Their love and encouragement sustained me through the process.

Last in order but first in importance, I wish to thank God, the original creative Person. I believe that the joy we experience in being creative is because we bear His image. To Him be the glory.

-Joel C. Adams

In memory of Randy Pausch,
whose vision made this book possible.

Chapter 1
Getting Started with Alice

The computer programmer . . . is a creator of universes for which he [or she] alone is the lawgiver. . . . Universes of virtually unlimited complexity can be created in the form of computer programs. Moreover, systems so formulated and elaborated act out their programmed scripts. They compliantly obey their laws and vividly exhibit their obedient behavior. No playwright, no stage director, no emperor, however powerful, has ever exercised such absolute authority to arrange a stage or a field of battle and to command such unswervingly dutiful actors or troops.

JOSEPH WEIZENBAUM

If you don't know where you're going, you're liable to wind up somewhere else.

YOGI BERRA

Louis, I think this is the beginning of a beautiful friendship.
RICK (HUMPHREY BOGART) TO CAPTAIN RENAULT (CLAUDE RAINS), IN *CASABLANCA*

Objectives

Upon completion of this chapter, you will be able to:

❑ Design a simple Alice program
❑ Build a simple Alice program
❑ Animate Alice objects by sending them messages
❑ Use the Alice `do in order` and `do together` controls
❑ Change an object's properties from within a program
❑ Use different Alice views to position objects near one another

Screenshots from Alice 2 © 1999–2013, Alice 3 © 2008–2013, Carnegie Mellon University. All rights reserved. We gratefully acknowledge the financial support of Oracle, Electronic Arts, Sun Microsystems, DARPA, Intel, NSF, and ONR.

Welcome to the fun and exciting world of computer programming! In this chapter, we are going to build our first computer program using **Alice**, a free software tool for creating virtual worlds.

Developing programs to solve problems is a complex process that is both an art and a science. It is an art in that it requires a good deal of imagination, creativity, and ingenuity. But it is also a science in that it uses certain techniques and methodologies. In this chapter, we're going to work through the *thought process* that goes into creating computer software.

If you can manage it, the very best way to read this book is at a computer, doing each step or action as we describe it. In this way, you will be engaging in *active learning*, which is a much better way to learn than by trying to absorb the ideas through passive reading.

1.1   Getting and Running Alice

1.1.1   Downloading Alice

Alice can be freely downloaded from the Alice Web site at *http://alice.org*. From the main page, choose Get Alice 3.1 (or a newer version) from the Downloads menu, and the site will display a page of links allowing you to download the version of Alice that is appropriate for your computer. Clicking the link for a Windows computer begins the transfer of an installer file named *Alice3_Installer…Windows.exe* to your computer. On a MacOS computer, the file is named *Alice3_Installer…macosx.tgz*. Save this file to your computer's desktop.

1.1.2   Installing Alice

Alice 3 provides an Alice Installer Wizard to guide you through the steps of installing Alice 3 on your computer. To launch it, begin by double-clicking the file that was downloaded to your desktop. Then, do the following depending on whether you're working on a MacOS computer or a Windows computer:

- On a MacOS computer, double-click the downloaded file to extract the *Alice Installer* package from that file; once this new file appears on your desktop, double-click it to run the Alice Installer Wizard. It will install Alice in an *Alice 3* folder in your computer's *Applications* folder.
- On a Windows computer, this runs the Alice Installer Wizard. It will create an *Alice 3* folder in *C:\Program Files* in which it installs Alice.

If the Alice installer does not create a shortcut on your desktop and you wish to have one, navigate to the *Alice 3* folder and locate the file named *Alice* (*Alice.exe* or *Alice.bat* in Windows). In MacOS, select the file and choose File->Make Alias to create an alias for that file; in Windows, if the shortcut does not automatically appear on your desktop, right-click the file, and from the menu that appears, choose Create Shortcut to create a shortcut to *Alice.exe*. Drag the resulting alias/shortcut to your desktop and rename it *Alice*, so that you can launch Alice conveniently.

1.1.3   Running Alice

To start Alice, just double-click the *Alice* icon on your desktop. Congratulations, you are now running Alice!

1.2   Program Design

Programming in Alice is similar to *filmmaking*, so let's begin with how a film is put together.

When filmmakers begin a film project, they do not begin filming right away. Instead, they begin by *writing*. Sometimes they start with a short prose version of the film called a treatment; eventually, they write out the film's dialog in a longer form called a screenplay. Regardless, they always begin by *writing*, to define the basic structure of the story their film is telling.

A screenplay is usually organized as a series of **scenes**. A scene is one piece of the story the film is telling, usually set in the same location. A scene is typically made up of multiple **shots**. A shot is a piece of the story that is told with the camera in the same position. Each change of the camera's viewpoint in a scene requires a different shot. For example, if a scene has two characters talking in a restaurant, followed by a closeup of one of the character's faces, the view showing the two characters is one shot; the closeup is a different shot.

Once the screenplay is complete, the filmmaker develops **storyboards**, which are drawings that show the position and motion of each character in a shot. Each storyboard is like a blueprint for a shot, indicating where the actors stand, where the camera should be placed with respect to them, and so on. (You may have seen storyboards on the extras that come with the DVD version of a film.)

Creating an Alice program is much like creating a film, and modern computer software projects are often managed in a way that is quite similar to film projects.

1.2.1   User Stories

A modern software designer begins by writing a prose description, from the perspective of a person using the software, of what the software is to do. This is called a **user story**. For example, here is a user story for the first program we are going to build:

> When the program begins, Alice and the White Rabbit are facing each other, Alice on the left and the White Rabbit on the right. Alice turns her head and then greets us. The White Rabbit also turns and greets us. Alice and the White Rabbit introduce themselves. Alice and the White Rabbit simultaneously say "Welcome to our world."

A user story provides several important pieces of information:

- A basic description of what happens when the user runs the program.
- The *nouns* in the story—for example, Alice or the White Rabbit. These correspond to the **objects** we need to place in the Alice world. Objects include the characters in the story as well as background items like plants, buildings, and vehicles.
- The *verbs* in the story—for example, "turns" or "says." These correspond to the *actions* we want the objects to perform in the story.
- The chronological *flow* of actions in the story. This tells us what has to happen *first*, what happens *next*, what happens *after that*, and so on. The *flow* thus describes the *sequence of actions* that take place in the story.

By providing the objects, behaviors, sequence of actions, and description of what the program will do, a user story provides an important first step in the software design process, upon which the other steps are based. The user story is to a good software product what the screenplay is to a good film.

It is often useful to write out the flow of a story as a numbered sequence of objects and actions. For example, we can write out the flow for the Alice and White Rabbit user story as shown in Figure 1-1.

Scene: Alice is on the left, the White Rabbit is on the right.

1. Alice turns her head toward the user.
2. Alice greets the user.
3. The White Rabbit turns to face the user.
4. The White Rabbit greets the user.
5. Alice introduces herself.
6. The White Rabbit introduces himself.
7. Alice and the White Rabbit say "Welcome to our world."

FIGURE 1-1   First flow (algorithm)

© Cengage Learning 2015

A **flow** is thus a series of steps that precisely specify (in order) the behavior of each object in the story. In programming terminology, a flow—a sequence of steps that solves a problem—is called an **algorithm**.

1.2.2   Storyboard-Sketches

When they have completed a screenplay, filmmakers often hire an artist to sketch each shot in the film. For each different shot in each scene, the artist creates a drawing (in consultation with the filmmaker) of that shot, with arrows to show movements of the characters or the camera within the shot. These drawings are called storyboards. When completed, the collection of storyboards provides a graphical version of the story that the filmmaker can use to help the actors visualize what is going to happen in the shot, before filming begins.

The progression of storyboards thus serves as a kind of cartoon version of the story, which the filmmaker uses to decide how the film will look, before the actual filming begins. By first trying out his or her ideas on paper, a filmmaker can identify and discard bad ideas early in the process, before time, effort, and money are wasted filming (or in our case, programming) them.

In a similar fashion, the designers of modern computer software draw sketches of what the screen will look like as their software runs, showing any major changes that occur. Just as each distinct shot in a film scene requires its own storyboard, each distinct screen in a computer application requires a different sketch, so we will call these **storyboard-sketches**. Because our first program has just one scene, it has just one storyboard-sketch, as shown in Figure 1-2.

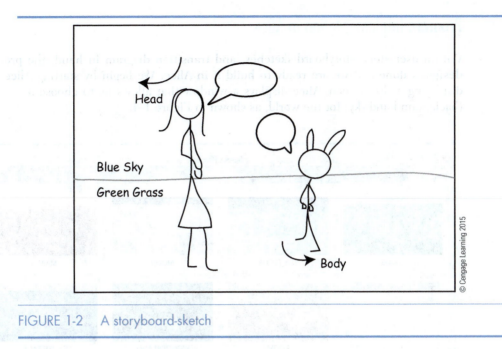

FIGURE 1-2   A storyboard-sketch

In Alice programming, the storyboard-sketches provide important information for the programmer about each object visible on the screen, including:

- Its **position** (the object's location in the 3D world)
- Its **pose** (the positions of its limbs, if it has any)
- Its **orientation** (what direction it is facing)

Storyboard-sketches also indicate where Alice's `camera` object should be positioned, whether it is stationary or moving during the shot, and so on.

1.2.3   Transition Diagrams

When a program has multiple scenes, it has multiple storyboards. When all the storyboard-sketches are completed, they are linked together in a **transition diagram** that shows any special events that are required to make the transition from one sketch to the next. In a movie, there are no special events, so the transition diagram is a simple linear sequence, as shown in Figure 1-3.

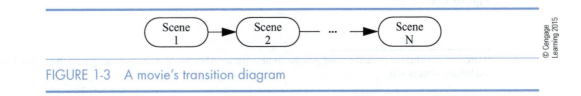

FIGURE 1-3   A movie's transition diagram

1.3   Program Implementation in Alice

With a user story, storyboard-sketches, and transition diagram in hand, the program's **design** is done and we are ready to build it in Alice. We begin by starting Alice. After displaying a title screen, Alice displays a window that allows us to choose a Template (background and sky) for the world, as shown in Figure 1-4.

FIGURE 1-4   Alice's template worlds

You can also get this window to appear by clicking Alice's File menu and then choosing New or Open. Double-click the template you want to use (we will choose the Grass template), and Alice will create a pristine[1] three-dimensional world for you, using that template, as shown in Figure 1-5. (Your screen may look slightly different.) To help you find your way around, labels for the various areas in Alice have been added to Figure 1-5.

---

[1]Here and elsewhere, we use the word *pristine* to describe an Alice world in its beginning state, before we have added any objects to it.

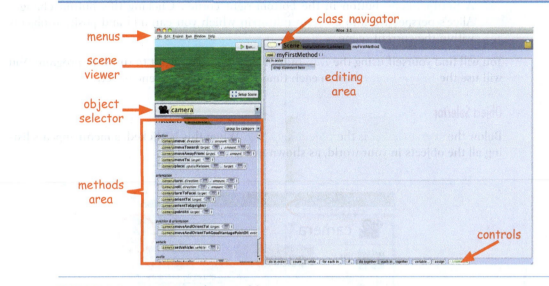

FIGURE 1-5   A pristine Alice world

1.3.1   Alice's Integrated Development Environment (IDE)

Menus

At the top of the Alice window are six menus:

1. **File** lets you load, save, and print your Alice programs (as well as other operations).

2. **Edit** lets you undo, redo, cut, copy, and paste. Tip: Any time you make a mistake, use the keyboard shortcut **Command-z** (**Ctrl-z** on Windows) to undo it.

3. **Project** lets you manage the objects in your project and retrieve statistics about it.

4. **Run** lets you run your project.

5. **Window** lets you change the current perspective (see later in this chapter), view your project's history or its memory usage, or change your preferences.

6. **Help** lets you report bugs, suggest improvements, request features, and access information about your specific version of Alice.

Scene Viewer

Below Alice's menus is the scene viewer, which provides you with a viewport into the 3D world you are creating. The scene viewer contains two controls:

1. A **Run** button in the upper-right corner. Clicking this button runs the program associated with the current world.

2. A Setup Scene button in the bottom-right corner. Clicking this button changes Alice's perspective into a scene editor in which you can add and position objects within the current scene.

You will find yourself using the Run button every time you want to run your program. You will use the Setup Scene button each time you build a new scene or set.

Object Selector

Below the scene viewer is the object selector. When this is clicked, a menu appears listing all the objects in your world, as shown in Figure 1-6.[2]

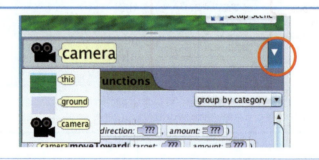

FIGURE 1-6 **Object selector** listing the objects in a world

Even in a pristine world, this menu contains several objects: **this**, which refers to the scene or world we are creating; the **ground** (or whatever kind of surface you chose) in your scene, and the **camera**. As we shall see, any of these objects can be moved or reoriented. For example, the **camera** can be moved within the world, as required by the scenes and shots in our user story. The **camera** position determines what is seen in the scene viewer. In Section 1.3.2, we will see how to modify the **camera**'s initial position and orientation.

It doesn't make much sense to move the ground, although we may wish to change it, for example, from grass to snow or sand or the moon or whatever. We'll see how to do this in Section 2.2.2.

Methods Area

The methods area lies below the scene viewer and object selector. It has two tabbed panes: the Procedures pane, the Functions pane, and the Properties pane. Whenever an object is selected in the object selector, the following occurs:

• The Procedures pane lists the messages we can send to animate that object.
• The Functions pane lists the messages we can send to get information from that object.

---

[2]In Figure 1-6 and subsequent figures, we use a red circle to indicate a mouse-click, a red line to indicate a mouse-drag, and a red arrowhead to indicate a mouse-drop action.

Take a moment to click through these panes, to get a feel for the things they contain. We'll present an overview of them in Section 1.4.

Editing Area

To the right of the scene viewer and methods area is the editing area, the place where we will edit or build the program that controls the animation. As can be seen in Figure 1-5, above the editing area is a class navigator containing a yellow hexagon. To its right are two tabs, of which the tab named myFirstMethod is selected. In a pristine world, this method is *empty*, meaning it contains no *statements*. Very shortly, we will see how to build our first program by adding statements to this method.

At the bottom of the editing area are controls (do in order, count, while, for each in, if, and so on) that can be used to build Alice statements. We will introduce these controls one by one, as we need them, throughout the next few chapters.

1.3.2 Program Language

Before we begin programming, you may want to alter the *language* in which Alice displays the program. We will use the notation Window > Preferences > Programming Language > Java as a shorter way of saying "Click the Windows menu, then the Preferences choice on that menu, then the Programming Language choice on the submenu, and then Java on the sub-submenu," as shown in Figure 1-7.

FIGURE 1-7   Choosing the Java language

Since Java is a popular programming language, we will be displaying our programs using Alice's Java language option. This will let us begin becoming familiar with the Java programming language. If you want your programs to look consistent with those in the text, please make certain Java is the language that is selected.

1.3.3 Adding Objects to Alice

Once we have a pristine world, the next step is to populate it with objects and build the scene(s) in our user story. First, click the Setup Scene button in the scene view. Alice will change to its Setup Scene perspective and display its scene editor, as shown in Figure 1-8.

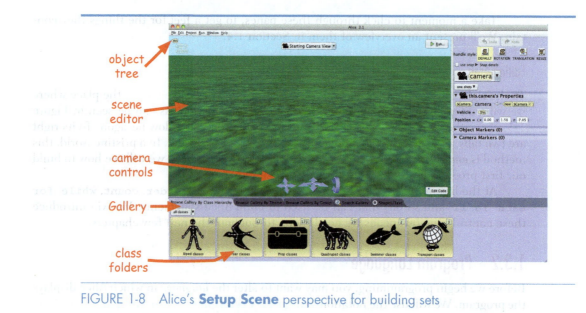

object tree

scene editor

camera controls

Gallery

class folders

FIGURE 1-8   Alice's **Setup Scene** perspective for building sets

In the upper-left corner of the scene editor, Alice lists the various objects in the 3D world, which Alice gives the name **this**. This list of objects is called the object tree, and in a pristine world, the object tree contains just the **ground** and **camera** objects.

At the bottom-center of the scene editor is a set of three blue-arrow control buttons, which let you change the position and orientation of the camera. More precisely, these buttons let you reposition the camera within the 3D world by panning left, right, up, or down; zooming left, right, in or out; and angling the camera up or down. For example, in Figure 1-9, we have used the right-most blue arrow control to change the camera angle so that the sky fills the top two-thirds of the screen.

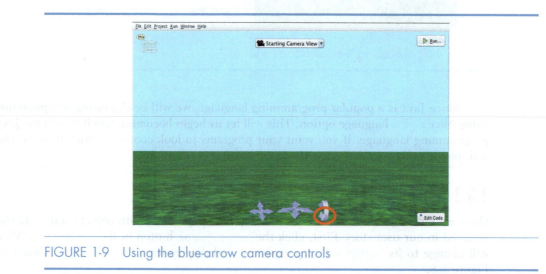

FIGURE 1-9   Using the blue-arrow camera controls

At the bottom-right of the scene editor is an Edit Code button. Clicking this button will return you to Alice's code-editing perspective. But don't click this button yet; we are still building our scene!

Below the scene editor is Alice's Gallery, which provides a vast assortment of classes we can use to build objects for our scenes. A class can be thought of as a blueprint from which an object is constructed. The classes in the Gallery are organized hierarchically, according to their structure:

- The **Biped classes** folder contains classes for things that walk on two legs, such as different kinds of **Person**, and classes **Alien**, **MadHatter**, and **WhiteRabbit**.
- The **Flyer classes** folder contains classes for things that have wings (and usually fly), such as **Chicken**, **Falcon**, **Flamingo**, and **Toucan**.
- The **Prop classes** folder contains classes for things that are inanimate, such as bookcases, coffee tables, sofas, and tables. Many of these props are organized into sub-folders.
- The **Quadruped classes** folder contains classes for things that walk on four legs, such as **Camel**, **Cow**, **Dalmatian**, and **Wolf**.
- The **Swimmer classes** folder contains classes for things that swim, including: **Fish** classes, such as **ClownFish** and **Shark**; and **MarineMammal** classes, such as **Dolphin** and **Walrus**.

Both of the objects in our user story—Alice Liddell and the White Rabbit—are bipeds. At it happens, there is a **WhiteRabbit** class in the **Biped classes** folder. We can use it to create a **whiteRabbit** object in our scene by clicking the **WhiteRabbit** class and dragging it to the appropriate position in our scene editor window. When we do this, Alice displays a golden outline—a **bounding box**—that indicates the model's dimensions and location, as shown in Figure 1-10.

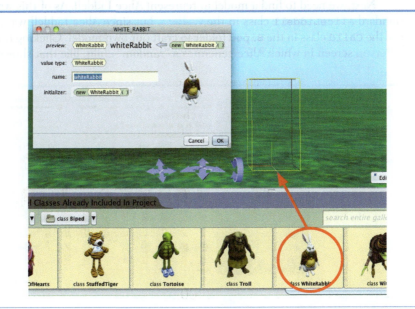

FIGURE 1-10   Dragging a model into the scene viewer window

When we drop the model there, Alice displays a dialog box listing the properties of this model, as can be seen in Figure 1-10. When we click its OK button, the `whiteRabbit` model appears in our scene editor, as shown in Figure 1-11.

FIGURE 1-11   The `whiteRabbit` model in our scene

Note that in addition to appearing in the world, a `whiteRabbit` object is now listed in the object tree in the upper-left corner of the world window. Note also that as we clicked on the `Biped` folder, Alice added a button for that folder in the area between the scene editor window and the Gallery. These buttons allow you to navigate back "up" to the Gallery and "down" to its other folders, when necessary.

Next, we need to find a model to represent Alice Liddell. As of this writing, there is no standard `AliceLiddell` class in the Gallery, but since Alice Liddell was a person, we can use the `Child` class in the `Biped` folder to craft our own model. Clicking this class brings up a Person screen in which Alice generates a "random" child, like that shown in Figure 1-12.

FIGURE 1-12   The `Person` screen for crafting models of people

This screen provides numerous controls that let us choose the person's life stage (toddler, child, teen, adult, or elder), the person's gender, and the person's skin color. Below that are four tabs: one for the person's Outfit, one for its Top/Bottom, one for its Hair/Hat, and one for its Face. The Outfit tab lets you choose its clothing. The Top/Bottom tab lets you mix and match tops and bottoms and choose how fit or unfit the person is. The Hair/Hat tab lets you choose the person's hair color and its hair and/or hat style. The Face tab lets you choose the shape of the person's face and its eye color.

Using this screen, we can craft a model for Alice Liddell. Since the illustrations of *Alice in Wonderland* depict Alice as a young blonde woman from Victorian England, we might model her as a female child with lighter skin, blonde hair with pigtails, blue eyes, and wearing the outfit shown in Figure 1-13.

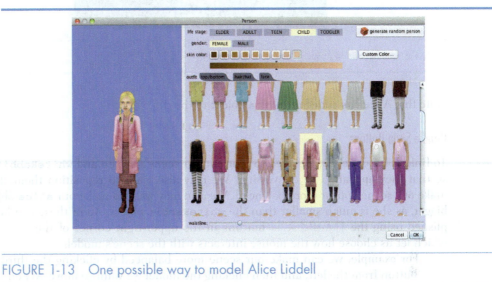

FIGURE 1-13   One possible way to model Alice Liddell

When we are satisfied with our person's appearance, we can click the OK button, and Alice will display a dialog box listing the person's attributes, where we can specify the person's name. We will use this to rename our person **alice**, as shown in Figure 1-14.

FIGURE 1-14   `Create Person` dialog box

When we click its OK button, Alice creates an instance of the Child class—also known as an object—named **alice** into our scene, as shown in Figure 1-15.

FIGURE 1-15   An **alice** object in our scene

Note that Alice has added an **alice** object to the object tree

Handle Style Buttons

To finish off our scene, we need to reorient our scene's **alice** and **whiteRabbit** objects so that they appear to be conversing. We may also want to reposition them slightly to make our scene appear more balanced. We also may want to make our **alice** object a bit bigger, as she is much smaller than the **whiteRabbit** object. All of these can be accomplished using the Handle style buttons in the upper-right corner of the scene editor, which let us choose how the mouse interacts with the scene's models.

For example, we can make our scene more balanced by clicking the third Handle style button from the left, and then clicking the model we want to move. When we do so, three yellow axis-arrows appear, which we can use as handles to reposition the model, as shown in Figure 1-16.

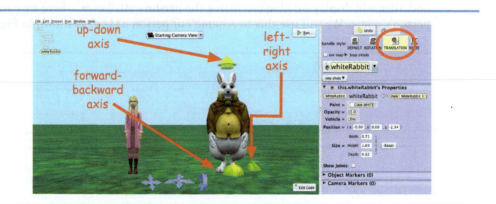

FIGURE 1-16   Repositioning an object using axis-handles

We call the axis to a model's sides the *left-right* axis, the vertical axis the *up-down* axis, and the axis in front of a model the *forward-backward* axis, as can be seen in Figure 1-16.[3]

In Figure 1-16, we have used these axis-handles to make our scene more balanced by clicking on our models' left-right axes and dragging to the left until they are positioned about one third of the distance from each edge of the scene.

Note that you can also move an object up or down using the up-down axis-handle. We will not use that feature here, but you should feel free to experiment with these axis-handles until you are comfortable with their use.[4] If you make a mistake, remember that you can always use the *Undo* button!

To reorient our objects so that they appear to be conversing, we can use the first (left-most) Handle style button. When this button is clicked, a yellow ring appears at the selected object's base. To rotate an object, click the object and then drag left or right on its rotation ring, as shown in Figure 1-17. Experiment with this until **alice** and the **whiteRabbit** are facing each other as if conversing.

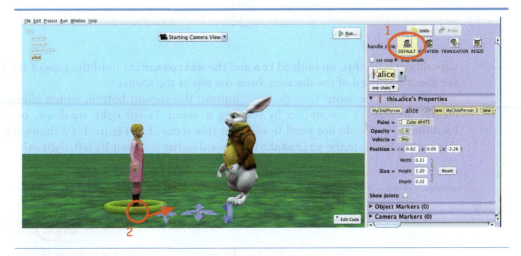

FIGURE 1-17   Rotating an object using its rotation ring

Finally, to resize **alice** so that she is as big as the **whiteRabbit**, we can use the right-most Handle style button. With this button selected, a diagonal handle appears above the selected object that lets us make the object bigger or smaller while keeping its proportions the same. In Figure 1-18, we use this to make our **alice** model larger.[5]

---

[3]Computer scientists and mathematicians usually call these the x, y, and z axes.

[4]The blue-arrow camera controls sometimes stop working; likewise, the object's axis-handles, rotation rings, and other controls sometimes freeze. If this happens, just save your work and restart Alice to solve the problem.

[5]If you are unable to see the diagonal handle, the handle is likely hidden behind the model. To see if this is the case, rotate the model 180 degrees (one half turn), then select the Handle style button to resize the model and see if the diagonal handle appears. If so, use it to resize the model and then rotate the model back to the desired orientation. Otherwise, you may have to rotate the camera up to bring the handle into view.

FIGURE 1-18   Resizing an object

Experiment with this, on both **alice** and the **whiteRabbit**, until the tops of their heads are about one third of the distance from the top of the scene.

There is one more Handle style button: the second button, which allows you to change an object's orientation by rotating it about its *left-right*, *up-down*, or *forward-backward* axis. We do not need to use it in this scene, but Figure 1-19 shows the use of this button to rotate the **whiteRabbit** forward—that is, about its left-right axis.

FIGURE 1-19   Changing an object's orientation

Feel free to experiment by clicking this button and then dragging your mouse over the axes that appear. You can always use the *Undo* button to undo what you have done.

Properties

An object's **properties** are internal characteristics that determine the object's appearance and behavior when you run your program. To the right of the scene editor and beneath the Handle style buttons, Alice displays the Properties of the currently selected object, as can be seen in Figure 1-19. These include an object's Paint, its Opacity, its Name, its Vehicle, its Position, and its Size. Feel free to experiment with these settings, to see what they do. (You can always use Alice's Edit > Undo mechanism if you make a mistake.)

To illustrate, if our story contained the White Rabbit's ghost as a character, we could add a `WhiteRabbit` object named `whiteRabbitGhost` to our scene and change its Opacity property to 40 percent, so that 60 percent of our world's light passes through him. The result would be a spooky translucent `whiteRabbitGhost` in our program.

We will see how to use other Properties in the coming chapters.

Using Different Views

By default, the scene editor displays the scene viewer from the **camera**'s perspective. However, trying to position two objects in close proximity to each other (e.g., trying to position a person on the back of a horse) can be difficult, because the scene viewer's default perspective is quite limited. When building a scene, Alice lets you choose alternative views that include the Starting Camera View, the Layout Scene View, plus views from the Top, Side, and Front of the scene.

To choose a different view, change to the Setup Scene perspective, click the box near the top center of the scene viewer, where it says Starting Camera View, and choose one of the views. Figure 1-20 shows the Layout Scene View.

FIGURE 1-20   One of the alternative view options

As can be seen, this view provides an alternative perspective into the scene that allows us to better see how the characters are positioned with respect to each other. In this view, clicking the use snap checkbox will superimpose a virtual grid over the ground, allowing us to see how well our characters are positioned. This helps us see that the White Rabbit is further from the camera than Alice Liddell; we might want to move him so that he and Alice Liddell are better aligned. The characters can be moved within the scene using the mouse, as described earlier.

Note that unlike the Starting Camera View, the `camera` is visible as an object at the bottom of the scene in the Layout Scene View. Because the `camera` is visible, it can be repositioned using the mouse in this view, unlike the Starting Camera View.

From the Top, Side, and Front views, the blue-arrow controls at the bottom of the world window can be used to zoom in or out or to pan from side to side. These are very useful when you shift to a view and the characters you expected to see are not in view. When this happens, just click one of the arrows and drag left, right, up, or down until the characters become visible.

Rule of Thirds

There is a useful guideline to keep in mind when designing or laying out a scene. It is called the **Rule of Thirds**, and this is how it works: Imagine a 3 × 3 tic-tac-toe grid laid over your scene. The scene will be more visually interesting if its main features—its characters, their heads, the horizon, and so on—are positioned on the lines or intersections of this grid.

Most photographers and directors follow this rule when composing their shots. To illustrate, we can click the scene's Run button and imagine a 3 × 3 grid superimposed on the scene, as shown in Figure 1-21.

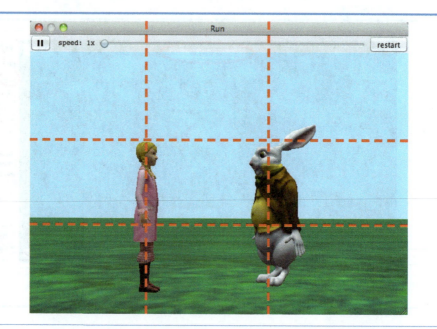

FIGURE 1-21   Imaginary 3 × 3 grid of the Rule of Thirds

As can be seen above, we need to make both **alice** and the **whiteRabbit** a bit taller in order for their heads to actually be at the intersections of the lines. Because Alice's characters "speak" using speech bubbles, we also must leave room for those bubbles. Feel free to experiment with the scene until it seems to be well-balanced, but leave room at the top for the speech bubbles.

We are almost ready to animate our scene. Before we do, let's review some key concepts.

The items in the Gallery are not objects but are like blueprints that Alice uses to build objects. Such blueprints are called *classes*. Whenever we drag a class from the Gallery into the scene viewer, Alice uses the class to build an *instance* of the class—an object—for the world.

For example, when we dragged the **WhiteRabbit** class into the scene, Alice added a new **whiteRabbit** object to the scene and listed it in the object tree. If we were to drag the **WhiteRabbit** class into the world again, Alice would again use the class to create an object for the world, but we would need to give this new object a different name, such as **whiteRabbit2**. Feel free to try this; you can always delete **whiteRabbit2** or any object in the object tree by right-clicking it[6] and selecting delete from the context menu that appears.

The key idea is that each object is made from a class. Even though the world might contain ten **whiteRabbit** objects, there would still be just one **WhiteRabbit** class from which all of the **whiteRabbit** objects were made.

To distinguish objects from classes, Alice follows the "camel case" convention: for *class* names, the first letter of each word in the name is capitalized (e.g., **Child**, **WhiteRabbit**); *object* names are similar, but they always begin with a lowercase letter (e.g., **alice**, **whiteRabbit**). The resulting names have "humps" like a camel, which is why this is called "camel case".

If you decide to change the name of an object, you can always rename it by (1) right-clicking the object's name in the object tree, and (2) choosing Rename... from the menu that appears. Alice will display a dialog box in which you can type a different name for the object. Alice will then update all statements that refer to the object so that they use the new name.

With the objects **alice** and **whiteRabbit** in place, we are almost ready to begin programming, so click the Edit Code button in the bottom-right corner of the scene editor. In Alice, programming is accomplished mainly by:

1. Selecting the object (or the part of the object) to be animated in the object selector box.

2. Dragging the message you want to send that object (or part) from the methods area (usually the Procedures tab) into the editing area.

This effectively adds statements to the program that animate the selected object.

1.3.4 Accessing Object Subparts

In our user story, the first action is that Alice Liddell should seem to see us (the user) and turn her head toward us. To make this happen, we start by choosing **alice** in the object

---

[6]If you are on a Macintosh that does not have a right mouse button, hold down Control while clicking the normal mouse button.

selector, which selects our **alice** model. However, the user story says that Alice Liddell is to turn her head. To select that part of her, we drag to the arrow at the right of the **object selector** menu entry for **alice**. This causes a menu of methods to access **alice** joints to be displayed, from which we can choose the **getHead()** method, as shown in Figure 1-22.

FIGURE 1-22   Accessing an object's parts

As you can see, Alice persons have many joints (and there are more under the Other SBiped Joints option at the bottom of the menu). By selecting and animating different joints of a person's body, complex animations can be created. When we select a method to retrieve a joint of an object, Alice adjusts the methods area to indicate the Procedures and Functions for that joint.

Because the steps in a flow or algorithm need to be performed in a specified order, Alice initializes the **myFirstMethod()** method in the editing area with a **do in order** control, as is shown in Figure 1-23.

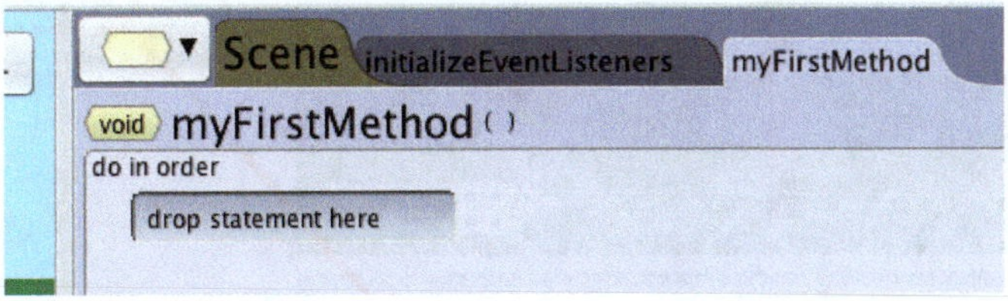

FIGURE 1-23   The **do in order** control in **myFirstMethod()**

The **do in order** control is a structure within which we can place program statements. As its name suggests, any statements we place within the **do in order** will be performed in the order they appear, top to bottom. The **do in order** control has additional convenient features that we will explore in later chapters.

1.3.5   Sending Messages

Much of Alice programming consists of sending **messages** to objects.

You can animate an object with a desired behavior by sending the object a message that asks the object to perform that behavior.[7]

In programming, messages that produce a behavior are called **methods**. Methods that animate an object without producing a value are called **procedures**. Not too surprisingly, these can be found under the Procedures tab of the methods area.

To illustrate, Step 1 of our algorithm in Figure 1-1 is to make Alice Liddell's head turn to look at the user. To accomplish this, we can send Alice Liddell's head the **pointAt()** message and specify the **camera** as the thing to which her head is to point. With **alice.getHead()** selected in the object selector, we scan through the procedures in the methods area until we see **pointAt()**. We then click the **pointAt()** method, drag it into the space below the **do in order** in the editing area, and drop it.

The **pointAt()** message requires that we specify a target—the object at which Alice Liddell's head is to point. When we drop the **pointAt()** method in the editing area, Alice displays a menu of the objects in your scene, from which we can choose the **camera** as the target, as shown in Figure 1-24.

---

[7]It should go without saying, but if you send the right message to the wrong object, you will not get the desired behavior!

FIGURE 1-24   Dragging the `pointAt()` message

When we select the **camera**, Alice updates the editing area, as shown in Figure 1-25.

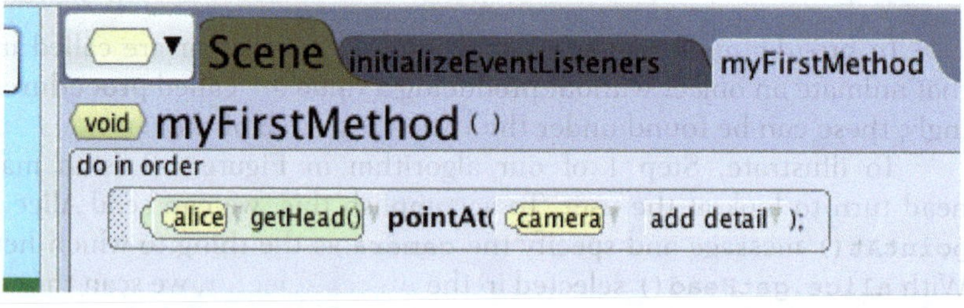

FIGURE 1-25   Our first message

It is worth mentioning that the statement in Figure 1-25 consists of *two* messages. Reading left to right, the statement first sends our **alice** object the **getHead()** message; this method returns her head. The **pointAt(camera)** message is then sent to the head object returned by the **getHead()** message, so that only our model's head will turn towards the camera. Objects like `alice` are thus composed of *joints*, which are themselves objects (e.g., her *pelvis, spine base, spine middle, spine upper, neck, head*). A given object's joints can be selected using the object selector menu, as was shown in Figure 1-22.

1.3.6 Testing and Debugging

If you now click the Run button in the scene viewer, you should see `alice`'s head turn and seem to look at you (the user)! Figure 1-26 shows the end result.

FIGURE 1-26   Alice Liddell looks at the user

As can be seen, our one-statement program causes `alice`'s head to turn toward the user, but the rest of her body remains as it was. (If you are not at a computer doing this interactively, compare Figure 1-26 to Figure 1-24 to see the effect of sending `alice.getHead()` the `pointAt(camera)` message.)

By clicking the Run button, we are **testing** the program, to see if it produces the desired result. If the program does something other than what we wanted, then it contains an **error** or **bug**. Finding and fixing the error is called **debugging** the program. If you have followed the steps carefully so far, your program should have no bugs, so let's continue. (If your program does have a bug, compare your editing area against that shown in Figure 1-25 to see where you went wrong.)

1.3.7   Programming the Other Actions

We can use similar steps to accomplish actions 2, 3, 4, 5, and 6 of the algorithm in Figure 1-1 by sending **pointAt()** or **say()** messages to **alice** or the **whiteRabbit**. When we send an object the **say()** message, Alice displays a menu from which we can select what we want the object to say. To customize the greetings, select the Custom TextString... menu choice; then, in the dialog box that appears, type what you want the object to say. After a few minutes of clicking, dragging, dropping, and typing, we can have the partial program shown in Figure 1-27.

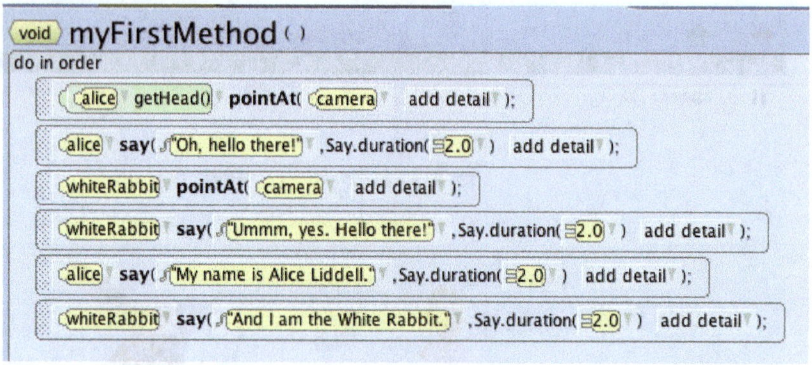

---

void myFirstMethod ( )

do in order

   (alice   getHead()   **pointAt(** camera   add detail);

   alice   **say(** ♪"Oh, hello there!" ,Say.duration(2.0)   add detail);

   whiteRabbit   **pointAt(** camera   add detail);

   whiteRabbit   **say(** ♪"Ummm, yes. Hello there!" ,Say.duration(2.0)   add detail);

   alice   **say(** ♪"My name is Alice Liddell." ,Say.duration(2.0)   add detail);

   whiteRabbit   **say(** ♪"And I am the White Rabbit." ,Say.duration(2.0)   add detail);

FIGURE 1-27   A partial program

By clicking on the add detail button to the right of a message in the editing area, we can customize that message. For example, in Figure 1-27, we have increased the duration attribute of each **say()** message to two seconds to give the user sufficient time to read what the character says.

For **say()** messages, set the duration to 2–3 seconds per line of text being displayed to give the user time to read what is being said.

1.3.8   Statements

Most of the lines in the program have the same basic structure:

```
object.message(value); add detail
```

In programming terminology, such a line is sometimes called a **statement**. A computer program consists of a collection of statements, the combination of which produces some desirable behavior. The basic structure shown above is common in Alice, and it is what we will use most often.

The **do in order** control is also a statement; however, it is a statement that controls *how other statements are performed* (i.e., one at a time, from top-to-bottom).

1.3.9   The Final Action

We are nearly done! All that is left is the final step in our algorithm, in which Alice Liddell and the White Rabbit simultaneously say "Welcome to our world." It should be evident that we can accomplish this in part by sending **say()** messages to **alice** and the **whiteRabbit**. For both objects, the value accompanying the **say()** message should be the same value: **Welcome to our world**.

As we have seen, the **do in order** control performs the first statement, then the next statement, then the next statement, and so on. This is sometimes called **sequential execution**, meaning the statements are executed or performed in order or *in sequence*. Sequential execution means that if we were to send **alice** the **say()** message, and then send the **whiteRabbit** the **say()** message, the message to the **whiteRabbit** will not be performed until after the **message** to **alice** has finished.

To achieve the effect specified in our user story, we must send **say()** messages to **alice** and the **whiteRabbit** *simultaneously*. We can accomplish this using the **do together** control, located at the bottom of the editing area. To use this control, we click **do together**, drag it upward into the editing area, and drop it below the last statement in the program, producing the program shown in Figure 1-28.

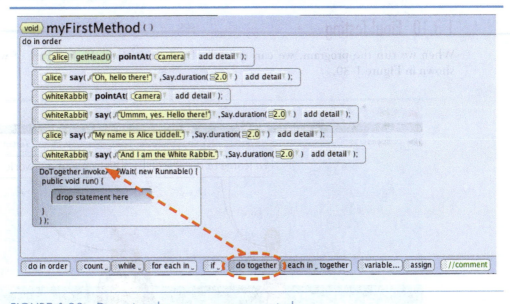

FIGURE 1-28   Dragging the do together control

The **do together** control is another Alice statement. Like the **do in order** control, it has a form that is different from the **object.message()** structure we saw previously. When the program performs a **do together** statement, all statements within the **do together** are performed simultaneously, so it should provide the behavior we need to finish the program.

Using the same skills we used earlier, we can send **say()** messages to **alice** and to the **whiteRabbit**. However, now we drop these messages inside the **DoTogether** statement, yielding the final program, which is shown in Figure 1-29.

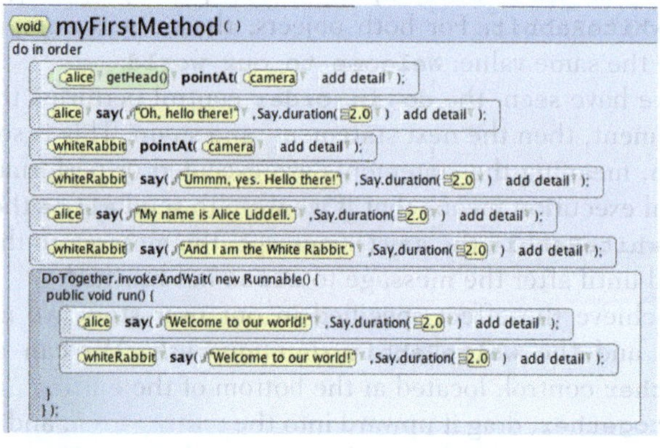

FIGURE 1-29   Our first program

1.3.10 Final Testing

When we run the program, we can view the final animation, the last part of which is shown in Figure 1-30.

FIGURE 1-30 Alice Liddell and the White Rabbit speaking together

We saw earlier that the Alice **do in order** statement performs the statements within it *sequentially*. By contrast, the **DoTogether** statement performs the statements it contains **simultaneously** or **concurrently**.

1.3.11 Saving and Reopening Your Work

To save your work in a file, choose File > Save As... and a standard dialog box will appear in which you can enter a name under which to save your project. Alice 3 files are saved with a *.a3p* extension.

As of this writing, you cannot open an Alice file by double-clicking its icon. Instead, you should (if necessary) launch Alice and then use File > Open... to open the file. Alice will display a tabbed dialog box; if your file is not listed under the My Projects or Recent tabs, choose the File System tab, and then click the Browse button to navigate to your file.[8] When you have located your file, click the OK button and Alice will open the file.

1.3.12 Software Engineering Process

The approach we just used to create our first program is an example of a methodical, disciplined way of creating computer software. The process consists of the following steps:

---

1. Write the *user story*. Identify the nouns and verbs within it. Organize the nouns and verbs into a *flow* or *algorithm*.

2. Draw the *storyboard-sketches*, one for each distinct shot in your program, and create a *transition diagram* that relates them to each other. If you have some users available, use your sketches to walk them through your program. Take seriously any improvements they suggest. Using their feedback, update your user story and algorithm, as necessary.

3. For each noun in your algorithm: add an *object* to your Alice world.

4. For each verb in your algorithm:

    a. Find a *message* that performs that verb's action and send it to the verb's object. (If the object has no message that provides that verb's action, we'll see how to build our own methods in Chapter 2.)

    b. Test the message sent in Step 4a, to make sure it produces the desired action. If not, either alter how the message is being sent (with its add detail attributes) or find a different message (and if you cannot find one, build your own).

Steps 1 and 2 of this process are called **software design**. Steps 3 and 4—in which we build the program and then verify that it does what it is supposed to do—are called **software implementation** and **software testing**. Together, software design, implementation,

---

[8]If the Browse button cannot be seen, drag the right edge of the dialog box to the right to make it wider.

and testing are important parts of **software engineering**—a methodical way to build computer programs.

We will use this same basic process to create most of the programs in this book. You should go through each one of these steps for each program you write, because it will help you create better-crafted programs.

1.4   Alice's Methods Area

As we mentioned earlier, Alice's methods area provides two tabbed panes. Whenever an object is selected in the object selector, these two panes list the procedure and function messages that can be sent to that object. In this section, we provide an overview of this methods area.

1.4.1   The Procedures Tab

Click the Procedures tab of the methods area, and you will see the behavior-generating messages that you can send to the object in the object selector. Figure 1-31 shows some of the procedural messages that we can send to many Alice objects by scrolling within this list; a complete list is given in Appendix A.

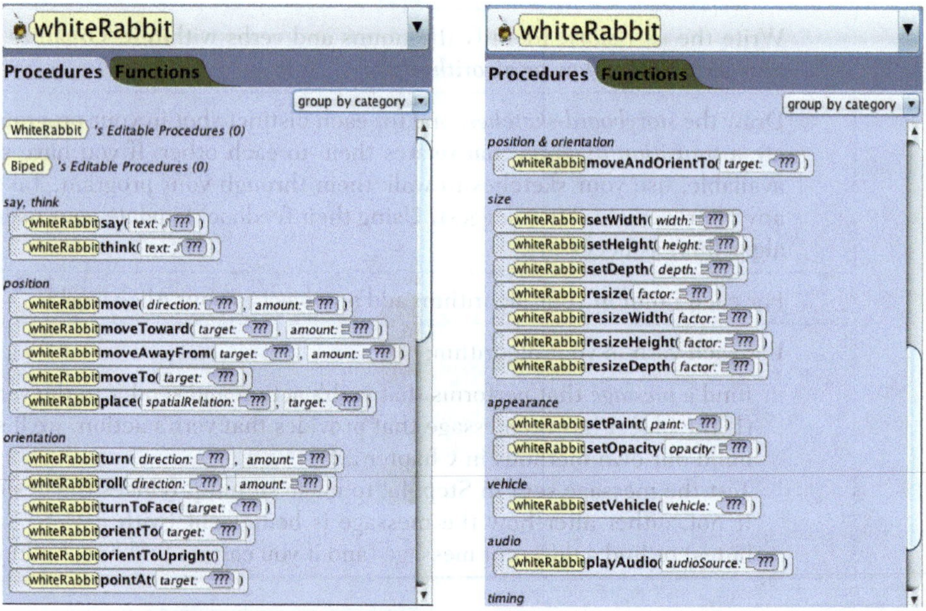

FIGURE 1-31   Scrolling through the **Procedures** pane

These messages provide a rich set of operations that, together with the `do together` and `do in order` controls, let us build complex animations. Because we can send these messages to nearly any Alice object, they allow us to build worlds containing dancing animals, talking trees, and just about anything else we can imagine! As always, feel free to experiment with these methods to see what they do.

The `resize()` message is especially fun, as it lets our program change an object's Size property. For example, `resize(2)` makes an object grow to be twice as big; `resize(0.5)` shrinks it to half size.

The `setOpacity()` message is also fun, as it lets our program change an object's Opacity property. For example, setting an object's Opacity to `0.0` makes the object invisible; setting it to `1.0` makes it fully visible, and setting it to a value between `0.0` and `1.0` makes the object translucent.

It is important to note that the Properties area in the scene editor view only lets us change an object's properties *before* our program begins running. By contrast, procedures like `resize()` and `setOpacity()` let *our program* change an object's properties *while the program is running*, and change them as many times as we want.

Scene Procedures

If we choose `this` (our world or scene object) from the object selector, there are special procedural messages there, some of which are shown in Figure 1-32.

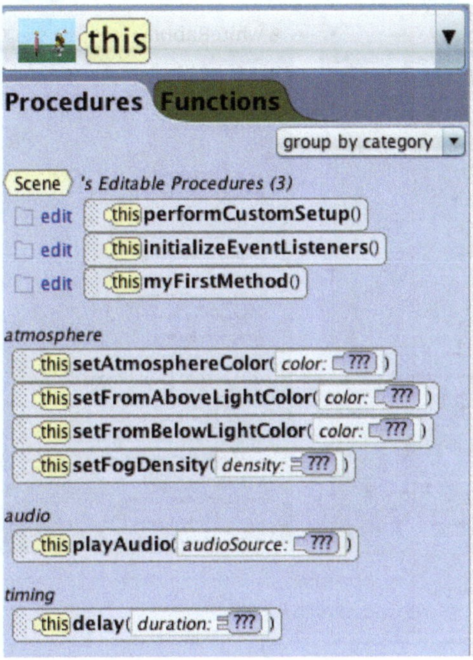

FIGURE 1-32   Some **Scene** procedures

Of special interest in these scene methods are the `myFirstMethod()` and `performCustomSetup()` procedures. As we have seen, `myFirstMethod()` is where we place the statements that animate our story. The `performCustomSetup()` can be used to position objects or the camera before the story begins. When you click the Run button, any statements in the `performCustomSetup()` method are performed; then the statements in `myFirstMethod()` are performed.

For example, to ensure that all of a story's characters are in their starting positions when the story begins, we could right-click the `performCustomSetup()` method, choose performCustomSetup from the context menu that appears to begin editing this procedure, and then drag in statements that move the characters to their starting positions, like actors taking their places before the curtain rises. We will see a convenient way to do this positioning in the next chapter; any activities that are needed to set up the scene can be performed using this method.

Feel free to experiment with the remaining methods; they can be used to create some interesting atmospheric effects, play music, and pause a scene.

1.4.2   The Functions Tab

If we click the Functions tab in the methods area, we will see the list of functions or "question messages" that we can send to the object selected in the object selector. Figure 1-33 shows most of these; a complete list is given in Appendix A.

FIGURE 1-33   The `Functions` pane

Functions are messages that we can send to an object to retrieve information from it. Put differently, the Functions tab lists the messages that we can send to an object to access one of its joints or "ask it a question."

Most Alice objects have functions that let us ask the object about its:

- Joints, assuming the object has joints (not all do)
- Size (its *height*, *width*, or *depth*, and how these compare to another object)
- Proximity to another object (i.e., how close or how far away the other object is)
- Spatial relation to another object (*position* or *orientation* with respect to the other object)
- **Point of view** (*position* and *orientation* within the world)

Many of these functions refer to an object's bounding box (or one of its edges). For example, an object's height, width, and depth are actually the dimensions of its bounding box.

General vs. More Specialized Functions

As can be seen in Figure 1-33, the messages listed in the Functions tab are general **Biped** functions, in the sense that they can be sent to any object whose class is in the Biped area of the Gallery. Many of these functions can be used to retrieve the values of an object's properties or joints. For example, all **Biped** objects have heads, so the **getHead()** function can be used to access a given **Biped** object's **Head** joint.

By contrast, there are other function messages that are more specialized. For example, the **WhiteRabbit** class provides specialized functions like **getLeftEarTip()** and **getTail()** that allow those joints of a **WhiteRabbit** object to be accessed. When present, such class-specific functions can be accessed using the object selector, as shown in Figure 1-34.

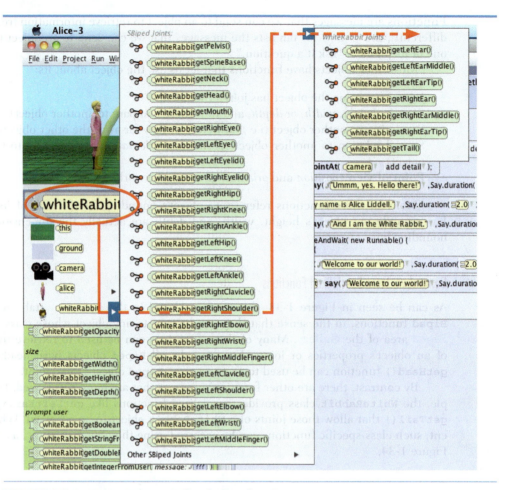

FIGURE 1-34   Accessing specialized class functions

There are additional general functions that can be accessed by selecting the Other SBiped Joints option at the bottom of the first-level menu shown in Figure 1-34.

Scene Functions

Alice also provides a group of function messages we can send to our Scene. If we use the object selector to select the object named **this**, then the Functions tab displays these functions, as shown in Figure 1-35.

FIGURE 1-35   The **Scene Functions** pane

These allow us to access the various objects in our story, access its atmospheric properties, get input from the user, and other things. We will see how to use some of these messages in the coming chapters.

1.5   Running Example: Design

Big projects can seem overwhelming at first. To help you learn how to handle a large project and make use of the ideas to come, we are going to build a project over the next few chapters. The project is to use Alice to make a short animated movie. The title of this movie is *Tim the Wizard Has a Bad Day*. As you might guess from the title, the movie is about a wizard named Tim.

A very rough outline for this project is as follows:

A title screen displays *Tim the Wizard Has a Bad Day.*

Scene 1: Tim is a bored wizard, working in his garden outside his castle. A neighbor stops by to warn him about the local ogres.

Scene 2: Outside their cave, three ogres scheme to "get" Tim.

Scene 3: Outside Tim's castle...

Shot a: The ogres appear and threaten Tim.

Shot b: Tim decides how to respond.

Shot c: Tim defeats the ogres.

Shot d: A dragon appears, circles Tim's castle several times, and settles on its wall.

Shot e: Tim approaches the dragon, who is mute. After asking many yes-or-no questions, Tim learns that a group of pixies have been plotting against him.

Scene 4: Outside the pixie lair, the queen pixie gives a rousing speech and orders her pixies to "go get" Tim.

Scene 5: Back outside Tim's castle...

Shot a: The pixies appear. Tim initially repels them, but when a giant pixie appears, Tim is distracted, allowing the other pixies to overwhelm him.

Shot b: The pixies carry Tim away to the Pixie Queen's court.

Scene 6: Tim is brought to the court of the Pixie Queen, who has another surprise in store for him.

From this outline, we can see that our story has a total of six scenes. At least two of those scenes have multiple shots, meaning the camera will change its position within the scene. The sequence of scenes and shots can be used as a flow or algorithm for our story.

Note that this is just an outline; we are free to modify or add to it as new ideas occur to us. The important thing is to outline the basics of what you want to happen, because that will form the structure of the story and provide an initial idea of how many scenes and shots the story will have.

Once we have an outline, we can proceed to fill in the details by writing user stories for each scene. For example, we might write the user story for Scene 2 as follows:

> Three ogres are standing outside their cave, in the desert. The first shouts, "WE GET WIZARD TODAY!" The second ogre shouts, "YEAH!" The third ogre says, "Okay." The first ogre shouts, "WE GIVE HIM NASTY SURPRISE." The second ogre shouts, "YEAH!" The third ogre says, "Okay." The first ogre looks at the third ogre and shouts, "YOU NOT SHOUTING!" and then "YOU HAVE BAD ATTITUDE!" The second ogre shouts, "YEAH!" The third ogre says, "Whatever." The first ogre shouts, "WE GO NOW!" The second ogre shouts, "YEAH!" The third ogre says, "Ok." The three ogres disappear into the ground.

Once we have written the user stories and specified in detail what will happen in each scene or shot, we draw a storyboard-sketch for each scene, using the Rule of Thirds to organize that scene.

To illustrate, Figure 1-36 shows storyboard-sketches for shots 3a and 3b of our story. The first storyboard frames the scene for shot 3a, showing the ogres menacing the wizard, with the castle in the background. The second storyboard frames the scene for shot 3b, with the camera zooming in on the wizard as he decides how to respond to the ogres' provocations.

FIGURE 1-36   Two of the storyboard-sketches for our story

Once we have sketched storyboards for all of our scenes, we are ready to begin using Alice to build and animate the scenes. In the next chapter, we begin doing so.

1.6   Chapter Summary

❑ The user story describes the behavior of a computer program.

❑ Storyboard-sketches indicate the appearance of each of the program's scenes.

❑ Transition diagrams relate the storyboard-sketches to one another.

❑ A flow or algorithm provides a concise summary of the user story.

❑ The basics of using Alice include how to add an object to a world; how to set its initial position, orientation, and pose; how to animate an object by sending it a message; how to select an object's parts; how to change an object's properties; and how to send multiple messages simultaneously.

1.6.1   Key Terms

Alice	procedure
algorithm	property position
bounding box	properties
bug	Rule of Thirds
class	scene
concurrent execution	sequential execution
debugging	shot
design	simultaneous execution
error	software design
flow	software engineering
function	software implementation
message	software testing
method	statement
object	storyboard-sketches
orientation	testing
point of view	transition diagram
pose	user story
position	

Programming Projects

1.1 Modify the world we created in Section 1.3 so that, after Alice Liddell and the White Rabbit introduce themselves, Alice Liddell tells the user she and the White Rabbit would like to sing a duet, after which they sing a simple song, such as *Mary Had a Little Lamb*. Have Alice Liddell and the White Rabbit sing alternate lines of the song, the lyrics for which are provided here:

Verse 1. Mary had a little lamb, little lamb, little lamb. Mary had a little lamb, its fleece was white as snow.	Verse 2. And everywhere that Mary went, Mary went, Mary went. And everywhere that Mary went, the lamb was sure to go.
Verse 3. It followed her to school one day, school one day, school one day. It followed her to school one day, which was against the rules.	Verse 4. It made the children laugh and play, laugh and play, laugh and play. It made the children laugh and play, to see a lamb at school.

© Cengage Learning 2015

1.2 Finish the story we animated in Section 1.4.1, so that the story ends with the **whiteRabbit** disappearing and **alice** saying, "Now where has he gone this time?"

1.3 Proceed as in 1.2, but go to a site that provides royalty-free sound effects, such as *http://www.pacdv.com/sounds/index.html*. There, locate and download a sound effect that makes a popping noise. Modify the program using the **playAudio()** method so that the popping sound occurs at the same time as the **whiteRabbit** disappears.

1.4 Using any two characters from the Gallery, design and build a program in which one tells the other a knock-knock joke. (If you don't know any knock-knock jokes, see *www.knock-knock-joke.com.*) Make your story end with both characters laughing.

1.5 Using class **MyPerson**, build a superhero named **resizer** who can alter his or her size at will. Build a story in which **resizer** demonstrates his or her superpowers to the user by growing and shrinking. Make sure that **resizer** tells the user what he or she is going to do before doing it.

1.6 Build a scene containing one of the animals (e.g., one of the rabbits). Write a program that makes the animal hop once, as realistically as possible (i.e., legs extending and retracting, head bobbing). Bonus: download sound effects and send your animal **playAudio()** messages so that an appropriate "thump" sound is played as it leaves the ground, a "whoosh" sound is played while it is in the air, and a "thud" sound is played when it lands.

1.7 Build a scene containing a character and a tree. Using **move()** and **turn()** messages, write a program that makes the character walk around the tree.

1.8 Choose a person from the Gallery. Then build a world containing your person and a sports prop (e.g., a baseball or a basketball). Write a program in which your person uses the item for that sport (e.g., pitches the baseball or dribbles the basketball).

1.9 Choose one of your favorite movie scenes that contains just two or three characters. Use Alice to create an animated spoof of that scene, substituting Alice characters for the characters in the movie.

1.10 Write an original short story (10–20 seconds long), and use Alice to create an animated version of it. Your story should have at least two characters, and each character should perform at least five actions that combine to make an interesting story.

1.11 *Mules* is a silly (and confusing!) song the lyrics for which are shown below. (It is sung to the tune of *Auld Lang Syne.*) Build a world containing a camel (or a different relative of a mule) and a person. Build a program that animates the person and camel appropriately while the person "sings" the lyrics to the song. For example, the person should point to the different legs (front or back) as he or she sings about them, move to the back of the camel when the song calls for it, and get kicked as the sixth line is sung.

On mules we find two legs behind, and two we find before. We stand behind before we find, what the two behind be for!	When we're behind the two behind, we find what these be for. So stand before the two behind, behind the two before!

© Cengage Learning 2015

Chapter 2
Methods

Great things can be reduced to small things, and small things can be reduced to nothing.

CHINESE PROVERB

Weeks of programming can save you hours of planning.

ANONYMOUS

When do you show the consequences? On TV, that mouse pulled out that cat's lungs and played them like a bagpipe, but in the next scene, the cat was breathing comfortably.

MARGE SIMPSON (JULIE KAVNER), IN "ITCHY AND SCRATCHY LAND," THE SIMPSONS

Objectives

Upon completion of this chapter, you will be able to:

❑ Build scene methods to help organize a story into scenes and shots
❑ Build class methods to elicit desirable behaviors from objects
❑ Use markers to reposition the camera for different shots within a scene
❑ Understand how an object's position, orientation, and point of view are determined

In the last chapter, you saw how to design and build computer programs. You also saw how Alice lets us build programs that consist of *statements*, in which we often send *messages* to *objects*. Finally, you saw that Alice provides a rich set of predefined messages that we can send to objects, to create programs that generate fun and interesting animations.

Alice's predefined messages provide an excellent set of *basic operations* for animation, but these basic operations are *all* that are predefined. So there are no predefined methods to elicit many of the behaviors we might want Alice objects to exhibit. For example, a wolf should be able to walk, trot, run, and wag its tail, but there are no predefined methods for these behaviors in Alice's `Wolf` class. A falcon should be able to flap its wings and fly, but `Falcon` and the other subclasses of class `Flyer` do not provide methods for such behaviors.

When an Alice class does not provide a method for a behavior we need, Alice lets us create a new method to provide the behavior. After we have created the method, we can send the corresponding message to the object to elicit the desired behavior.

There are actually two quite different reasons for building your own methods. One reason is to divide your story into smaller pieces to keep it more manageable and organized. A second reason is to provide an object with a behavior it needs but does not already have. In this chapter, we examine both approaches. As we shall see, the motivations, thought processes, and circumstances are quite different for these two approaches.

2.1   Scene and Shot Methods

As we mentioned in Chapter 1, films (and by extension, animations) are often divided into **scenes**, and each scene makes up a piece of the story that takes place on a particular set. Scenes can be further divided into **shots**, with each shot consisting of the scene's set and whatever characters are in the shot, filmed from a particular camera position. When a film crew has finished one shot, it begins work on the next one. When all the shots for a particular scene are finished, the shots are combined to form the scene, which is then complete. Work then begins on the next scene.

So scenes and shots provide a logical and convenient way to break a big film project down into smaller, more manageable pieces. We can use the same approach to program in Alice. By organizing your user story into a series of scenes and organizing each complex scene into a series of shots, you can work through the story shot by shot and scene by scene and thereby avoid being overwhelmed by the size of the project. This approach, in which you solve a "big" problem by (1) breaking it into "small" problems, (2) solving each "small" problem, and (3) combining the "small" problem solutions into a solution to the "big" problem, is called **Divide and Conquer**. You conquer the big problem by dividing it into smaller subproblems that are easier to solve. Once you have solved all the subproblems (which may themselves require Divide and Conquer to solve), you combine those subsolutions into a solution to the big problem.

2.1.1 Running Example: Methods for Scenes

To illustrate how this approach can be used in Alice, remember that the user story we designed in Section 1.6 began with a title screen, followed by six scenes. When we first start Alice (even before we have added any objects to the world), we can organize our Alice program to reflect the scene structure of our user story. To create a method that performs our first scene,[1] we first select the tab for the **Scene** class above the editing area and then click the Add Scene Procedure button, as shown in Figure 2-1.

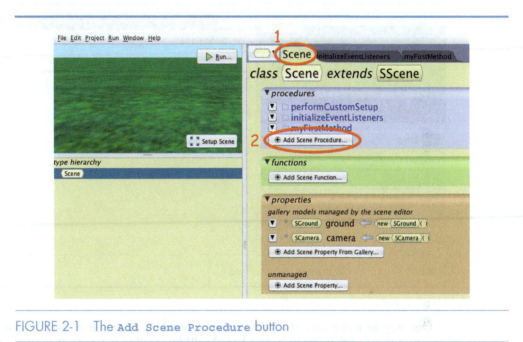

FIGURE 2-1   The **Add Scene Procedure** button

As you can see, the **Scene** class contains three predefined methods[2] one of which is **myFirstMethod**, which is where our program starts when we click the **Run** button.

Clicking the Add Scene Procedure button pops up an Add Scene Procedure dialog box into which we can type the name we wish to give the new method. A method name should usually be (1) a *verb* or *verb phrase* and (2) descriptive of what it does. Because we are creating a method to perform our first scene, we will enter the name **doScene1**.

Method names should begin with a lowercase letter and contain no spaces. If a name consists of multiple words, capitalize the first letter of each word after the first.

---

[1]We will write a method to do our title screen in Section 6.4.

[2]Object-oriented programmers use the word *method* to describe the code that runs when you send an object a message. There are two kinds of methods: those that return a value and those that do not. Methods that return a value are called *functions*. In Alice 3, methods that return no values are called *procedures*.

When we click the Add Scene Procedure dialog box's OK button, two things happen:

1. Alice creates a new pane in the editing area, labeled **doScene1**, containing an empty definition for our **doScene1()** method.

2. Alice adds **doScene1()** to **Scene**'s list of procedures in the methods area.

These two changes are highlighted in red in Figure 2-2.

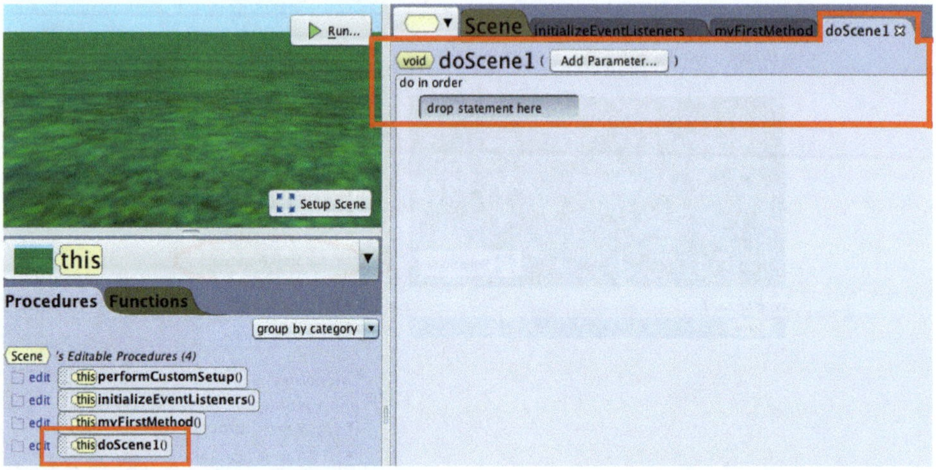

FIGURE 2-2   A new **doScene1()** method

One way to make sure that the method is working is to select the **camera** in the object selector and then make it do a barrel roll[3] by sending it a **roll()** message within **doScene1()**, with the values shown in Figure 2-3.

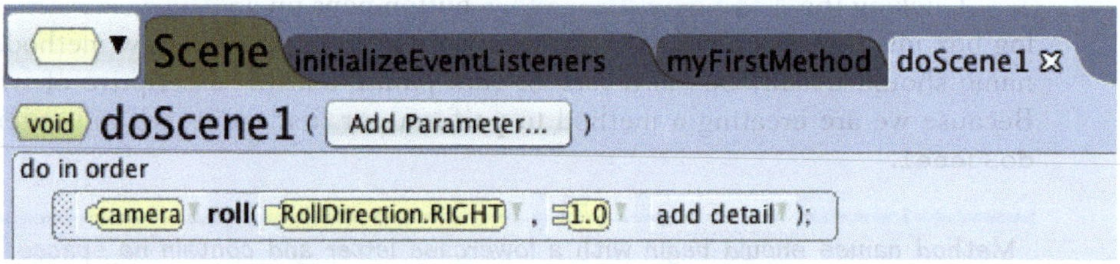

FIGURE 2-3   A simple method test

-----

[3]If you dislike testing **doScene1()** by making the **camera** roll, you can instead test it by the **setAtmosphereColor()** method to test the atmosphere to a different color.

If we do this and then click Alice's Run button, nothing happens. The problem is that although we have *defined* a new **doScene1()** method, there are no statements in our program that send the corresponding **doScene1()** message. Our **myFirstMethod()** method is empty, and because that is where the program begins running, we need to send the **doScene1()** message in **myFirstMethod()**.

Every message must be sent to an object, which raises the question: To which object do we send the **doScene1()** message? Because **doScene1()** is a **Scene** method, we must send the **doScene1()** message to a **Scene** object.

When our program begins running, Alice creates a **Scene** object and sends it the **myFirstMethod()** message. Alice's name for that **Scene** object is **this**, so to send it the **doScene1()** message, we select **this** in the object selector above the methods area, click on the tab for **myFirstMethod()** in the editing area, and then drag the **doScene1()** message from the methods area into the **doInOrder** statement in the editing area, giving us the (short) program shown in Figure 2-4.

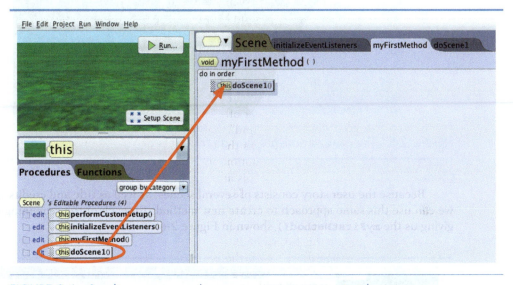

FIGURE 2-4   Sending our scene the **doScene1()** message inside **myFirstMethod()**

Now, when we click Alice's Run button, **myFirstMethod()** begins running. It sends the **doScene1()** message to **this**, which sends the **roll()** message to the **camera**, telling it to roll 1.0 complete rotation to the right. If we've done everything correctly, we will see the **camera** do a barrel roll, which we have captured partway through in Figure 2-5.

FIGURE 2-5   The `camera` partway through a barrel roll

Because the user story consists of several scenes, as well as title and credits screens, we can use this same approach to create new methods for each of the remaining scenes, giving us the **myFirstMethod()** shown in Figure 2-6.

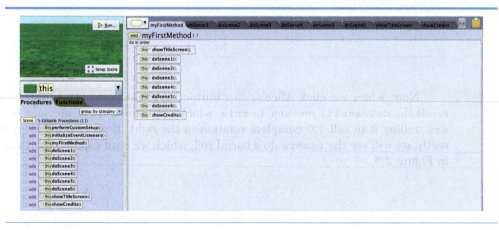

FIGURE 2-6   Scene methods outlining our project

Inside each new **doScene** method, we can send the **camera** another **roll()** message, or a **turn()** message, or some other message to generate a different visual effect. Clicking Alice's Run button should then display the effects of those messages in order. This is a simple way to test that all the new methods are being invoked properly. When we are confident that all these methods are working correctly, we can replace the **roll()** statements in each scene method with the statements needed to animate that scene. So this approach lets us work on our individual scenes *independently*. It also lets us work on them in whatever order we choose.

2.1.2   Running Example: Methods for Shots

We have just seen how a big, complicated project can be divided into smaller, easier-to-program scenes. But a scene itself may be very complicated! In such situations, complex scenes can be further divided into simpler (easier-to-program) *shots*. One good rule of thumb is: If you must use the scroll bar to view all the statements in a scene method, divide it into two or more **shot methods**.

Long methods tend to be complicated and error prone, and their length can make it harder to find errors. If you keep your methods short, you'll be less likely to make a mistake; and if you do make one, you can find it more easily, because you'll be able to see the entire method at once, without having to scroll down and up.

To illustrate this idea, recall that Scene 1 and Scene 2 of our running example are reasonably simple. It may be possible to implement them in a method that requires no scrolling. However, Scene 3 is more complicated; according to our design, building it will require five different shots. We can use an approach similar to what we did in the last section to create a method for each shot. To be consistent, we might name these methods **doShot3a, doShot3b, doShot3c, doShot3d,** and **doShot3e**.

As before, we select the tab for class **Scene** above the editing area and click the Add Scene Procedure button. (You may want to close the tabs of scenes we are not working on.) In the Add Scene Procedure dialog box, we name the new method **doShot3a**. As before, Alice (1) updates the editing area with a new pane that contains an empty definition for the new method, and (2) adds the new procedure method to the list of **Scene** procedures in the methods area. To test that it works, we can again send the **camera** object a **roll()** message. To distinguish a shot method, we might have our camera roll left instead of right; and because we have five shots in this scene, we might have each one roll the camera one-fifth (0.2) of a rotation, as shown in Figure 2-7.

FIGURE 2-7   Testing a shot method

We can then click on the `doScene3` tab in the editing area, delete the `camera.` `roll()` message from `doScene3()`, select `this` from the object selector: box in the details area, and finally drag the `doShot3a()` message from the details area into the method, yielding the `doScene3()` definition found in Figure 2-8.

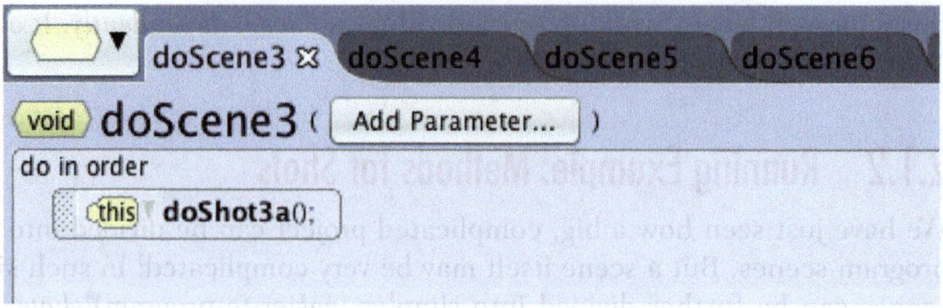

FIGURE 2-8   Calling a shot method from a scene method

If we repeat this for each of the four remaining shots in the scene, we get the definition of `doScene3()` shown in Figure 2-9.

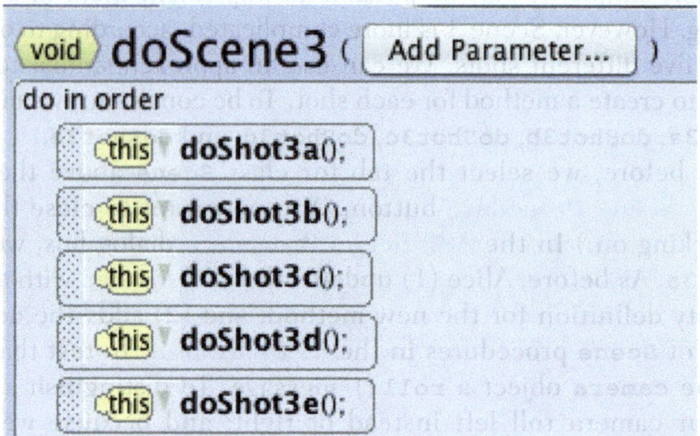

FIGURE 2-9   A scene method built from several shot methods

If, in keeping with Figure 2-7, each of these shot methods also rolls the **camera** one-fifth (0.2) of a rotation to its left, then the **camera** should do a complete 360-degree rotation when our `doScene3()` method is performed. That provides an easy way to make sure that each of our shot methods is being invoked correctly.

We can use this same approach for each of the multi-shot scenes in the story and lay out its entire structure in advance. By doing this, we create a **framework** within which we can place the animations for specific scenes. The good thing about this approach is that we can work on the animations for one scene in isolation from all of the other scenes. In other words, we can develop each scene or shot independently from the others. For example, when we are ready to work on Scene 3, we can add statements to each of the five shot methods to produce the animation required for that shot. When each is complete, our animation of Scene 3 will be complete!

In a story with many scenes and shots, this approach produces a tab above the editing area for each scene or shot, leading to visual clutter. When you are not working on a given scene or shot, you can close its method by selecting its tab and then clicking the X in the tab to the right of its name. You can reopen that method later by clicking the tab for class **Scene** above the editing area, locating the method you want to edit, clicking the down-arrow to the left of its name, and choosing Edit from the context menu that appears. This same menu can be used to rename or delete a method.

A different, faster way to edit methods that we have defined is to right-click an invocation of that method in the editing area and then choose its name from the context menu that appears. This often provides the fastest way to switch from editing one method to editing another, so practice it a few times to become familiar with it.

If we were to draw a diagram of the structure of our program (minus the title and credits screens for now), it would look like what is shown in Figure 2-10.

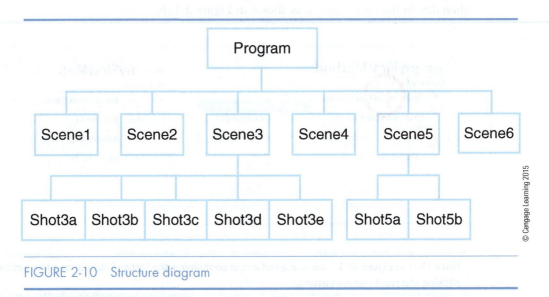

FIGURE 2-10   Structure diagram

© Cengage Learning 2015

A diagram or program like this can have as many pieces and levels as necessary to make your project manageable. If a shot is complicated, it can be further subdivided into *pieces*, which can be broken down into *parts*, and so on.

Scene and shot methods reflect the structure of the story we are telling and therefore belong to the program we are building. As such, they are properly stored in the **Scene** class, since it represents our program as a whole. If you look at the object tree in the scene editor closely, you will see that all the non-**this** objects in a world—including the **ground**, **camera**, and anything else we add to the program—are parts of the program, which Alice calls **this**. More precisely, **this** refers to an object that Alice creates from class **Scene**. Because our scene and shot messages are stored in the **Scene** class, we send these messages to **this**, as was shown in Figures 2-8 and 2-9.

We will call methods that are stored in the **Scene** class **scene methods**, because they define messages that are sent to our program's **Scene** object, which is named **this**. If a method controls the behavior of *multiple objects* (as a scene does), it should usually be defined as a scene method.

2.1.3   Enabling and Disabling Methods

When we have laid out our story's structure and defined methods for each one of its scenes and shots, we can work on specific scenes or shots in isolation by *disabling* all the parts we are *not* working on. To illustrate, we can disable the **showTitleScreen()** message in our **myFirstMethod()** method by right-clicking that message in the editing area; Alice will display a context menu containing an attribute called Is Enabled, with a check mark by that attribute, as can be seen in Figure 2-11a below. Selecting Is Enabled from this context menu will "uncheck" that attribute and disable the message, which Alice will then dim in the editing area, as shown in Figure 2-11b.

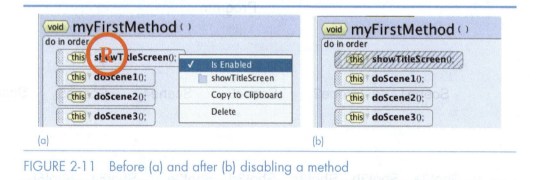

(a)   (b)

FIGURE 2-11   Before (a) and after (b) disabling a method

Note that in Figure 2-11 we use a red circle containing the letter R to denote the action of clicking the right mouse button.

When we click Alice's Run button and method **myFirstMethod()** is performed, only the messages that are enabled are actually performed; Alice "skips" any methods that are disabled. We can thus use this approach to disable all the messages in method **myFirstMethod()** except the one on which we are working. Then, when we click Alice's

Run button, only the method we are working on will be performed, and we do not have to spend valuable time waiting while Alice performs all the methods preceding the one on which we are working.

To re-enable a disabled message, use the same approach: Right-click the disabled method in the **editing area**, choose **Is Enabled** from the context menu that appears, and Alice will "re-check" that message, re-enabling it.

2.1.4   Running Example: Scene 1

The user story for Scene 1 of our story appears below.

Scene 1: Introduction

The scene begins with a wide-angle view of Tim the wizard's castle. The camera zooms in on Tim, who is standing in front of his castle. There are two trees there, and the left tree is half the size of the other. Tim thinks, "I planted these trees at the same time. This one sure needs some help." A woman walks on-screen from the left and says, "Hi Tim. What's my favorite neighbor up to today?" Tim replies, "Hi Ann. Nothing special. I was just looking at my trees and noticed this one could use a boost." Tim casts a spell and the tree doubles in size. Ann says, "Wow—that is so handy!" Tim replies, "That's my exciting life as a wizard: helping trees grow." Ann says, "Speaking of excitement, I came over to tell you that I heard the ogres beating their drums last night." Tim says, "Hmmm, I wonder what has riled them up." Ann says, "I don't know, but watch out for them. They can be nasty sometimes." Tim says, "Thanks for the warning." Ann says, "You're welcome. Bye-bye." Ann turns and leaves the way she came.

The introductory scene of a user story is very important, because it has to introduce the story's characters to the viewer. So we thus craft this scene carefully to communicate to the user that: (a) Tim grows trees near a castle, presumably his castle; (b) Tim has a neighbor named Ann, and he is her favorite neighbor; (c) Tim has magical powers, which he will use to help a struggling tree; (d) Tim is bored; and (e) there are ogres living nearby who seem to be stirred up about something. By writing this scene carefully, we "set the stage" for the rest of our story.

It is easy to turn this user story into an algorithm of numbered steps for this scene, so we will leave that as an exercise for you, the reader.

Using our storyboards, we can build a set for this scene by going to the **Gallery** and using class **Biped > Adult** for our characters Tim and Ann, using class **Prop > CastleGate** and **Prop > CastleWall** to build Tim's castle and using class **Prop > WonderlandTree** for Tim's trees.

Using the techniques presented in Section 1.3.2, we might build the set shown in Figure 2-12.

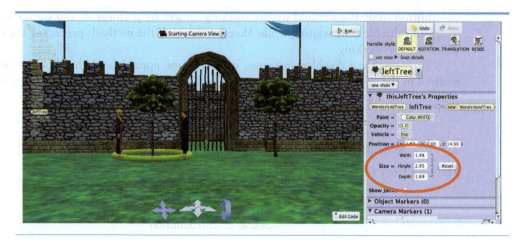

FIGURE 2-12   Setting the stage for Scene 1

To make the left tree appear stunted, we might shrink the `leftTree` to half of its current size. We do this by changing the `leftTree`'s Size settings, which are circled in red in Figure 2-12. By default, a tree's height is 2.95; if we change this property to 1.47 for the `leftTree`, it will shrink by 50 percent.[4]

Ann is supposed to be off-screen; she walks to this position after the scene begins. One way to position her offscreen is to right-click her name in the object-tree, choose ann > procedures > move > MoveDirection.BACKWARD > Custom Decimal Number... from the context menu, and then choose a minimal distance to move her offscreen, such as 5. This will position her that distance "back" from where we want her to end up when she walks on-screen. Then, when it is time for her to appear in the scene, we just have to make her walk forward that distance.

With Ann positioned offscreen, we can proceed to animate the scene, most of which is straightforward. One issue is that the camera needs to zoom in at the beginning of this scene. We will see how to do this in the next section.

Another issue is that Ann is supposed to walk on-screen near the beginning of the scene and offscreen at the end of the scene, and class `Adult` does not offer a method to make our characters walk realistically. For now, we will just use the predefined `move()` method to move her to the correct position; we will see how to build a `walk()` method in Chapter 4.

Another issue is that Tim does not have a method to cast a spell that will make a tree grow. We will see how to do this in Chapter 3.

For each of these issues, we have inserted **comments** to remind us where these messages should go, as shown in Figure 2-13. Comments are notes for when a human reads a method. The computer ignores them when performing the method, so we can insert a comment any time one will be useful. In addition to reminders like the one in Figure 2-13, comments are often used to document or explain tricky sections of a program.

---

[4]By default, the dimensions are linked, so that changing one dimension changes the others proportionally. This is what you want most of the time; if you want to change just one dimension of an object, click the links to the left of the `Reset` button.

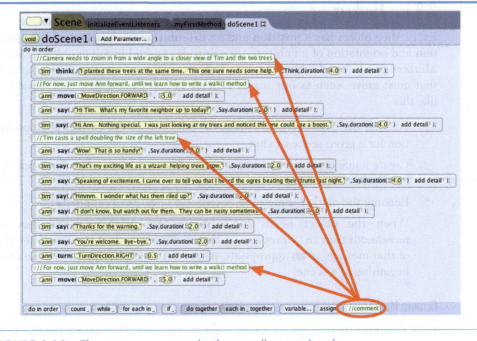

FIGURE 2-13 The doScene1() method, partially completed

Figure 2-13 shows a "rough cut" of our scene, which means most of the functionality is there but it needs further polishing and refinement. To complete this scene, we will need to build a **walk()** method for Ann and build a **castGrowSpell()** method for Tim. We will see how to build these methods in the next two chapters, so for now, let's see how to make our camera zoom in at the beginning of this scene.

2.2 Alice Tip: Using Markers

Stories are made up of multiple scenes, which are often divided into shots; each shot is a piece of a scene filmed with the camera in a different position. We have also seen that Alice places a **camera** object in every world. This raises the question: How do we move the camera from one scene to another, or from one position to another position within a scene?

We can move the **camera** "manually" using the blue-arrow camera controls in the scene editor to position it for a given scene. But that doesn't help us when we need to move the camera within a scene, as we must do at the beginning of **doScene1()**. It also doesn't help us when our program needs to move the camera between scenes.

Because the **camera** is an Alice object, most of the standard Alice messages can be sent to it. So we could use a set of simultaneous **move()**, **turn()**, and other motion-related messages to position the camera at the beginning of each scene or shot method. However, getting such movement-messages exactly right requires lots of tedious trial and error. Thankfully, Alice provides a better way, as we will see next.

2.2.1 Markers

Every Alice object has a **position** and an **orientation** in the 3D world. To save the position and orientation of an object, Alice provides special invisible objects called **markers**. Markers can be used with any kind of object, but they are especially useful for objects that must move, such as our story's characters and the `camera`. The basic procedure is like this:

1. Position the object (e.g., the `camera`) until it is in the correct position and orientation for a given scene or shot.

2. Create a marker at the object's position. This marker has the same position and orientation as that object.

3. Rename the marker something descriptive (e.g., `cameraShot3a`).

4. When the object needs to move to that position, send that object the `moveAndOrientTo()` message, with the marker as its target, and set the duration of that message to an appropriate value—for example, 0, to move the `camera` at the beginning of a scene.

Camera Markers

Let's illustrate these steps by using them to position the `camera` for the first scene of our running example. In the scene editor, we use the blue-arrow controls to back the camera up until we can see the entire castle. Next, we click the down-arrow next to the Properties of the currently selected object to hide it; then we click the right-arrow next to Camera Markers, as shown in Figure 2-14a. This reveals the Camera Markers buttons shown in Figure 2-14b.

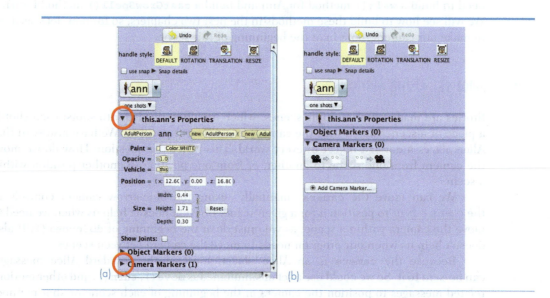

FIGURE 2-14 Locating (a) and using (b) using the Markers buttons

When we click the Add Camera Marker... button, Alice displays a dialog box in which we can give the marker a name (and color). Because this marker is for the camera's position in Scene 1, we name it `cameraScene1`. When we click the dialog box's OK button, Alice creates a marker for the camera's current position and orientation, accomplishing Steps 2 and 3 of the procedure. The marker is also added to a list directly above the Add Camera Marker... button, as shown in Figure 2-15.

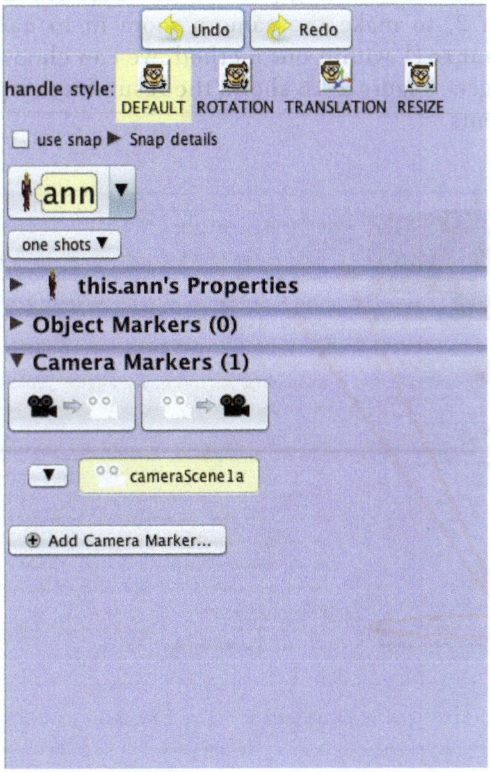

FIGURE 2-15   The list of markers

Note that there are two buttons below the Camera Markers label. These allow the camera or the marker to be easily repositioned. For example, if we move the camera elsewhere (perhaps to set up another scene) and want to move it back to this marker, clicking the left button moves the camera to the selected marker. If we move the camera and decide we want to move this marker to the camera's new position, clicking the right button moves the currently selected marker to the camera's current position.

Note also that there is an Object Markers area in Figures 2-14 and 2-15. This area lets us create a marker at the current position of the object that is currently selected in the object tree. We will use this area shortly.

Before we leave the scene editor, let's create a marker at the place where we want the camera to be at the end of its zoom. We first use the blue-arrow controls to manually zoom the camera forward until it is positioned as shown in Figure 2-12. Then we use the Add Camera Marker... button to drop a marker and label the new marker **cameraScene1b**.

Since we have already marked the camera's positions for the beginning of Scene 1, we can then perform Step 4 by returning to the code editor view, selecting the **camera** in the object selector, locating the **moveAndOrientTo()** message, and then dragging it to the beginning of our **doScene1()** method twice—once, with duration 0, to set the camera's starting position at **cameraScene1a**, and then a second time, with duration 2, to make the camera zoom in to **cameraScene1b**. When we drop **moveAndOrientTo()** within our method, we can choose the appropriate marker from the list of targets. Figure 2-16 shows the result after replacing our first comment with these statements.

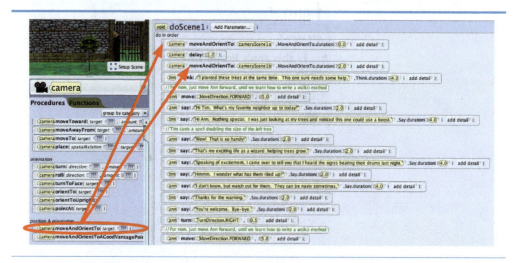

FIGURE 2-16   Using **moveAndOrientTo()** to set the camera's position and orientation

As appears in Figure 2-16, we set the duration of the first statement to 0 seconds, so that the camera will take its starting position "instantly" at the beginning of the scene, and we set the duration of the second statement to 2 seconds to zoom in more gradually. We also send our scene a **delay(1.0)** message between these two **moveAndOrientTo()** messages, as otherwise the "zoom" will happen too abruptly when the scene begins.

After doing this, we can now run our program and observe the camera zooming in at the beginning of our scene. Furthermore, we can use the blue-arrow controls to move the camera anywhere we wish. No matter where we reposition it in the 3D world, the camera will always instantly return to its marker at the beginning of Scene 1.

Object Markers

Just as we have used the scene editor to create a marker for positioning the camera at the beginning of a scene, we can also use the scene editor to create a marker for positioning characters using the Add Object Marker.... button under the Object Markers area.

To illustrate, even though we will likely be moving Tim and Ann as our story progresses, we can use markers to make sure they are always "in position" at the beginning of Scene 1. Using the Add Object Marker... button in the scene editor, create markers at Tim's and Ann's current positions, and give them appropriate names, such as `timScene1` and `annScene1`. Then send Tim and Ann `moveAndOrientTo()` messages at the beginning of `doScene1()`, using their markers to ensure that they are "in position," and set the duration of each message to 0.

Now that we know how to position the camera and characters, we are ready to test `doScene1()`, making sure everything (except the tree growing) works correctly. When it is satisfactory, we can proceed to Scene 2.

2.2.2   Scene 2: The Ogres

Scene 2 of our outline has three ogres who are scheming about Tim. We might construct a user story for this scene as follows:

Scene 2: The Ogres.

Three ogres stand in the desert, their cave in the background. The first ogre shouts, "TODAY WE GET WIZARD!" The second ogre shouts, "YEAH!" The third ogre says, "Ok." The first ogre shouts, "WE GO NOW, WE SURPRISE HIM!" The second ogre shouts, "YEAH!" The third ogre says, "Ok." The first ogre turns to the third ogre and shouts, "YOU HAVE BAD ATTITUDE!" The second ogre shouts, "YEAH!" The third ogre says, "Whatever." The first ogre shouts, "WE GO NOW!" The second ogre shouts, "YEAH!" The third ogre says, "Ok." The three ogres simultaneously disappear into the ground.

Turning this user story into an algorithm is easy, so we leave it as an exercise.

Using our storyboards, we can build a set for this scene. One thing we must decide is where in our 3D world to build this set. We can build it pretty much anywhere, provided it is off-camera when we are viewing the other scenes.

One approach that works well for large projects is to use the blue-arrow controls to move the camera somewhere in our world that cannot be seen from Scene 1 and build the scene there.

For smaller projects, another approach is to right-click the camera in the object tree and use the procedures choice from the context menu to send the camera a `turn()`

message, giving it an angle just large enough to ensure that everything from Scene 1 is off-camera.[5] We can then build our new scene there. It is often enough to turn the camera as little as 90 degrees (0.25 rotations) or 45 degrees (0.125 rotations) for a new scene. Figure 2-17 shows this approach.

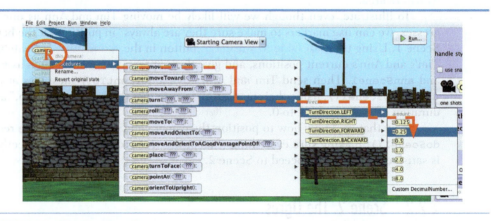

FIGURE 2-17   Sending the camera a `turn()` message via the context menu

When we choose an angle to turn the camera (e.g., 0.25), the camera turns as specified. If you make a mistake or want to try a different value, you can always use Edit > Undo or **Command-z** (**Ctrl-z** on Windows) to undo it, and then try again.

You can use this same context menu to send the camera a **moveAndOrientTo()** message in order to make it move to the position and orientation of a specific marker or object. That can be useful when you are working on one scene and want to jump to a different scene to work on it.

Note also that any object in the object tree can be manipulated this way, not just the camera. If an object should disappear off-camera, or if you add an object to a scene and it appears off-camera, one way to "find" that object is to send it a **moveAndOrientTo()** message, with an on-camera object as the target of the message. The missing object will then move to the position and orientation of the chosen object.

Regardless of whether we use this approach, the approach using blue-arrow camera controls, or some combination of these, once we have our **camera** positioned appropriately for a new scene, we can drop a marker there and then use the **moveAndOrientTo()** message at the beginning of that scene's method to position the camera appropriately. Take a moment and do this for Scene 2.

Using our storyboard, we might then build the set for Scene 2 as shown in Figure 2-18, using class **Prop classes > Cave** for the ogres' cave and instances of class **Biped classes > Ogre** for each of the ogres.

---

[5]Alice calls this invocation of a procedure via the context menu a "one shot" procedure invocation. These can also be invoked in the scene editor using the one shots button above the Properties area.

FIGURE 2-18   The set for Scene 2

Because the ogres appear in both Scene 2 and Scene 3, we will need to move them between the scenes. To make sure they begin Scene 2 in the correct starting positions, take a moment to drop a marker for each of them, so that we can send each of them a **moveAndOrientTo()** message at the beginning of **doScene2()**.

When we have finished building the scene, we return to the code editor and begin animating our scene. To do this, we first edit the **myFirstMethod()** method, disabling **doScene1()** and enabling **doScene2()** so that we can work on it in isolation, as shown in Figure 2-19.

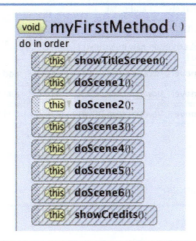

FIGURE 2-19   Enabling **doScene2()**

Next, we edit the `doScene2()` method, dragging in and dropping the messages and statements that will produce the desired animation. Figure 2-20 shows one possibility.

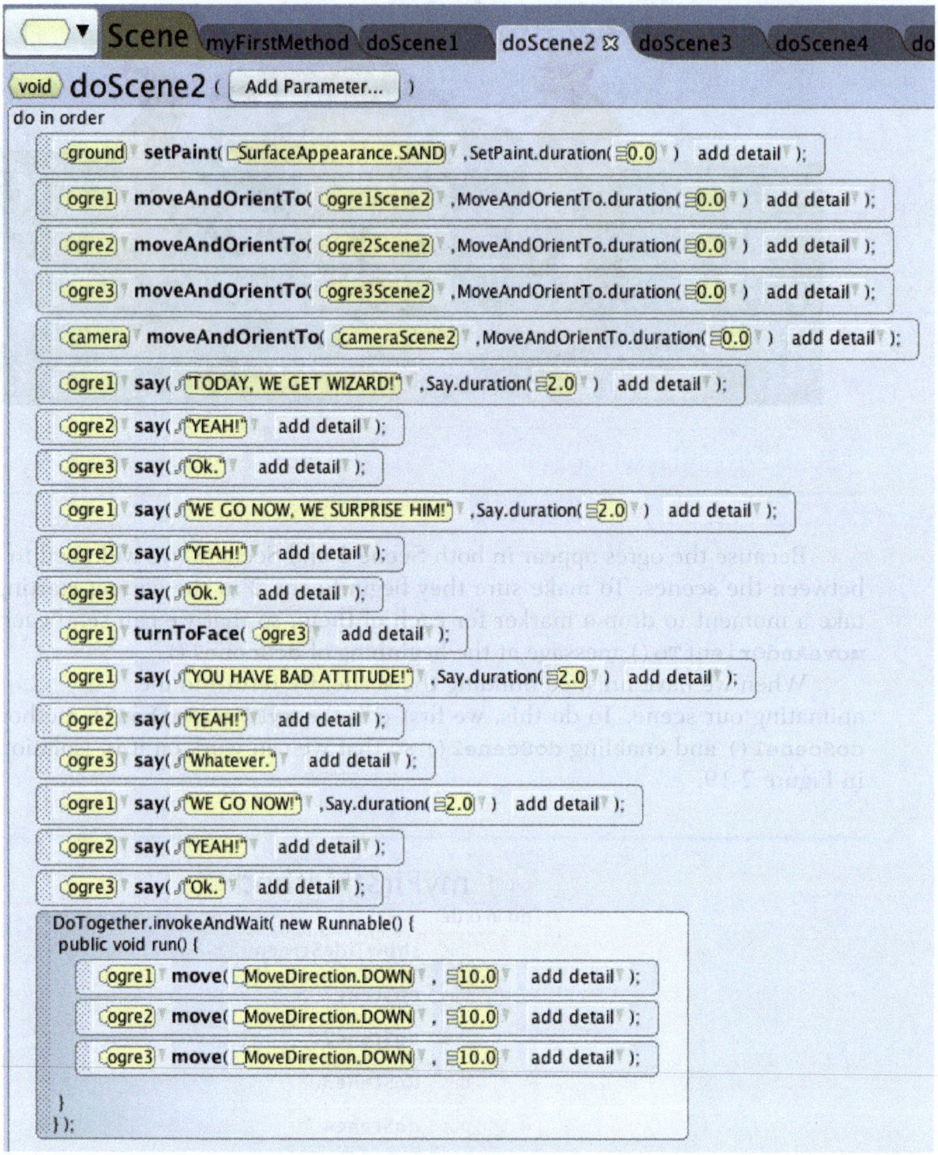

FIGURE 2-20   Animating Scene 2

The only new thing in this scene is the very first statement, which changes the appearance of the ground from the grassy appearance shown in Figure 2-18 to the sandy desert appearance shown in Figure 2-21.

FIGURE 2-21   The sandy ground

The **ground.setPaint()** method can be used to change the ground's appearance between more than 20 different options, including different types of grass, deserts, swamps, jungles, the ocean floor, and the surface of the Moon. This method can be found by selecting the **ground** in the object selector and then choosing the Procedures tab. Because our user story had this scene taking place in the desert, we tried both **DESERT** and **SAND** and then chose **SAND** because it offered better contrast to the ogres and their cave.

Next, we run our program and test that **doScene2()** animates correctly. When we are satisfied with it, we can enable **doScene1()** in method **myFirstMethod()** and ensure that the two scenes animate correctly together. Don't worry if the transition from Scene 1 to Scene 2 seems too abrupt. In Chapter 6, we will learn how to smooth out these transitions when our project is nearly complete.

When we have made sure that both **doScene1()** and **doScene2()** work satisfactorily both individually and together, we are ready to continue on to Scene 3.

2.3   Class Methods for Object Behaviors

An alternative to the scene method is the **class method**, which is used to define a behavior for a given type of object. Where a scene method usually controls the behavior of several different types of objects (e.g., each character in a scene), a class method primarily controls the behavior of just one type of object—the object to which the corresponding message will be sent.

2.3.1   Beginning Scene 3

Scene 3 begins with the ogres appearing at the wizard's castle. We might write the first part of the user story as follows:

> Scene 3: Back at the wizard's castle, only it and the trees are in sight.
>
> Shot 3a: The three ogres appear out of the ground simultaneously. The first ogre shouts, "WIZARD GONE! WE TRASH CASTLE!" The second ogre shouts, "YEAH!" The third ogre puts his finger to his lips and says, "Ssshhhh! Not so loud!" The first ogre turns to the third ogre and shouts, "WHY YOU SO NEGATIVE?" The second ogre shouts, "YEAH!" Before the third ogre can reply, the wizard materializes among them.

We can reuse our Scene 1 set for this scene; the trees and castle will help the viewer realize we are back in the same place again. To move the camera back there, we can switch to the scene editor, right-click the camera, and use the context menu to send the camera a **moveAndOrientTo()** message with our **cameraScene1b** marker as its target. Then, to set up the scene, we just have to (1) get the ogres into the right positions for them to emerge from the ground, and (2) hide Tim.

Positioning the three ogres is a bit tricky, but we can use an approach similar to how we positioned Ann in Scene 1. The basic idea is to first position the ogres where we want them to end up, and then work backwards from there:

1. We start by moving the ogres to where they will be *after* they emerge from the ground.

2. Using the context menu, we move each of them *down* (underground) 10 units.

3. We create a marker for each of them at that underground position.

If we follow these three steps, then at the beginning of Scene 3, we can send each ogre a **moveAndOrientTo()** message to move it from its position at the end of Scene 2 to the markers we created in Step 3. Then we can easily make them appear out of the ground at the beginning of Scene 3 using **move()** messages to move them *up* 10 units.

To get the ogres into position, we can right-click each of them in the object tree and then use the context menu to send each of them a **moveAndOrientTo()** message, with **tim** as the target. That will get them into the same scene as the castle and Tim. Then we can position them inside the scene, as shown in Figure 2-22.

FIGURE 2-22   Setting the stage for Scene 3

From that point, we can position the ogres by using the same right-click context menu to **move()** each of them *down* 10 units. Then we can drop a marker at each ogre, taking care to give each ogre's marker a helpful descriptive name, such as **ogre1Scene3**.

Now that we have marked the ogres' starting positions for Scene 3, we are ready to start animating the scene. To do so, we return to the code editor and, in method **myFirstMethod()**, disable **doScene1()** and **doScene2()** as well as enable and edit **doScene3()**. There, we can add statements to the method that change the appearance of the ground back to **GRASS**, hide Tim by setting his opacity to 0, then tell each of the ogres to **moveAndOrientTo()** their Scene 3 markers, and, finally, tell the **camera** to **moveAndOrientTo()** its Scene 1 marker, all with a duration of 0, as shown in Figure 2-23.

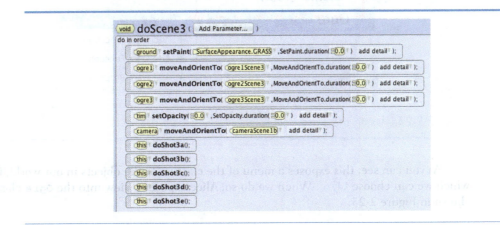

FIGURE 2-23   The **doScene3()** method

Now that we have set the stage for Scene 3, we are ready to begin animating Shot 3a. The only tricky part is that our user story calls for **ogre3** to put his finger to his lips as he is saying, "Shhh. Not so loud!" This is a complicated behavior, so we will build a new method to perform the gesture, as we describe next. What we want to do is send **ogre3** a message to tell him to perform this behavior. Because there is no predefined method to produce this behavior, we will define one, called **doShush()**.

2.3.2   Building a Class Method

Methods are stored within classes, so to send a message to an object, we must create a method in that object's class. In this case, our object is **ogre3**, whose class is **Ogre**. To create a method in class **Ogre**, we first click on **Scene** in the class navigator, and then choose **Ogre** from the menu,[6] as shown in Figure 2-24.

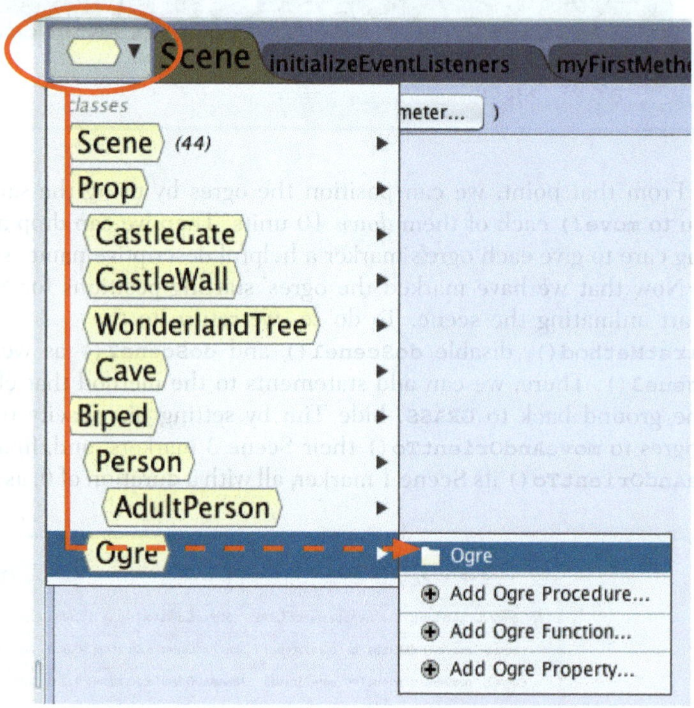

FIGURE 2-24   Using the class navigator

As you can see, this exposes a menu of the classes for the objects in our world, from which we can choose **Ogre**. When we do so, Alice exposes a view into the **Ogre** class, as shown in Figure 2-25.

---

[6]It is actually a bit faster if we choose **Add Ogre Procedure...** instead of **Ogre**, but we are choosing **Ogre** so that we can view its class in Figure 2-25.

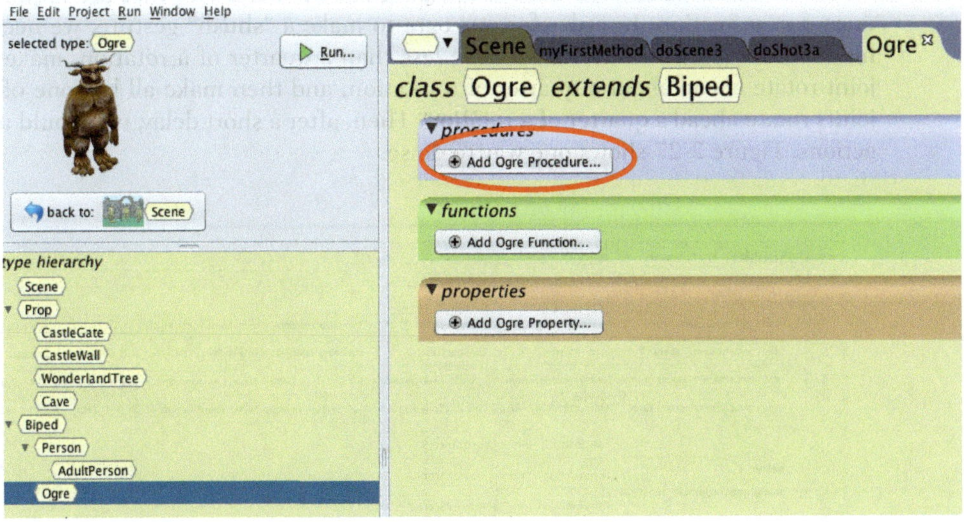

FIGURE 2-25   Class `Ogre`

To create a new procedural method, we click the Add Ogre Procedure... button, and then Alice will display an Add Ogre Procedure dialog box in which we can enter the name of our method. When we type `doShush` and press the OK button, Alice creates a new blank method named `doShush()` and adds `this.doShush()` to the Procedures tab in the methods area, as can be seen in Figure 2-26.

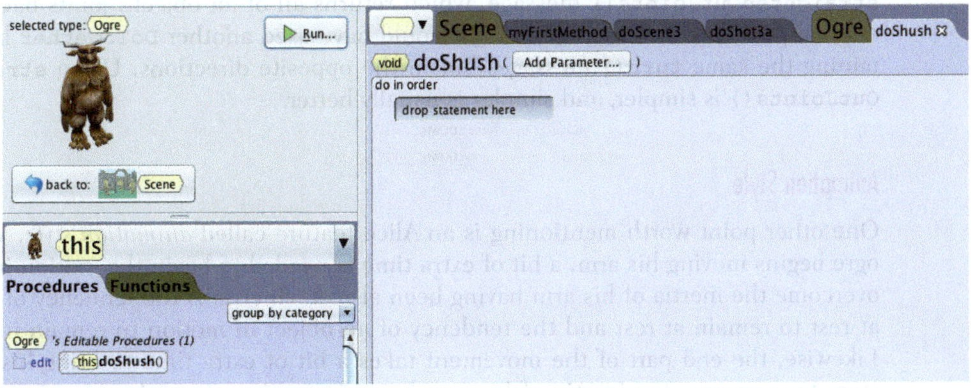

FIGURE 2-26   A blank class method

Inside this blank method, we can program the behaviors that are required to produce our animation. In order for our ogre to make a "shush" gesture, we need to make his shoulder joint rotate ahead a little less than a quarter of a rotation, make his elbow joint rotate ahead about a quarter of a rotation, and then make all but one of his finger joints rotate ahead a quarter of a rotation. Then, after a short delay, we should undo those actions. Figure 2-27 shows one way to do so.

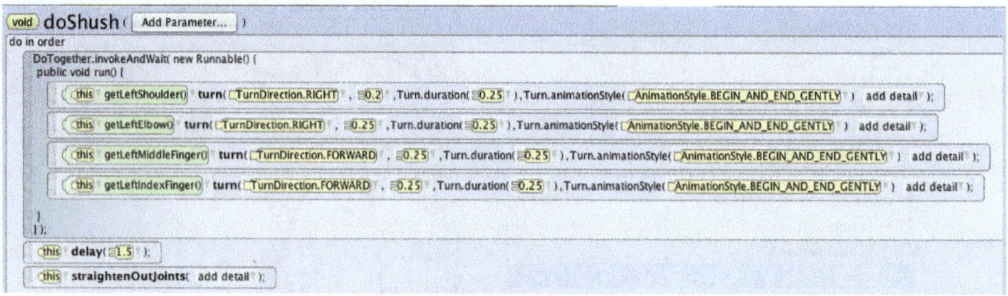

FIGURE 2-27   A class method to make a "shushing" gesture

The **DoTogether** block contains the special messages that are needed to make the "shush" gesture. More precisely, we use the object selector to select the ogre's left shoulder and then send it a **turn()** message that causes it to move in the right way. Then we do the same thing with the ogre's left elbow, left index finger, left middle finger, and left pinky finger. We have chosen to animate the ogre's left arm, because it is closest to the camera in our scene, as you can see in Figure 2-22.[7]

After a short pause, we need to undo that gesture. For this, we have used the **straightenOutJoints()** message, which returns all of an object's joints back to their original positions and orientations. We could have used another **DoTogether** block containing the same **turn()** messages but in the opposite directions. Using **straightenOutJoints()** is simpler, and simpler is usually better.

Animation Style

One other point worth mentioning is an Alice feature called *animation style*. When our ogre begins moving his arm, a bit of extra time is needed to begin the motion in order to overcome the inertia of his arm having been at rest. (Inertia is the tendency of an object at rest to remain at rest and the tendency of an object in motion to remain in motion.) Likewise, the end part of the movement takes a bit of extra time to bring his arm to a stop, to overcome the inertia of his arm being in motion. To make an animation seem

---

[7]Note that this "shush" gesture has our ogre hold his ring finger to his lips instead of the more customary index finger. As of this writing, the current version of Alice (3.1.85.0) does not include a getRingFinger() method. Being unable to access our ogre's ring finger, we leave it straight and rotate his other fingers. Hopefully this issue will be fixed in a future Alice release.

more realistic, many of Alice's standard statements provide four different animationStyle options under the add detail button:

1. BEGIN_AND_END_ABRUPTLY—The statement will begin and end without any delays.

2. BEGIN_GENTLY_AND_END_ABRUPTLY—A slight delay will be introduced so that the statement will begin slowly, but it will end with no delay.

3. BEGIN_ABRUPTLY_AND_END_GENTLY—The statement will begin with no delay, but a slight delay will be added at the end to make the ending more gradual.

4. BEGIN_AND_END_GENTLY—Slight delays will be added at the beginning and the end, so that the statement both starts and finishes more gradually.

The animationStyle you choose should depend on the complexity of the behavior you are animating. The guideline we follow is as follows:

- If a complete movement can be accomplished with a single message or statement, use BEGIN_AND_END_GENTLY, as this will simulate the extra time needed to overcome inertia at the beginning and end of the movement.
- When a movement requires a sequence of statements, use BEGIN_GENTLY_AND_END_ABRUPTLY for the first statement, BEGIN_AND_END_ABRUPTLY for the middle statements, and BEGIN_ABRUPTLY_AND_END_GENTLY for the last statement. This will ensure that the first part of the movement begins gradually but ends with no hesitation, the middle parts of the movement occur without any hesitations, and the final part of the movement begins with no hesitation but ends gradually. The result will be a more natural and realistic-seeming movement.

To illustrate, in Figure 2-27, the "shushing" animation consists of two movements: one in which the ogre's hand rises to his lips and another in which his hand returns to his side. The first movement consists of multiple statements that behave as one statement, because they are in a **DoTogether** block. In the same way, the second movement consists of a single **straightenOutJoints()** statement. In keeping with our guideline, we have used the BEGIN_AND_END_GENTLY style for both of these movements.

Testing

To test our method, we next open **doShot3a()** for editing, either by clicking its tab or by choosing **Scene** from the class navigator. The second approach takes us back to a screen listing all the methods for class **Scene**, from which we can edit **doShot3a()**. In that method, we can now send **ogre3** the **doShush()** message, which will invoke our method from Figure 2-27. Animating the rest of the shot described in our user story is fairly straightforward, as can be seen in Figure 2-28.

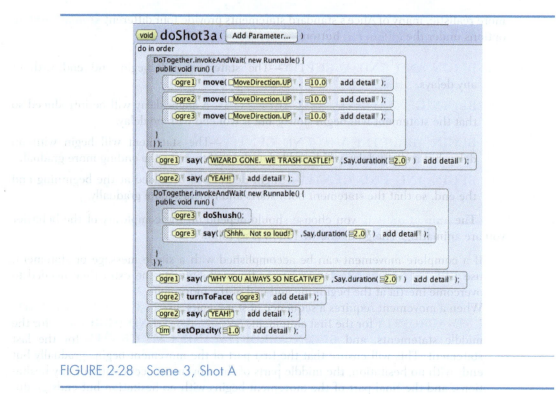

FIGURE 2-28 Scene 3, Shot A

Now, when we run **doScene3()** and it runs **doShot3a()**, the **doShush()** method that we defined in Figure 2-27 will be invoked, and we can test it to make sure that it produces the behaviors we desire. It takes a bit of trial and error to make the fingers turn in the correct directions and with the right amounts, but when we are done, we will have a reasonable-looking "shushing" gesture.

Note also that to make Tim materialize at the end of the shot, we set his Opacity property to 1.0, using the **setOpacity()** method. Recall that we had set his Opacity to 0.0 near the beginning of Scene 3 (see Figure 2-23) to make him initially invisible. By default, the duration of this method is 1 second; we can make him appear slower or faster by changing that message's add detail > duration.

The approach we have used here to create the "shushing" behavior illustrates an important idea in computing, called **abstraction**. The idea is that whenever we want to do something complicated, such as have one of our ogres make a shushing gesture, we create a new method to perform that behavior. By doing so, we hide that complexity inside the method; invoking the new method gives us an easy way to produce that complex behavior.

Another thing to remember is that when we animate the behavior of a single object, that animation should be defined as a class method.

Methods that affect the behavior of a *single object* should be defined as class methods in that object's class.

A final thing to realize is that because we defined the `doShush()` method in class `Ogre`, and because each of our three ogres is an instance of this class, we could now send the `doShush()` message to *any* of our three ogres.

> A class method defines a message that can be sent to any instance (object) of that class.

It is for this reason that we did not put the `say("Shhhh. Not so loud!")` message inside the `doShush()` method. Keeping the gesture separate from what the ogre says allows us to have different ogres make this gesture and say different things, making it more generally useful.

2.3.3 Building Scene 3, Shot B

We might write our user story for Shot 3b as follows:

> Shot 3b: Zoom in: a half-body shot of the wizard. He says,
> "Begone, ogres, or you'll be sorry!"

To begin this shot, we can use the controls in the scene viewer to manually position the camera where we want it to go. Also with these controls, we can zoom in and use the Rule of Thirds until we get a nice half-body shot of Tim, leaving space above his head for his dialog-balloon to appear, as shown in Figure 2-29.

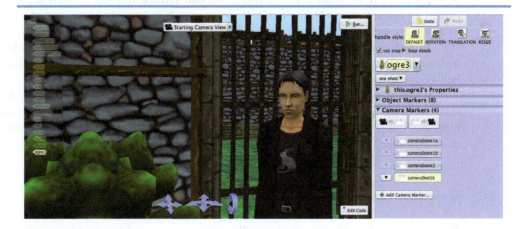

FIGURE 2-29 A half-body shot of the wizard

When we have the camera just where we want it, we again use the Add Camera Marker... button to drop a marker at the camera's current position. Because this is for Shot 3b, we name the marker `cameraShot3b`, as shown in Figure 2-29.

Thinking ahead, the third shot in Scene 3 is from the camera's original position, so we can reuse the **cameraScene1b** marker for that shot and avoid creating another marker.

Now that we have a marker for the second shot in the scene, we can turn our attention to programming the animation for that shot. Following our user story, this shot is simple to animate. Figure 2-30 shows one way to do it.

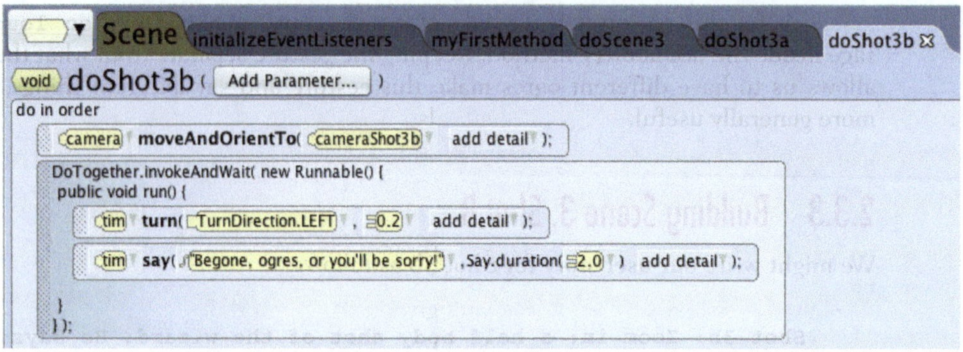

FIGURE 2-30   The `doShot3b()` method

By default, the duration of the **moveAndOrientTo()** method is 1 second, so the **camera** will take a full second to zoom in from the wide angle shot to the half-body shot of the wizard. If we want a faster zoom, we can reduce the duration (e.g., 0 seconds causes an instantaneous "jump cut"). If we want a slower zoom, we can set the duration to 2 or more seconds.

To test our work, we click the Run button. The first shot in Scene 3 is from the wide-angle view, and we see the ogres appear and speak. The camera then zooms in to the half-body view of Tim that is shown in Figure 2-29, and we see his dialog.

We have now seen one class method and several scene or shot methods. Building class methods is very common in object-oriented programming, so let's save our running example now, take a break from it for a while, and practice building some other class methods.

2.4   More Class Methods

To practice creating class methods, we'll open up a new world and add a couple of people to it from class **Biped classes** > **Adult**, one male and one female. We'll call them Alex and Bess; we will also add an object from class **Biped classes** > **StuffedTiger** named Hobbes. We'll outfit our humans in exercise clothing, as shown in Figure 2-31.

FIGURE 2-31 Setting the stage for class methods

2.4.1 Example 1: Bowing

In some cultures, people greet one another by bowing. The actors in a play and the musicians in a concert often bow at the end of the performance. Martial artists bow to one another at the beginning and end of a match. A king or queen's subjects bow to their sovereign. Because it is a fairly simple behavior and can be used in a variety of ways, we will build a **bow()** method that will cause any of our three characters to bow.

Suppose that Scene 1 of our user story begins with Alex bowing to Hobbes, then Hobbes bows back, and finally Bess bows to the camera. The idea is to build a method so that we can achieve this behavior by performing the following statements:

```
alex.bow();
hobbes.bow();
bess.bow();
```

Because these messages are being sent to objects, we need to define **bow()** as a class method.

As before, we begin creating a class method by going to the class navigator, which lists the classes **Scene**, **Biped**, **Person**, **AdultPerson**, and **StuffedTiger**, as shown in Figure 2-32.

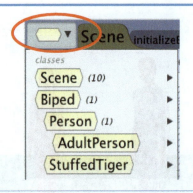

FIGURE 2-32   Using the class navigator

The question is: Which of these classes should we choose?

If we define our **bow()** method within class **Person** or **AdultPerson**, then we will be unable to send the **bow()** message to Hobbes because Hobbes is not a person. (Sorry, Hobbes!) Likewise, if we define our **bow()** method within class **StuffedTiger**, then we will be unable to send the message to Alex or Bess.

That leaves class **Biped**. Because **Person** and **StuffedTiger** are both specialized kinds of bipeds, classes **Person** and **StuffedTiger** inherit any methods, functions, or properties that are defined in class **Biped**. That means that if we define **bow()** in class **Biped**, then we will be able to send the **bow()** message to any object from class **Person**, **Alien**, **BigBadWolf**, ..., **StuffedTiger**, **Tortoise**, or **WhiteRabbit**.

In computing terminology, **Person**, **Alien**, ..., **WhiteRabbit** are **subclasses** of class **Biped**, and **Biped** is the **superclass** of **Person**, **Alien**, ..., **WhiteRabbit**. In the same way, class **Person** is the superclass of class **AdultPerson**, and **AdultPerson** is the subclass of **Person**, because it is a specialized kind of person. These relationships are often depicted using a hierarchical **class structure diagram**, as shown in Figure 2-33.

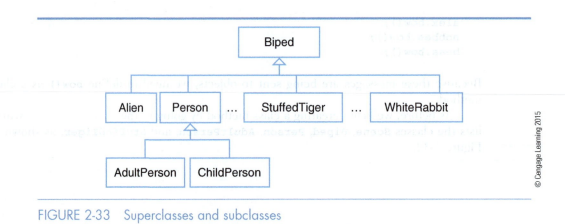

FIGURE 2-33   Superclasses and subclasses

The arrows in this diagram indicate the "is a special kind of" relationship, but don't worry too much about that. The key thing to understand at this point is that if we define the **bow()** method in class **Biped**, all the subclasses of **Biped** will inherit the method, allowing us to send a **bow()** message to objects from any of those classes.

We therefore choose class **Biped** from the class navigator, click the Add Scene Procedure... button, enter the name **bow** in the dialog box that appears, and click its OK button. Alice then creates a new blank method named **bow()**, to which we can add the statements to perform the "bowing" animation. Figure 2-34 shows one way to do this

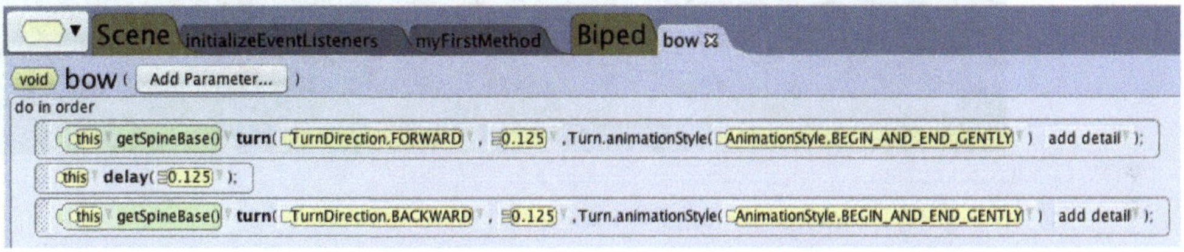

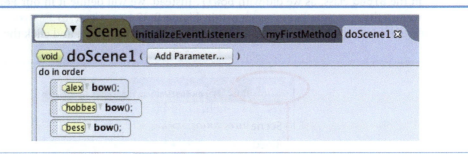

FIGURE 2-34   Animating a bow

Producing the "downward" part of the bow only required a single statement, so just one statement is needed to "undo" that behavior. Although we could have used the **straightenOutJoints()** method here (as we did in Figure 2-27), it is less advantageous when only a single statement has to be "undone."

To test our work, we can send **bow()** messages to our three objects inside a **doScene1()** method, as shown in Figure 2-35.

FIGURE 2-35   Testing our bow() method

With our test written, we can then invoke **doScene1()** in **myFirstMethod()** and then run our program to verify that the animation produces the correct behavior. Figure 2-36 shows the middle part of the animation.

FIGURE 2-36   Hobbes bowing to Alex

2.4.2   Example 2: Signalling "OK"

The **bow()** method in Figure 2-34 is pretty simple, but not all behaviors are this simple to animate. As an example, suppose that after doing some exercises in Scene 2, we want Scene 3 to have Bess ask, "Is everyone OK?" to which Hobbes replies, "I'm OK," and then Alex signals that he's okay using a hand gesture. Our task is create a **signalOK()** method that animates the "OK" hand gesture.

As can be seen in Figure 2-36, only our human models actually have fingers. As a result, if we refer back to Figure 2-33, it does not make sense to define the **signalOK()** method in the **Biped** class, as we did with **bow()**. Instead, we will define it in our **Person** class, so we use the class navigator as shown in Figure 2-37 to navigate to Person > Add Person Procedure…, enter **signalOK** as the name of the new method, and click the OK button.

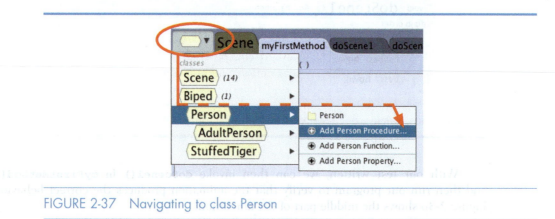

FIGURE 2-37   Navigating to class Person

As before, this will create a new empty method named **signalOK()** in which we can create the desired animation. If you begin with your right arm at your side and make the "OK" gesture with your right hand, you will see that:

- Your shoulder turns to its left slightly.
- Your elbow turns to its left about a third of a rotation.
- Your wrist rotates to the left a bit.
- Your index finger curls downward: the base joint turns forward slightly, while your middle joint turns forward about a third of a rotation.
- Your base and middle of the thumb move and rotate until the tips of your thumb and your index finger are touching.

All of these happen at the same time, making this a much more complex animation than bowing!

Since all of these must happen simultaneously, we might start by dragging a **DoTogether** block into our **signalOK()** method. Then we can proceed by selecting our person's right shoulder joint in the object selector, as shown in Figure 2-38.

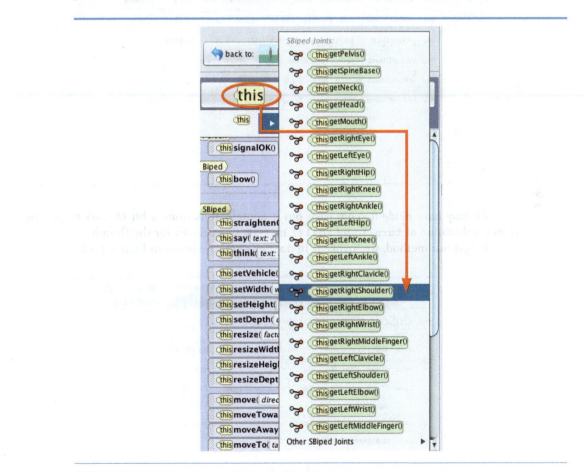

FIGURE 2-38   Accessing a Person's shoulder joint

With the right shoulder joint selected, we can drag a `turn()` message into our **signalOK()** method. We then do the same thing with the right elbow, the right wrist, the right index finger and its knuckle, and the right thumb and its knuckle. Figure 2-39 shows the completed method.

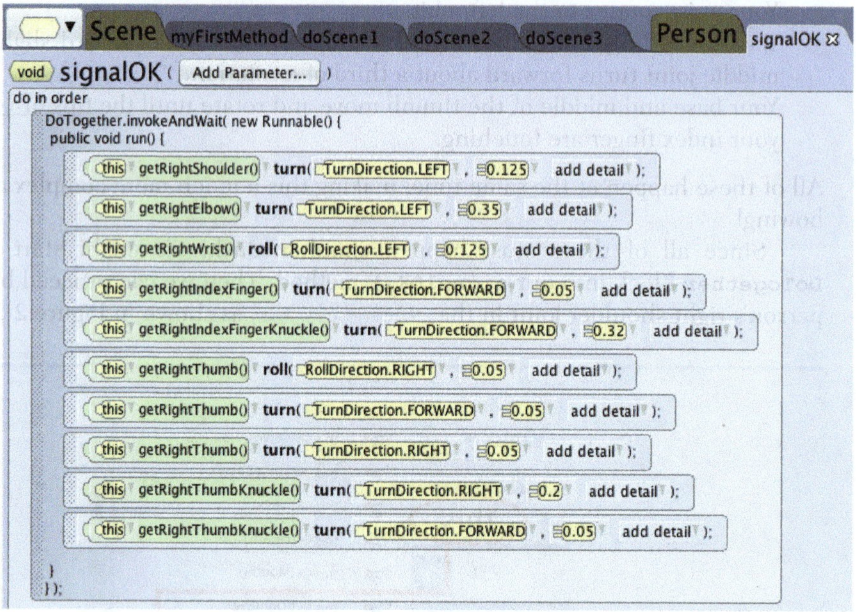

FIGURE 2-39   Signalling "OK"

We may have made it seem easy, but it actually took quite a bit of work to get the right combination of `turn()` and `roll()` messages, especially for the thumb.

To test our method, we invoke it in **doScene3()**, as shown in Figure 2-40.

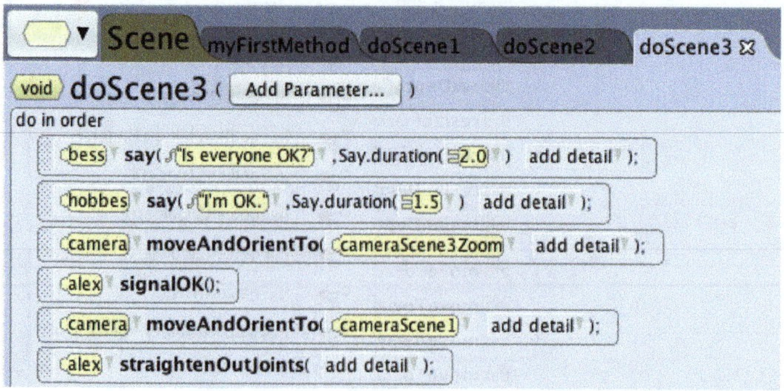

FIGURE 2-40   Invoking the `signalOK()` method

Note that we have added two markers for the camera: one for its original position and one that lets us zoom in on Alex when he makes the gesture. This method gives us a better view of Alex's hand when he makes the gesture, so that we can verify that we are animating his joints correctly.

Note also that we "undo" the OK gesture in **doScene3()**, rather than in the **signalOK()** method, because it leaves open the possibility of taking an action while Alex is still making the gesture. In this case, we are "unzooming" the camera; we might alternatively have Alex say, "Whew! I'm out of shape!" before we straighten out his joints.

Figure 2-41 shows the result of our work.

FIGURE 2-41   Alex making the OK gesture

Even seemingly simple movements can be complicated to animate. In the next chapter, we will see some other examples that are complicated. We will be reusing this example there, so be sure to save it before continuing.

2.5   Alice Tip: Reusing Your Work

Software developers like to say *work smarter, not harder*. One way to work smarter is to invest time in designing your algorithms. For example, by working out the steps and identifying the joints that move in making an "OK" gesture, actually building the **signalOK()** method took much less time than if we had just tried to code it.

Another way to work smarter is to *reuse work* that you've already done. The idea is that if you find yourself repeating actions that you have done previously, you can reuse what you did earlier by copying it and adapting the copy to the new situation. In the rest of this section, we examine two ways to reuse existing work.

2.5.1   Using the Clipboard

The clipboard icon located in the upper-right corner of the Alice window provides a way to work smarter in some situations. If you drag a statement from the editing area to the clipboard, Alice *cuts* that statement from the editing area. If you hold down the **Option** key (**Alt** on Windows) and drag a statement from the editing area to the clipboard, Alice *copies* that statement to the clipboard, leaving it intact in the editing area. You can accomplish the same copying action by right-clicking the statement and choosing Copy to Clipboard from the context menu that appears. Regardless of which way you do it, this copy operation can often be used to speed up program development.

Saving Yourself Time: Similar Operations

The clipboard can often be used to save yourself time when two algorithm steps or messages are similar. To illustrate, the **DoTogether** statements that we need to make the three ogres move down underground at the end of Scene 2 (see Figure 2-20) and to make them move up aboveground at the beginning of Shot 3a (see Figure 2-28) are very similar; they differ only in the directions they make the three ogres move. Rather than construct the **DoTogether** statement in Shot 3a the normal (time-consuming) way, we instead right-clicked that statement from Scene 2 and copied it to the clipboard, as shown in Figure 2-42.

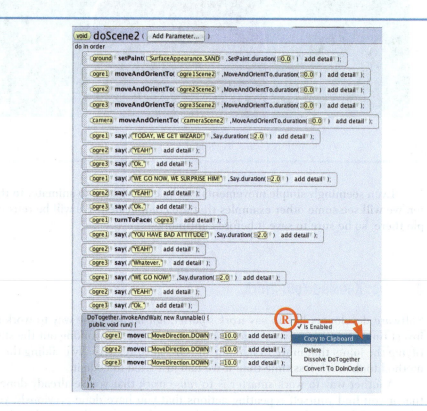

FIGURE 2-42   Right-clicking to copy a statement to the **clipboard**

When we select this choice, the clipboard turns from brown to white, indicating that a copy of the statement is now on the clipboard. We can then drag that statement from the clipboard back into the doShot3a() method definition, as shown in Figure 2-43.

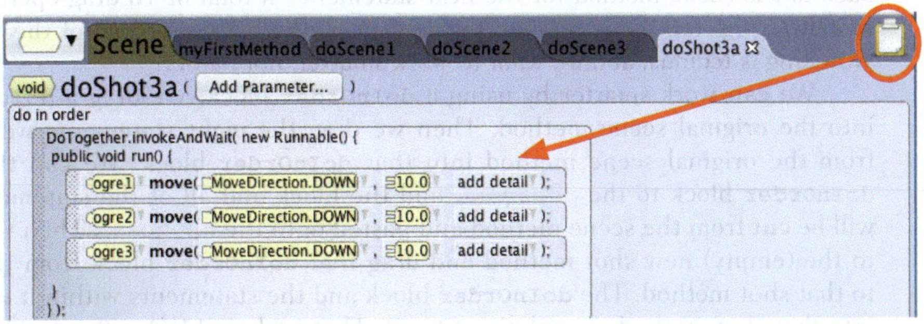

FIGURE 2-43   Dragging a statement from the clipboard to the editing area

To adapt these statements for Shot 3a (as shown in Figure 2-28), we just have to reverse the directions in the three move() messages (i.e., change each MoveDirection.Down to MoveDirection.UP). This takes much less time than dragging and building the statements one by one from the methods area.

In the same way, to create the second and third bow() messages in Figure 2-35, we copied the first bow() message to the clipboard, dragged the copy from the clipboard back into myFirstMethod(), and changed the recipient of the message from alex to hobbes. Then we repeated these steps to form the bow() message to bess. This was much faster and easier than building those two statements the usual way.

Taking the time to design an algorithm for each scene or shot will help you recognize these kinds of patterns or similarities, which will in turn save you time. If you find yourself redoing the same work more than once, there is usually a better way. Work smarter, not harder!

Dividing a Big Method into Smaller Methods

The clipboard can also be used to divide a too-large method into smaller methods. To illustrate, suppose you are building a scene method and are unable to view the entire method at once. Rather than waste time scrolling back and forth, you decide to break the scene method among two or more shot methods.

To split a scene method into two or more shot methods takes three steps:

1. Create the new (empty) shot methods.

2. Move statements from the scene method into those shot methods.

3. Invoke the shot methods in the scene method.

Steps 1 and 3 are straightforward, but Step 2 is new, so let's focus on it. To make this a bit more concrete, suppose we want to shift eight statements from a scene method to a shot method. We could do so one at a time: For each of the eight statements, we could drag (cut) the statement from the scene method to the clipboard, switch to the shot method, then drag the statement from the clipboard to the shot method, and then switch back to the scene method for the next statement—a total of 16 drag operations and 16 switches from the scene method to the shot method. However, all of this dragging and switching is tedious, and we want to work smarter, not harder!

We can work smarter by using a `doInOrder` block: We drag a `doInOrder` block into the original scene method. Then we drag the eight statements we want to cut from the original scene method into that `doInOrder` block. We can then drag the `doInOrder` block to the clipboard, and the block and all of the statements within it will be cut from the scene method and pasted onto the clipboard. Then we can switch to the (empty) new shot method and drag that `doInOrder` block from the clipboard to that shot method. The `doInOrder` block and the statements within it will be pasted into that shot method, completing Step 2. That took us 11 (1 + 8 + 1 + 1) drag operations and 1 scene-to-shot switch—five fewer drag operations and 15 fewer scene-to-shot switches!

When we complete Step 3, we will have reduced the number of statements in that scene method significantly. Shorter methods are easier to debug, so keeping your methods short is yet another way to work smarter, not harder!

2.6   Thinking in 3D

Most of us are not used to thinking carefully about the rules for moving around in a three-dimensional world any more than we're used to thinking carefully about grammar rules when we speak our native languages. However, to use Alice well and understand the effects of some of its methods, we do need to think about how objects move around in a 3D world, which is what the rest of this chapter is about.

Every object in a 3D world has the following two properties:

1. Position—An object's position determines its *location* within the 3D world.

2. Orientation—An object's orientation determines *the way it is facing* in the 3D world—that is, what is in front of and behind the object, what is to its left and right, and what is above and below it.

In the rest of this section, we will explore these two properties in detail.

2.6.1   An Object's Position

Imagine that you are the dolphin shown in Figure 2-44.

FIGURE 2-44 A dolphin

As you swim, you can move along any of the arrows shown in Figure 2-45.

FIGURE 2-45 The dolphin and 3D axes

You can make these arrows appear by clicking on an object in the scene viewer.

Each of these arrows (red [RIGHT-LEFT], green [UP-DOWN], and white+blue [FORWARD-BACKWARD]) is called an **axis**. Two or more of these arrows are called *axes*. Every Alice object has its own three axes, and the point where they meet is called the object's *pivot point*. For example, from a "downward-looking" angle, we might imagine the three axes of our three-dimensional world as shown in Figure 2-46.

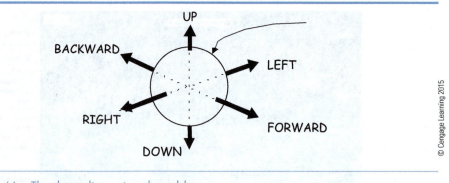

FIGURE 2-46   The three-dimensional world

Once we create a world and start adding objects to it, every object is located somewhere within that 3D world. An object's exact location with respect to the world's axes is called its **position**, a property we can access in the scene viewer, as can be seen in Figure 2-44.

To illustrate, the dolphin's x-position determines its location along the world's LEFT-RIGHT axis, its y-position determines its location along the world's UP-DOWN axis, and its z-position determines its location along the world's FORWARD-BACKWARD axis. We will call these three axes the *LR*, *UD*, and *FB axes*, respectively.

An object's position within a three-dimensional world thus consists of three numeric values—*lr*, *ud*, and *fb*—that specify its location measured using the world's three axes.[8]

Changing Position

To change an object's position, Alice provides the **move()** method (see Appendix A). When we drop Alice's **move()** method into the editing area, Alice displays a menu of the directions the object may move, shown in Figure 2-47.

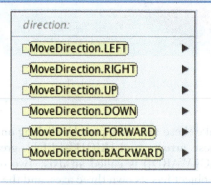

FIGURE 2-47   The directions an object may move

---

[8]These axes are usually called the X, Y, and Z axes, but we'll use the more descriptive LR, UD, and FB.

If you compare Figures 2-45 and 2-47, you'll see that Alice's **move()** message allows an object to move along any of that object's three axes:

1. Moving **LEFT** or **RIGHT** changes the object's location along its LR (red) axis.

2. Moving **UP** or **DOWN** changes the object's location along its UD (green) axis.

3. Moving **FORWARD** or **BACKWARD** changes its location along its FB (white-blue) axis.

Alice's **move()** message thus changes the *position* of the object to which the message is sent with respect to the world's axes, but the directional values that we specify for the movement (**LEFT**, **RIGHT**, **UP**, **DOWN**, **FORWARD**, and **BACKWARD**) are given with respect to *that object's axes*, not the world's axes.

2.6.2   An Object's Orientation

When an object moves, turns, or rolls, its axes move, turn, or roll with it. For example, if we send the dolphin of Figure 2-45 the message **turn(RIGHT, 0.25)** and then click the dolphin, the picture changes to that shown in Figure 2-48.

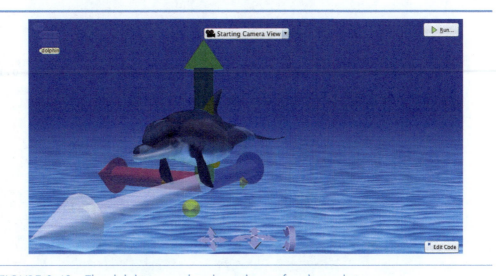

FIGURE 2-48   The dolphin turned to the right one-fourth revolution

If we now send the turned dolphin a message to **move(FORWARD, *someDistance*)**, the dolphin will move forward according to the new direction in which its FB axis points.

Yaw

If you compare the axes in Figure 2-45 and Figure 2-48 carefully, you'll see that a **turn(RIGHT, 0.25)** message causes the dolphin to *rotate* about its UD axis. A **turn(LEFT, 0.25)** message causes a rotation about the same axis, but in the opposite direction. If we were to position ourselves "above" the dolphin's green UD axis and look down, we might visualize the effects of **turn()** messages as shown in Figure 2-49.

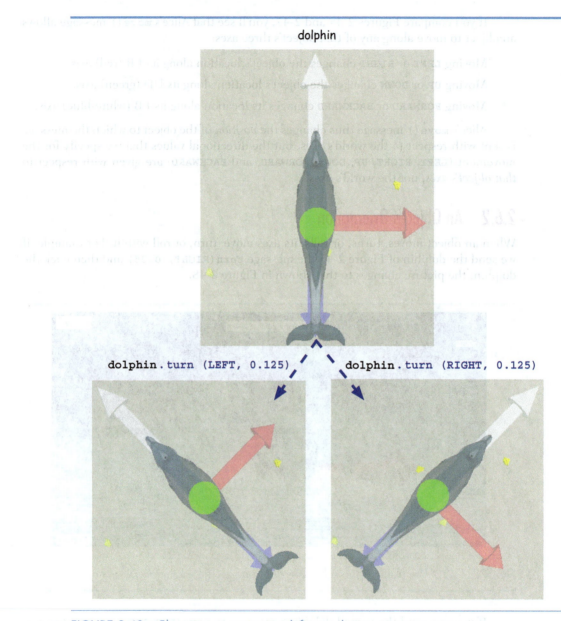

dolphin

dolphin.turn (LEFT, 0.125)   dolphin.turn (RIGHT, 0.125)

FIGURE 2-49   Changing yaw: turning left or right

In 3D terminology, an object's **yaw** is how much it has rotated about its UD axis from its original position. For example, when you shake your head "no," you are changing your head's yaw. Alice's **turn(LEFT, *someDistance*)** and **turn(RIGHT, *someDistance*)** messages change an object's yaw.

Pitch

We just saw that an object's yaw changes when it rotates around its UD axis. Because an object has three axes, it should be evident that we could also rotate an object around either of its other two axes. For example, if we wanted to orient the dolphin to dive toward the seabed, we could send it a **turn(FORWARD,** *someDistance***)** message; if we wanted it to climb toward the surface, we could send it a **turn(BACKWARD,** *someDistance***)** message. These messages cause an object to rotate about its LR axis, as shown in Figure 2-50.

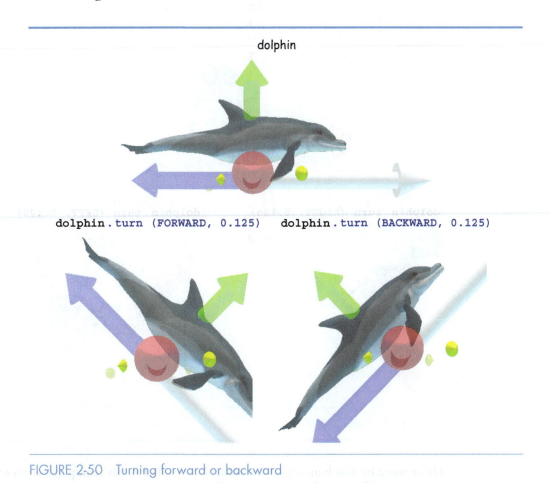

dolphin

dolphin.turn (FORWARD, 0.125)   **dolphin.turn (BACKWARD, 0.125)**

FIGURE 2-50 Turning forward or backward

An object's **pitch** is how much it has rotated about its LR axis from its original position. For example, when you shake your head "yes," you change your head's pitch. In Alice, a **turn(FORWARD,** *someDistance***)** or **turn(BACKWARD,** *someDistance***)** message changes an object's pitch.

Roll

An object can also rotate around its FB axis. For example, if we were to view the dolphin head-on and send it the `roll(RIGHT, 0.125)` or `roll(LEFT, 0.125)` message, it would rotate as shown in Figure 2-51.

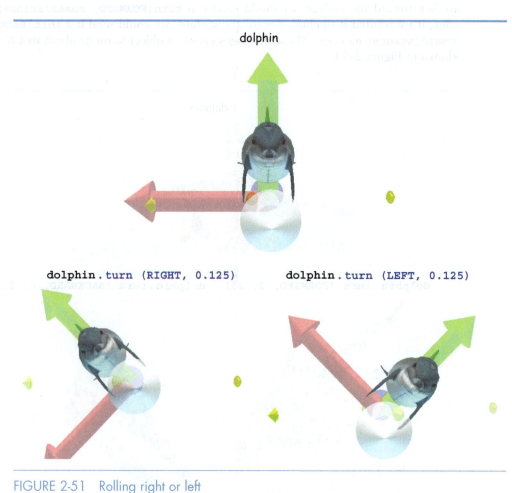

FIGURE 2-51   Rolling right or left

The amount by which an object has rotated about its FB axis (compared to its original position) is called the object's **roll**. In Alice, the `roll(LEFT, someDistance)` and `roll(RIGHT, someDistance)` messages change an object's roll.

An object's orientation is its combined yaw, pitch, and roll.

Just as an object's *position* has three numeric parts (*lr*, *ud*, and *fb*), an object's *orientation* has three numeric parts: yaw, pitch, and roll. An object's *position* determines where in the world that object is located; its *orientation* determines the direction the object is facing.

All of this matters because not only does each Alice object have its three axes, each *joint* in an Alice object has three axes, and the axes' orientations are generally different from the orientation of the object itself. For example, a **Person** has two shoulder joints, and the axes of each shoulder are oriented differently; each shoulder's blue BACKWARD axis points up, but the two shoulders' green UP axes point in opposite directions from one another, toward the person's sides. You can examine this by clicking the Show Joints checkbox in the scene editor and decreasing an object's Opacity property, as shown in Figure 2-52.

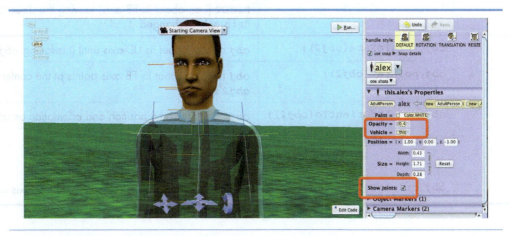

FIGURE 2-52   Viewing joint orientations

This difference in orientation is the reason that, in Figure 2-39, we sent Alex's right shoulder the **turn(LEFT)** message. Because that joint's FORWARD axis points in the same direction as Alex's DOWN axis, telling it to rotate **LEFT** from its perspective will make it rotate **FORWARD** from Alex's perspective.

2.6.3 Point of View

In Alice, an object's combined position and orientation is called that object's **point of view**. An object's point of view thus consists of six values: [(*lr*, *ud*, *fb*), (yaw, pitch, roll)]. Alice's **move()**, **turn()**, and **roll()** messages let you change any of these six values for an object, giving Alice objects *six degrees of freedom*.[9] Alice's **moveAndOrientTo()** message (see Appendix A) lets you set an object's point of view. The following table summarizes the information in this section.

---

[9]The phrase "six degrees of separation," which claims that any two living people are connected by a chain of six or fewer acquaintances, is derived from the phrase "six degrees of freedom." The "Six Degrees of Kevin Bacon" game, which is based on the idea that the actor Kevin Bacon and any other actor are linked by a chain of six or fewer film co-stars, is further derived from "six degrees of separation." See *www.cs.virginia.edu/oracle*.

Method	Behavior Produced
obj.move(*dir*,*dist*);	*obj* moves *dist* meters in direction *dir* = UP, DOWN, LEFT, RIGHT, FORWARD, or BACKWARD
obj.turn(*dir*,*revs*);	*obj* turns *revs* revolutions in direction LEFT, RIGHT, FORWARD, or BACKWARD (i.e., about its UD or LR axis) changing the direction its FB axis is pointing
obj.roll(*dir*,*revs*);	*obj* rotates *revs* revolutions in direction LEFT or RIGHT (i.e., about its FB axis) leaving the direction of its FB axis unchanged
obj.turnToFace(*obj2*);	*obj* rotates about its UD-axis until it is facing *obj2*
obj.pointAt(*obj2*);	*obj* rotates so that its FB axis points at the center of *obj2*'s axes
obj.moveAndOrientTo(*obj2*);	*obj* takes the same *position* and *orientation* as *obj2*
obj.orientTo(*obj2*);	*obj*'s *orientation* becomes that of *obj2* (*obj*'s *position* remains unchanged)
obj.orientToUpright();	*obj*'s *orientation* is changed so that its UD axis is perpendicular to the ground

2.7   Chapter Summary

❏ Scene and shot methods let us organize an Alice program by its scenes and shots.

❏ The approach can simplify problem solving.

❏ Class methods let us define new behaviors for an object.

❏ Subclasses inherit the methods and properties of their superclass.

❏ Camera and object movements can be simplified using markers and the moveAndOrientTo() message.

❏ In a 3D world, an object's position determines where the object is located in the world; its orientation is the object's combined yaw, pitch, and roll; and its point of view is its combined position and orientation.

2.7.1   Key Terms

abstraction

axis

class method

class structure diagram

comment

Divide and Conquer

framework

inherit

markers

orientation

pitch

point of view

position

roll

scene

scene method

shot

shot method

subclass

superclass

yaw

Programming Projects

2.1   Revisit the programs you wrote for Chapter 1. If any of them require scrolling to view all their statements, rewrite them using Divide and Conquer and scene or shot methods; remember, these statements can be viewed without scrolling.

2.2   The director Sergio Leone was famous for the extreme closeups he used of gunfighters' eyes in the showdown of "spaghetti western" movies like *For a Fistful of Dollars, The Good, the Bad, and the Ugly*, and *Once Upon a Time in the West*. Watch the "showdown" scene from one of these films (search YouTube for the film's title plus "showdown"). Then write a **doShot3b()** method for our running example, using Leone's camera techniques to heighten the drama of Tim's confrontation with the ogres.

2.3   Build an undersea world that contains a clownfish and a shark. Build a **swim()** method that makes each kind of fish swim forward 1 meter in a more or less realistic fashion. Build a program containing a scene in which a shark chases the clownfish and the clownfish swims to its giant cousin, a clownfish, which chases the shark away.

2.4   Choose a hopping animal from the Alice Gallery (e.g., a frog or a bunny). Write a **hop()** method that makes it hop in a realistic fashion. Add a building to your world, then write a program that uses your **hop()** method to make the animal hop around the building. Write your program using Divide and Conquer so that **myFirstMethod()** contains a minimal number of statements.

2.5   Build a world containing a flying vehicle (e.g., a helicopter). Build a class method named **loopDeeLoop()** that makes your flying vehicle move in a vertical loop. Then write a program that uses **loopDeeLoop()** to make your flying vehicle loop through the air.

2.6 *Boom, Boom, Ain't It Great to Be Crazy* is a silly song with the lyrics given below. Create an Alice program containing a character who sings this song. Use Divide and Conquer to write your program as efficiently as possible.

Verse 1. A horse and a flea and three blind mice sat on a curbstone shooting dice. The horse he slipped and fell on the flea. "Whoops," said the flea, "there's a horse on me." Boom, boom, ain't it great to be crazy? Boom, boom, ain't it great to be crazy? Giddy and foolish, the whole day through, boom, boom, ain't it great to be crazy?	Verse 2. Way down south where bananas grow, a flea stepped on an elephant's toe. The elephant cried, with tears in his eyes, "Why don't you pick on someone your size?" Boom, boom, ain't it great to be crazy? Boom, boom, ain't it great to be crazy? Giddy and foolish, the whole day through, boom, boom, ain't it great to be crazy?
Verse 3. Way up north where there's ice and snow, there lived a penguin whose name was Joe. He got so tired of black and white, he wore pink pants to the dance last night. Boom, boom, ain't it great to be crazy? Boom, boom, ain't it great to be crazy? Giddy and foolish, the whole day through, boom, boom, ain't it great to be crazy?	

© Cengage Learning 2015

2.7 Using appropriately colored **Shapes** from the Alice **Gallery**, build a checker board. Then choose an object or shape from the **Gallery** to serve as a checker. Build class methods named **moveLeft()**, **moveRight()**, **jumpLeft()**, and **jumpRight()** for the character. Then make copies of the object for the remaining checkers. Build a program that simulates the opening moves of a game of checkers, using your board and checkers.

2.8 Using any of the other persons with enough detail in the Alice **Gallery**, build a world containing a person. Using that person, build an aerobic exercise video in which the person leads the user through an exercise routine. Use scene and/or class methods in your program, as appropriate.

2.9 Using class **Wolf**, **Dalmation**, or a different dog class build a method that makes a dog wag its tail realistically. Then create a scene in which a person comes home and her dog greets her by barking and wagging its tail.

2.10 Write an original story consisting of at least two characters, three scenes, and markers to position your characters in the different scenes. Each scene should have multiple shots. Use scene and class methods to create your story efficiently.

Chapter 3
Variables and Expressions

*T*he first step towards wisdom is calling things by their right names.

OLD CHINESE PROVERB

*F*iguratively speaking, killing two birds with one stone may be good, but killing three, four, or even more birds with one stone is even better.

V. OREHCK III

*S*top! Who would cross the Bridge of Death must answer me these questions three, ere the other side he see.

THE BRIDGEKEEPER (TERRY GILLIAM), IN *MONTY PYTHON AND THE HOLY GRAIL*

Objectives

Upon completion of this chapter, you should be able to:

❑ Use variables to store values that can be used later in a method

❑ Use a variable to store the value of an arithmetic expression

❑ Use a variable to store the value produced by a function

❑ Use parameters to write methods that are more broadly useful

❑ Define and access property variables

❑ Use the `vehicle` property to synchronize the movements of two objects

❑ Create functions—messages that return a value to their sender

Screenshots from Alice 2 © 1999–2013, Alice 3 © 2008–2013, Carnegie Mellon University. All rights reserved. We gratefully acknowledge the financial support of Oracle, Electronic Arts, Sun Microsystems, DARPA, Intel, NSF, and ONR.

In Chapter 2, we saw how to define scene and class methods. In this chapter, we look at **variables**, which can make it easier to define methods. In computer programming, *a variable is a name that refers to a piece of the program's memory, in which a value can be stored, retrieved, and changed.*

Alice provides three kinds of variables, which we will examine in this chapter. The first kind is the **local variable**, which lets us compute and store a value within a method for later use. Local variables are created using the variable... control at the bottom-right of the editing area.

The second kind of variable is the **parameter**, which lets us write methods that are more broadly useful. Parameters are created using the Add Parameter... button, which is located inside the parentheses of Alice's programmer-defined methods.

The third and final kind of variable is the **instance variable** or **property**, which lets us store a characteristic of an object. Properties are declared in an object's class, so property variables can be created using the Add Property... button at the bottom of a class page, accessed via the class navigator.

In this chapter, we see how to create and use all three kinds of variables.

3.1   Local Variables

Local variables are names defined within a method that refer to program memory in which values can be stored. When we drag and drop the variable... control from the base of the editing area into a method, Alice displays a dialog box in which we can specify the *name* of the variable, the *type* of information we want to store in it, and its initial value. When we have told it these things, Alice reserves as much program memory as is needed for that type of information, associates the **variable name** with that memory, and gives it an initial value. These steps are called **defining a variable**. Local variables can be accessed only from within the method in which they are defined—they are *local* to it— and they must be defined before they are used; otherwise, an error will occur when the statement that uses the variable is performed.

One common use of local variables is to compute and store values that will be used later, especially values that will be used more than once. Another common use is to store values that the user enters. In the rest of this section, we present examples that illustrate these uses.

3.1.1   Example 1: Storing Computed Values

Suppose that in Scene 2 of a story, a young woman named Annie approaches a horse, stops an arm's length away, and reaches out her hand to touch the horse's nose. We might set up this scene by creating and positioning the characters shown in Figure 3-1.

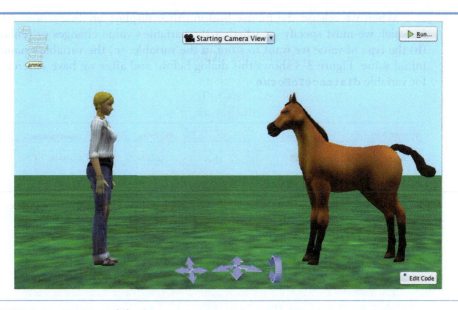

FIGURE 3-1   Annie and the horse

We first create a scene method named **doScene2()** for this scene, and invoke it in **myFirstMethod**. After doing that, we are ready to move Annie toward the horse inside **doScene2()**. We can move Annie by sending her the **move()** message; the question is, how far should we move her? Rather than use trial and error to determine the distance she should be moved, we will have our program compute that distance for us and store that distance in a variable. Then we will pass that variable to the **move()** message for the distance we want Annie to move.

Let's start by creating the variable, which we will call **distanceToHorse**. We can create this variable by dragging the **variable…** control from the bottom of the **editing area** into **doScene2()**, as shown in Figure 3-2.

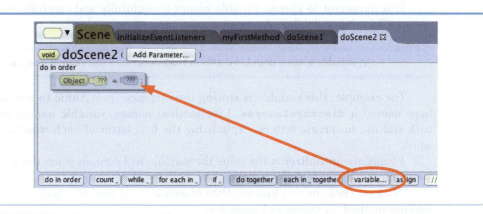

FIGURE 3-2   Creating a variable

When we release the mouse button, Alice displays an Insert Variable dialog box in which we must specify (a) whether the variable's value changes or remains constant, (b) the type of value we want to store in the variable, (c) the variable's name, and (d) its initial value. Figure 3-3 shows this dialog before and after we have entered these values for variable **distanceToHorse**.

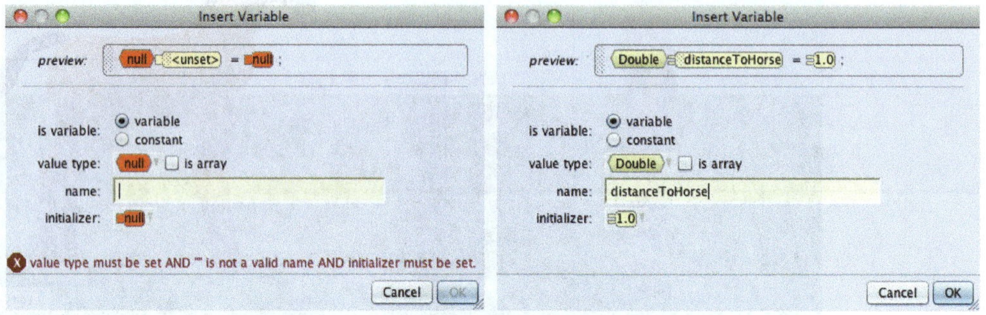

FIGURE 3-3   The **Insert Variable** dialog box, before and after

A variable's **type** describes the kind of value we intend to store in it. Alice provides four basic types:

1. **Double,** for storing decimal numbers (**–1.5**, **0.123**, **3.14159**, and so on)

2. **Integer,** for storing whole numbers (**-3**, **0**, **1**, **42**, and so on)

3. **Boolean,** for storing logical (**true** or **false**) values

4. **String,** for storing sequences of characters (**"hello"**, **"goodbye"**, and so on)

Since the distance we have to move is a decimal number, **Double** is the appropriate type for this variable.

It is important to choose variable names thoughtfully and carefully, because their names affect the readability of your program.

A variable's name should be a noun that describes the value it stores.

For example, this variable is storing the distance from Annie to the horse, so we have named it **distanceToHorse**. Like method names, variable names always begin with and use lowercase letters, capitalizing the first letter of each word after the first word.

Finally, the **initializer** is the value the variable will contain when the method starts. Common initializers include **0.0** and **1.0**.

After we click the OK button, Alice inserts a local variable declaration statement into our method, as shown in Figure 3-4.

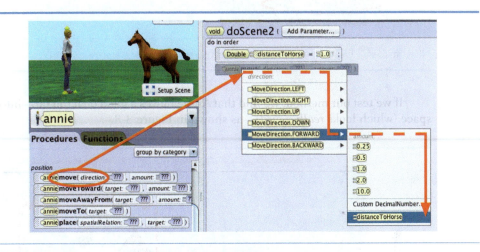

FIGURE 3-4   A local variable declaration statement

Now that we have declared this variable, let's send Annie the **move()** message. As appears in Figure 3-5, the variable **distanceToHorse** now appears as one of the options for how far Annie should move, so we choose it:

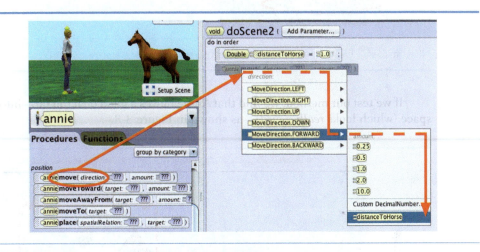

FIGURE 3-5   Choosing a variable when sending a message

When we release the mouse button, Alice completes the **move()** message using the value we have chosen. Figure 3-6 shows the resulting message:

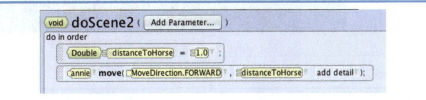

FIGURE 3-6   A message using a variable as an argument

Next, we have to compute the correct value in our **distanceToHorse** variable. After we select **annie** in the object selector, we click the Functions tab, drag the `getDistanceTo()` function on top of the 1.0 initializer in our variable declaration statement, and finally choose **horse** as the argument to the function, as appears in Figure 3-7.

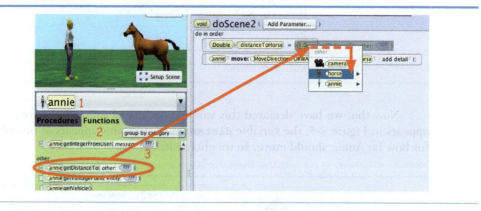

FIGURE 3-7   Using a function to initialize a variable

If we test our method, we find that Annie moves a good deal too far—into the horse's space (which looks *really* weird)—as shown in Figure 3-8.

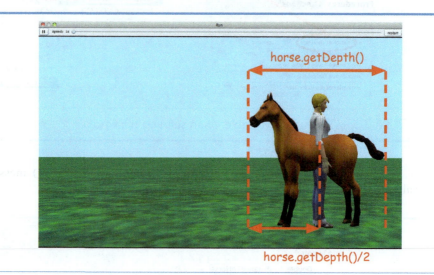

FIGURE 3-8   When Annie moves too far

The problem is that the **distanceTo()** function returns the distance from the *center* of one object to the *center* of the target object. We can fix this by first recognizing that the excess amount Annie has moved is one half the depth of the horse, as we have indicated in Figure 3-8, and then calculating and subtracting that amount from our **distanceToHorse** variable. One way to do this is to compute and store this distance in a new variable, called **halfHorseDepth**. To do so, we first declare the variable above the declaration of **distanceToHorse**, then select **horse** in the object selector, and then drag the **horse.getDepth()** function onto its initializer, producing the variable declaration statement shown in Figure 3-9.

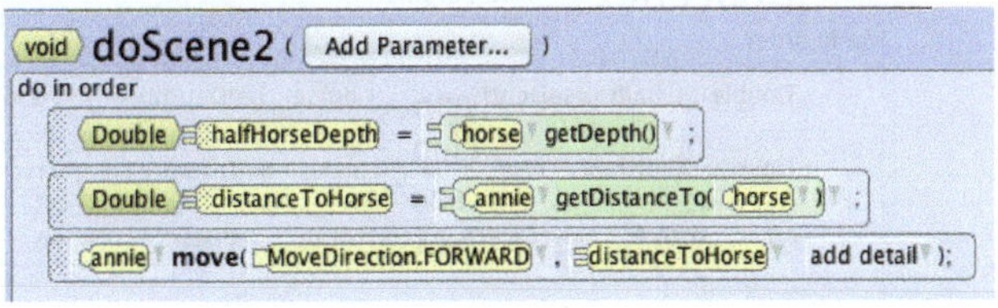

FIGURE 3-9   Declaring **halfHorseDepth**

Then, we click the down-arrow at the right end of the **halfHorseDepth** declaration statement, drag the mouse cursor to the Math menu choice, choose the division operator (/), and finally choose **2.0** as the denominator, as shown in Figure 3-10.

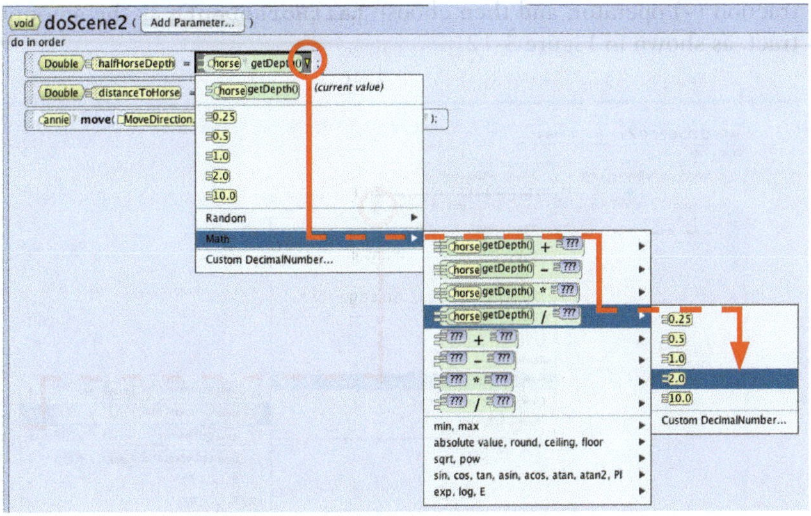

FIGURE 3-10   Dividing **horse.getDepth()** by 2.0

As appears in Figure 3-10, the Math menu choice provides a variety of options, including:

- The arithmetic addition (+), subtraction (-), multiplication (*), and division (/) operations
- Other mathematical functions, including minimum and maximum functions, decimal-to-integer conversion functions, square root and exponentiation functions, trigonometric functions, and logarithmic functions

These allow us to perform calculations that are useful in math and science.

When we release the mouse button, Alice updates our variable declaration statement, as shown in Figure 3-11.

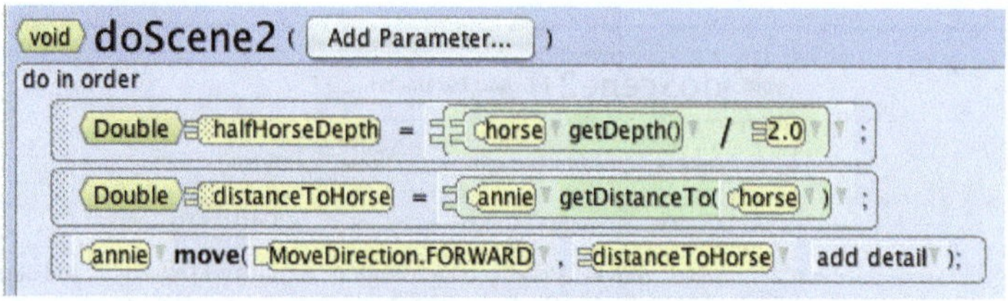

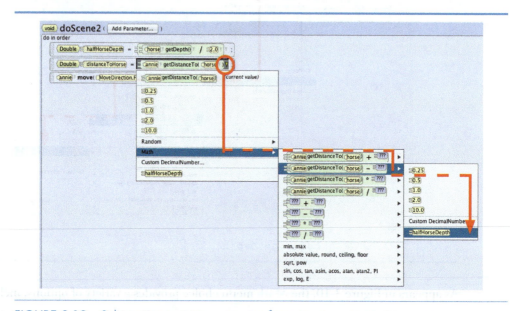

FIGURE 3-11   Updating the declaration of `halfHorseDepth`

When this statement is performed, our **halfHorseDepth** variable will be initialized to one half of the horse's depth.

Next, we want to subtract **halfHorseDepth** from the value we are computing in **distanceToHorse**. To do this, we click the down-arrow at the end of the **distanceToHorse** declaration statement, drag the mouse cursor to the Math menu choice, choose the subtraction (-) operator, and then choose **halfHorseDepth** as the amount we want to subtract, as shown in Figure 3-12.

FIGURE 3-12   Subtracting **halfHorseDepth** from **distanceToHorse**

When we release the mouse button, Alice updates the declaration statement, as shown in Figure 3-13.

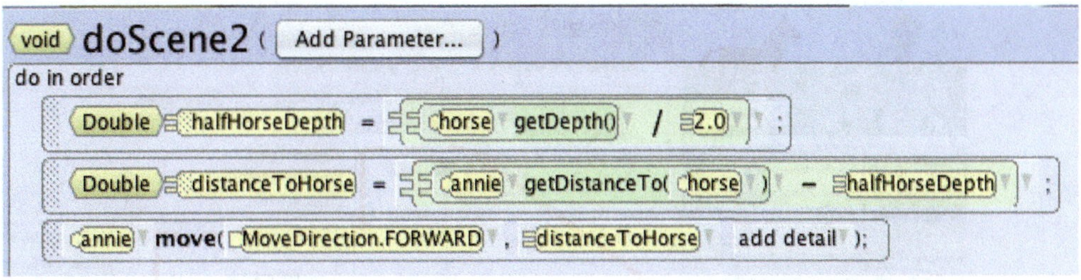

FIGURE 3-13   Correcting `distanceToHorse`

If we test our method at this point, we see that Annie actually moves to the horse, which lets us verify that the value in **distanceToHorse** is very close to correct.[1]

The final thing we need to do to solve the problem is move Annie the distance to the horse minus the length of her arm. To do this, we will compute and store Annie's arm length in a variable named **armLength**, and then pass **distanceToHorse – armLength** as the argument to the **move()** message. We begin by using the **variable . . .** control to declare the **armLength** variable before the **move()** message, as shown in Figure 3-14.

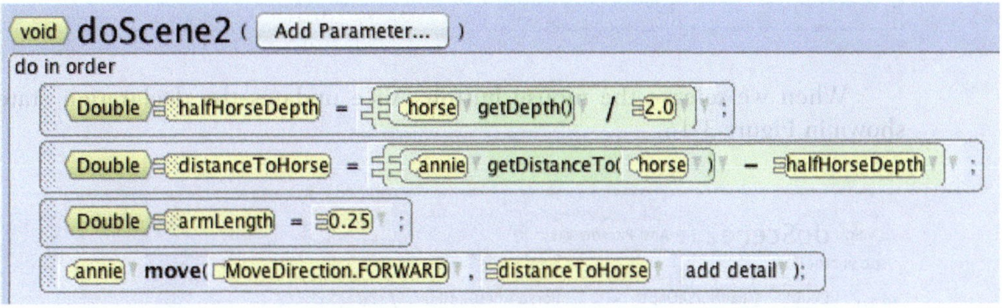

FIGURE 3-14   Declaring `armLength`

We can compute Annie's approximate arm length as the distance from her right shoulder to the knuckle on her right index finger. We therefore choose **annie.getShoulder()** in the object selector, drag the **getDistanceTo()** function onto the **armLength** initializer, and choose **annie.getRightIndexFingerKnuckle()** as the target, as shown in Figure 3-15.

---

[1]Actually, because the **annie.distanceTo(horse)** function returns the distance from Annie's center to the horse's center, the value in **distanceToHorse** is still off by half of Annie's depth. Fixing this is left as an exercise.

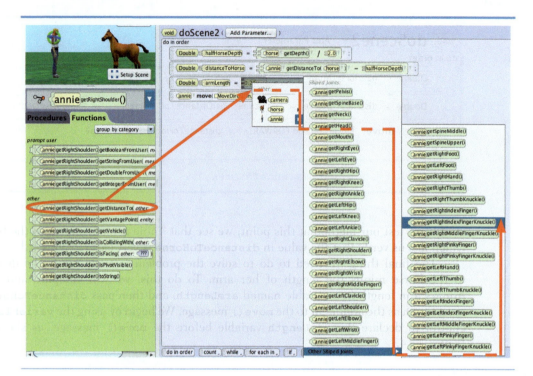

FIGURE 3-15   Calculating the length of Annie's arm

When we release the mouse button, Alice updates the declaration statement, as shown in Figure 3-16.

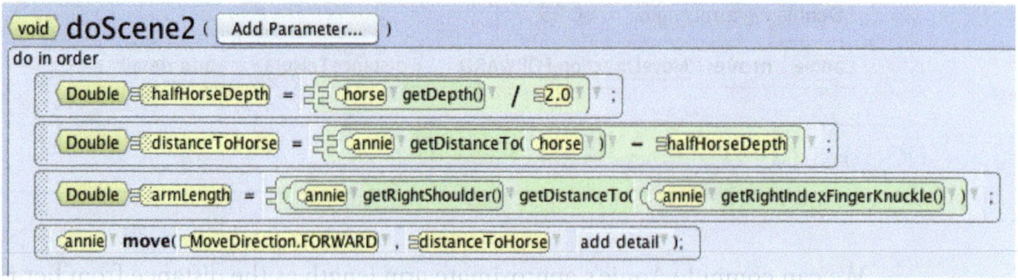

FIGURE 3-16   The updated `armLength` declaration

All that is left to do is subtract the value of **armLength** from **distanceToHorse** within the **move()** message. To do so, we click the down-arrow next to **distanceToHorse** inside the **move()** message, drag the mouse cursor to the Math choice, choose the subtraction operator, and choose **armLength** as the value we wish to subtract, as shown in Figure 3-17.

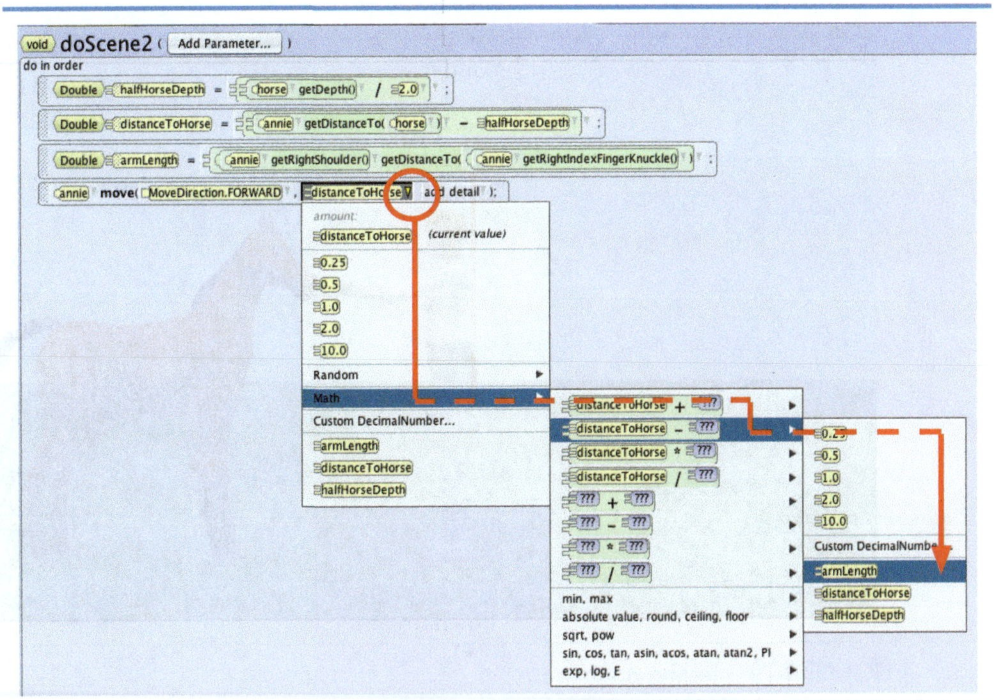

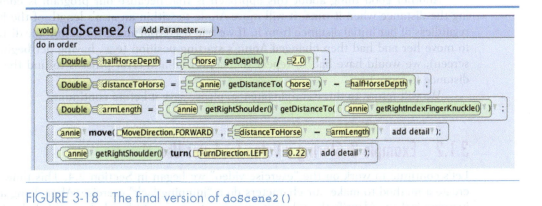

FIGURE 3-17   Altering the distance Annie moves

When we release the mouse button, Alice updates the **move()** message accordingly. If we then add a **turn()** message that moves Annie's hand to the horse's mouth, we get the final version of our scene method, as appears in Figure 3-18.

FIGURE 3-18   The final version of **doScene2()**

We then test our method to check our work, as shown in Figure 3-19.

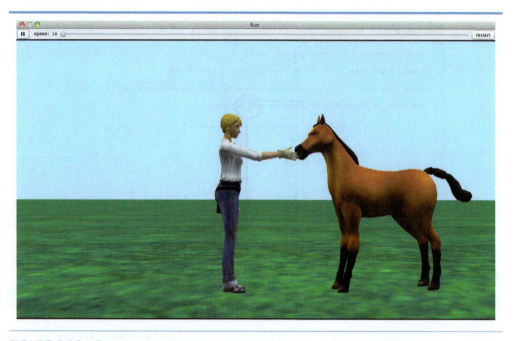

FIGURE 3-19   Testing `doScene2()`

In this example, we have learned how to declare variables, compute and store values in them, and use them in subsequent statements. If we choose descriptive names for our variables, these variable names indicate our program's logic step by step. This produces a program that is much more readable than if we had just used trial and error to find the right distance.

Another good thing about this approach is that because our program is computing the distance when it runs, it will move Annie to within an arm's length of the horse regardless of her initial distance from it. If we had used trial and error to find the distance to move her and had then changed Annie's starting position (e.g., having her begin off-screen), we would have had to repeat the same trial-and-error process to find the new distance to move her.

We will return to this example later, so please save it before continuing.

3.1.2   Example 2: Storing a Value for Later Use

Let's continue to work on the "exercise video" we began in Section 2.4. This time, let's create a method to make our characters do a "jumping jack" exercise. After doing a few jumping jacks to identify the relevant movements, we might break down this behavior in the following four steps:

To do one jumping jack, we:

1. Simultaneously move both of our arms halfway up, move both of our legs halfway out, and our body move up a bit.
2. Simultaneously move both of our arms the rest of the way up, both of our legs the rest of the way out, and move our body down a bit.
3. Simultaneously move both of our arms halfway down, move both of our legs halfway in, and move our body up a bit.
4. Simultaneously move both of our arms the rest of the way down, move both of our legs the rest of the way in, and move down our body a bit.

In forming this algorithm for jumping jack behavior, we have been deliberately vague, because we don't know the exact amount to move our arms or legs, or how far to move up and down. However, it should be evident that we move the same distance (either up or down) in Steps 1–4. Likewise, both of our arms move the same amount in Steps 1–4, and both of our legs move the same amount in Steps 1–4, but our arms and our legs move by different amounts.

Variables provide a means of dealing with such uncertainty. More precisely, we can define three variables—**halfArmMove**, **halfLegMove**, and **upDownDistance**—and then use them to specify the amounts by which our arms, legs, and body move in each of the four steps.

We begin by creating a new method named **doJumpingJack()** in the **Biped** class, as we saw in the last chapter. We can create all three of these variables using the variable... control, giving them initial values of **0.2**, **0.05**, and **0.25**, as shown in Figure 3-20.

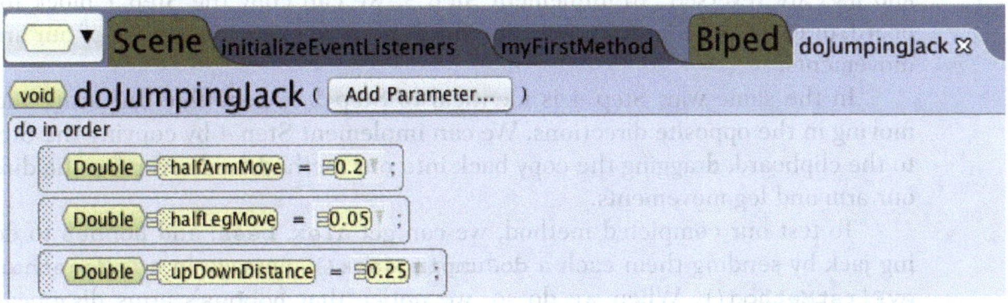

FIGURE 3-20 Declaring three variables

After we have declared these variables, we can use them as the arguments in messages to implement our jumping jack algorithm. Figure 3-21 shows Step 1 of our algorithm using these variables.

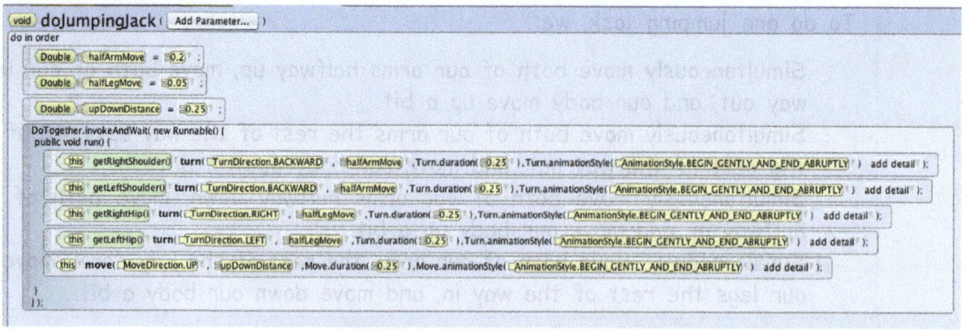

FIGURE 3-21   Step 1 of a jumping jack

Note that since a jumping jack takes about 1 second to perform, and since this is one of four steps, we have set the duration of each simultaneous animation to 0.25 seconds. Also, since this step is the beginning of a movement (i.e., with inertia to overcome at the beginning), we set the animationStyle of each message to BEGIN_GENTLY_AND_END_ABRUPTLY.

Step 2 is the same as Step 1, except that (a) we move ourselves DOWN instead of UP, and (b) we set each message's animationStyle to BEGIN_ABRUPTLY_AND_END_GENTLY, because this step is the end of a movement (i.e., with inertia to overcome at the end). Since these steps are so similar, we can "work smarter not harder" by copying our Step 1 block to the clipboard, dragging the copy back, and making the necessary changes.

Step 3 is identical to Step 1, except that the directions in which we move our arms and legs are reversed. To implement Step 3, we can copy the Step 1 block to the clipboard, drag the copy back into our method, and reverse the directions of our arm and leg movements.

In the same way, Step 4 is identical to Step 2, except that our arms and legs are moving in the opposite directions. We can implement Step 4 by copying the Step 2 block to the clipboard, dragging the copy back into our method, and reversing the directions of our arm and leg movements.

To test our completed method, we can get **alex**, **bess**, and **hobbes** to do a jumping jack by sending them each a **doJumpingJack()** message in a **DoTogether** block in **myFirstMethod()**. When we do so, we notice that **hobbes**'s arms disappear into his head! The problem is that our value for **halfArmMove** (**0.2**) is too large. We can easily fix this by changing the variable's initial value, as shown in Figure 3-22.

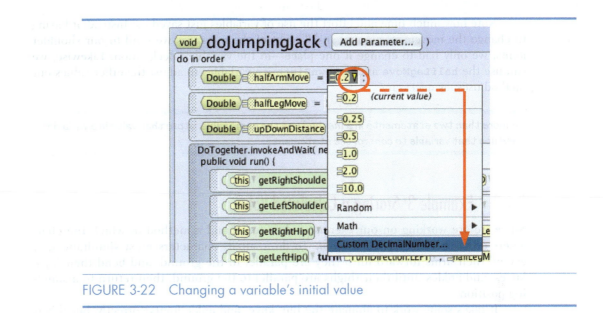

FIGURE 3-22   Changing a variable's initial value

This brings up a numeric keypad with which we can enter a smaller value, such as 0.15. Once we do that, we can re-run our program to see if our problem is fixed.

Figure 3-23 shows our method in action, after Steps 1 and 2 have been performed.

FIGURE 3-23   Testing doJumpingJack()

Note how much time and effort the use of variables just saved us! Instead of having to change the movement-amount in all eight of the messages we send to our shoulder joints, we only had to change it one place—in the variable's declaration. Likewise, we can use the **halfLegMove** and **upDownDistance** variables to adjust the other values our method uses, as necessary.

> If more than two statements in a method use the same value, store that value in a variable, and use that variable to control the statements.

3.1.3   Example 3: Storing a Calculated Value

Since we are working on our exercise video, let's build a method in which the characters do an exercise called a *squat*. To do a squat, characters must simultaneously extend their arms forward until they are parallel to the ground, and bend their hips, knees, and ankles until their thighs are parallel to the ground, then return to a standing position.

It takes some work to animate the hip, knee, and ankle joints correctly, but this is not especially difficult, as can be seen in Figure 3-24.

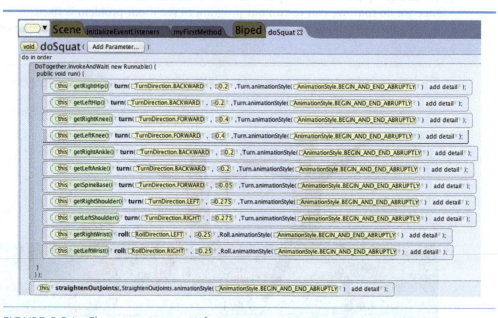

FIGURE 3-24   The joint animations for a squat

The problem is that when the characters bend their hips and knees, these statements cause their feet to leave the ground. Moreover, how far a character's feet are off the ground depends on its height, as can be seen in Figure 3-25.

FIGURE 3-25   Characters' feet leaving the ground

To fix this problem, we need to add a statement to the **DoTogether** block in Figure 3-8 that moves our characters *down* to compensate for their feet coming *up*. However, this is a challenge because the distance a character needs to move down depends on that character's size.

There are different ways to calculate this distance. One way is to recognize that the distance a character needs to drop is proportional to the length of the thighs. That is, when a character crouches so that the thigh is parallel to the ground, the change in height will be roughly the length of the thigh.

To make use of this observation, we might start by declaring a local variable named **dropDistance** with an initial value of **1.0** and use it as the distance in a **move()** message, as shown in Figure 3-26.

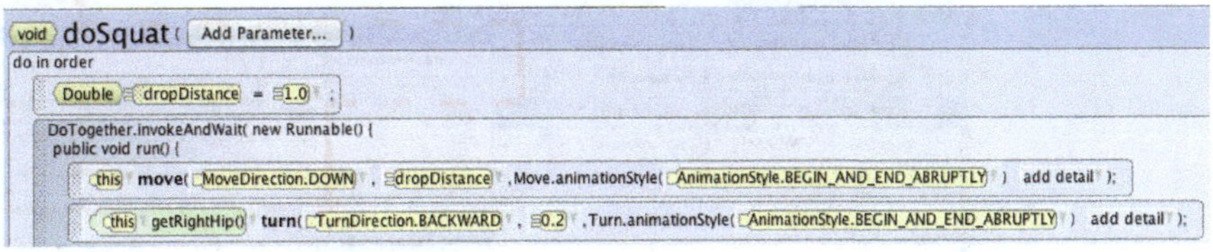

FIGURE 3-26   Declaring and using the **dropDistance** variable

To initialize this variable to the length of a character's thigh, we can use the **getDistanceTo()** function to calculate the distance from a character's hip to its knee. We first select **this.getRightHip()** in the object selector, choose the function tab, drag the `getDistanceTo()` function on top of the 1.0 initializer in the variable declaration statement, and finally choose `this.getRightKnee()` as the argument to the function, as shown in Figure 3-27.

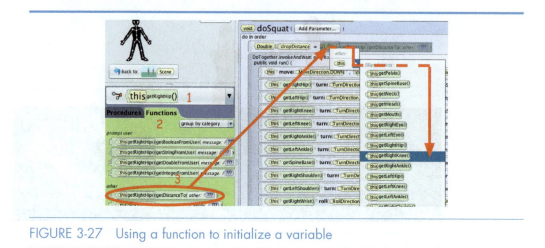

FIGURE 3-27   Using a function to initialize a variable

If we test our method by sending **alex**, **bess**, and **hobbes** the **doSquat()** message, we find that this distance is not quite enough to get our characters' feet back to the ground. To move them the rest of the way, we can modify this distance by a constant factor. To do this, we can click the down-arrow at the right end of the initializer, choose the Math menu option, choose the multiplication operator (*), and choose **Custom Decimal Number**, as shown in Figure 3-28.

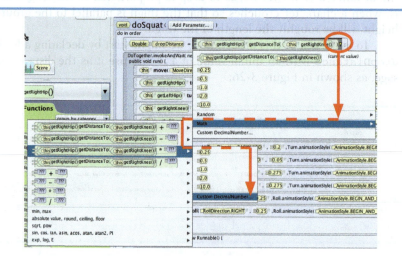

FIGURE 3-28   Using the **Math** operations

On the keypad that appears, we can enter a value between 1.0 and 2.0 and then test the results. We found that the value **1.4** seemed to work pretty well. Figure 3-29 shows the final method.

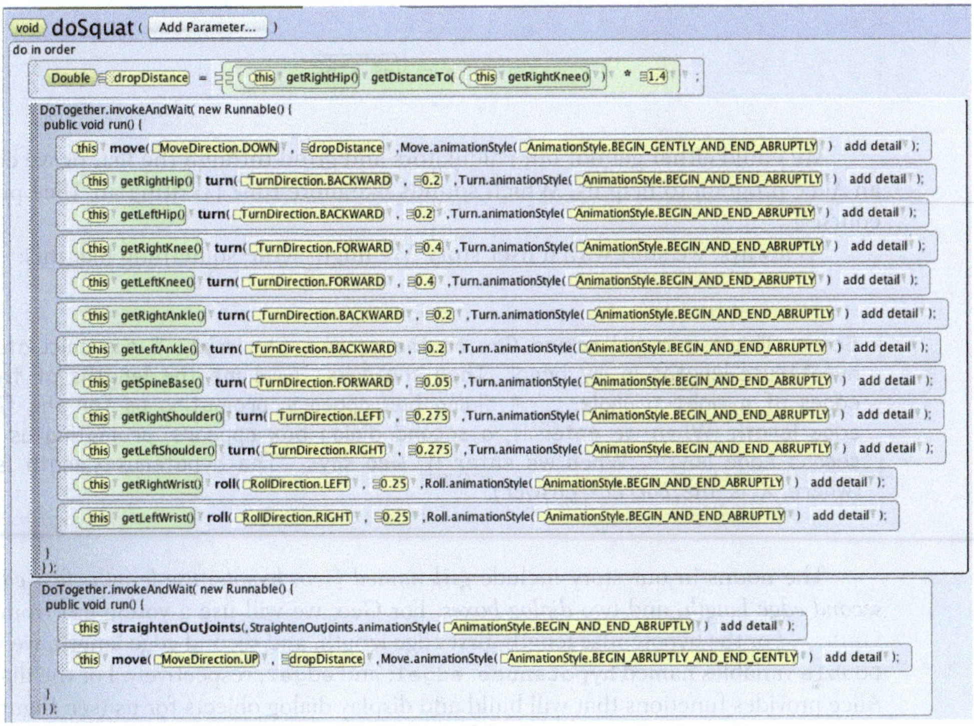

FIGURE 3-29   The doSquat() method

When we first wrote this method, we set the animationStyle of all 10 messages in the first block to BEGIN_GENTLY_AND_END_ABRUPTLY, and we set the two messages in the second block to BEGIN_ABRUPTLY_AND_END_GENTLY. However, with these settings, our characters' feet tended to sink into the ground because they were moving down at the same time as their joints were turning. As can be seen in Figure 3-29, we were able to improve the animation by keeping this animationStyle for the **move()** messages but setting the animationStyle of all the other messages in our method to BEGIN_AND_END_ABRUPTLY. This has the effect of giving the **turn()** messages a head start by delaying the **move()** messages slightly, which keeps the characters' feet from sinking into the ground.

Once you get used to using variables and functions, they often give you a much better way to control an animation, instead of choosing numbers by trial and error. Becoming familiar with the functions Alice provides can greatly simplify the solution of many problems!

3.1.4 Example 4: Storing a User-Entered Value

Another common use of variables is to store values that the user enters, for later use. To illustrate, suppose your geometry teacher gives you a list of right triangles' leg-lengths, and tells you to calculate each triangle's hypotenuse length using the Pythagorean Theorem:

$$c = \sqrt{a^2 + b^2}$$

We could either get out our calculators and grind through the list, or we could write an Alice program to help us. Which sounds like more fun? (Writing an Alice program, of course!)

As always, we start with a user story. We might write something like this:

> Scene: There is a girl named Geo on the screen. She says, "I can calculate hypotenuse-lengths in my head!" Then she says, "Give me the lengths of the two edges of a right triangle...." A dialog box appears, prompting us for the first edge length. When we enter it, a second dialog box appears, prompting us for the second edge length. When we enter it, Geo says, "The hypotenuse-length is X" (where X is the correct answer).

The nouns in our story include *girl named Geo, hypotenuse-length, first edge length, second edge length,* and two *dialog boxes.* For Geo, we will use a young girl from the Alice Gallery. For the hypotenuse length, first edge length, and second edge length, we will create **Double** variables named **hypotenuse, edge1,** and **edge2,** respectively. For the dialog boxes, Alice provides functions that will build and display dialog objects for us (see Figure 3-31).

Since the scene has just one object (Geo) and computing hypotenuses is her special gift, we will create a method named **computeHypotenuse()** in class **ChildPerson** to provide the desired behavior. Within this method, we declare the three **Double** variables and then begin programming the desired behavior. Using what we have seen so far, we can get to the point shown in Figure 3-30.

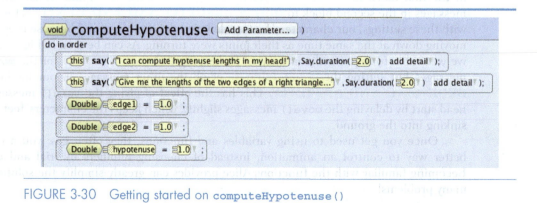

FIGURE 3-30 Getting started on **computeHypotenuse()**

But how do we get the value of **edge1** from the user? The answer lies under the Functions tab! If we click there and then scroll down a bit, we will find a **getDoubleFromUser()** function that we can drag over to replace the **1.0** initializer, as we have seen before. When we drop it on the **1.0**, Alice displays the menu of choices shown in Figure 3-31.

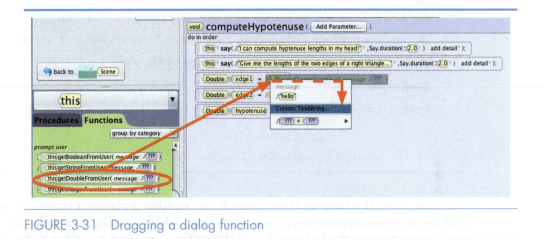

FIGURE 3-31   Dragging a dialog function

These choices are for the string we want the dialog to display in order to prompt the user to enter a value. Since we want the dialog box to ask for the length of one edge of a right triangle, we choose the Custom TextString... option. Alice then displays a dialog box in which we can enter the prompt that we want to appear, as shown in Figure 3-32.

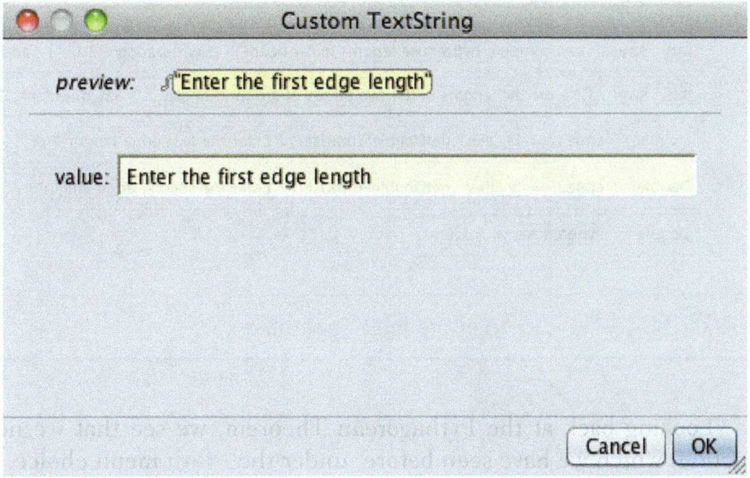

FIGURE 3-32   Customizing a dialog box's prompt message

When we click the OK button, Alice updates our declaration of **edge1**, as shown in Figure 3-33.

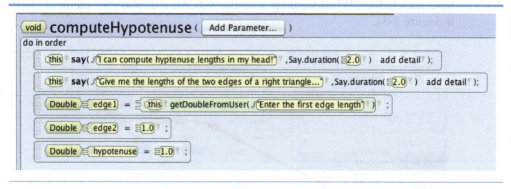

FIGURE 3-33   Setting a variable to a dialog box's result

Now, when the program flows through this variable declaration statement, it will send the **getDoubleFromUser()** message to **geo**, which will display a dialog box that asks the user to enter the first-edge length. When the user enters a number in that dialog box, the **getDoubleFromUser()** function will return that number, which will be used to give **edge1** its initial value.

We can use a similar approach to get the value for **edge2**, and once we have the two edge lengths, we are ready to compute the **hypotenuse** value. We get as far as shown in Figure 3-34 before we hit a snag.

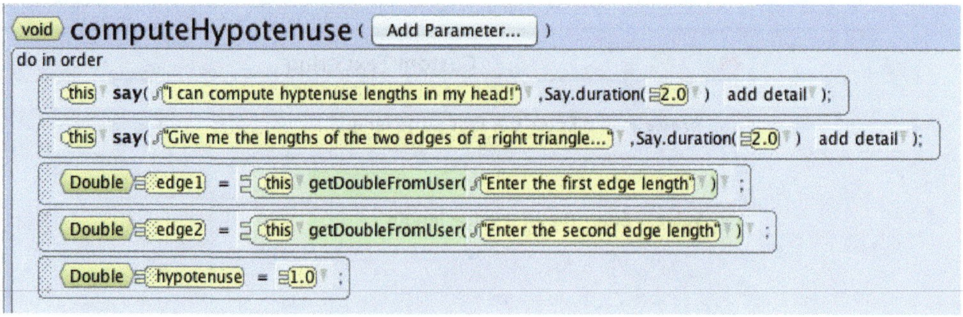

FIGURE 3-34   How to compute the hypotenuse

Looking back at the Pythagorean Theorem, we see that we need the square root function, which we have seen before, under the Math menu choice. We thus do the following: click the down-arrow at the end of the hypotenuse initializer; drag down to the Math choice; choose sqrt, pow; choose Math.sqrt(???); finally, since we must compute the square root of (edge1^2 + edge2^2), choose **edge1**, as shown in Figure 3-35.

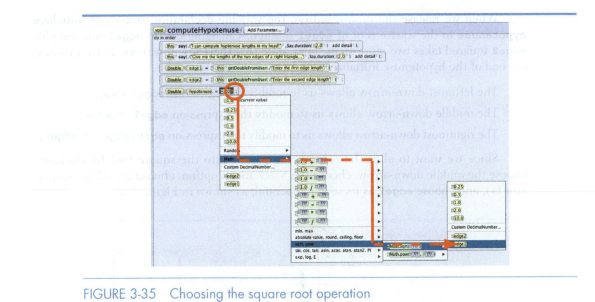

FIGURE 3-35   Choosing the square root operation

When we choose **edge1**, the resulting initializer sets the value of **hypotenuse** to the square root of **edge1**. To change this to **edge1²**, we can click the down-arrow immediately to the right of **edge1**, choose the Math menu option, choose the multiplication operator, and choose **edge1** as the second operand of the multiplication, as shown in Figure 3-36.

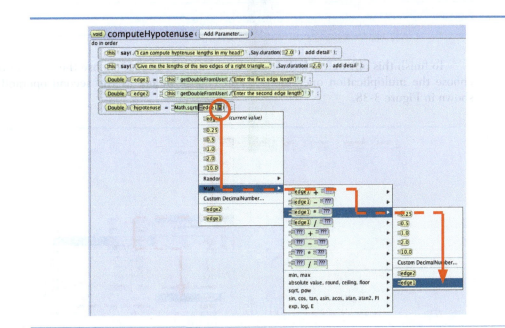

FIGURE 3-36   Computing the square root of **edge1²**

When we release the mouse button, the variable declaration statement initializes **hypotenuse** to the square root of **edge1** squared. Changing this to **edge1** squared plus **edge2** squared takes two more steps. First, note that there are now three down-arrows at the end of the hypotenuse initializer:

1. The leftmost down-arrow allows us to modify the rightmost **edge1** value.

2. The middle down-arrow allows us to modify the expression **edge1 * edge1**.

3. The rightmost down-arrow allows us to modify the expression **sqrt(edge1 * edge1)**.

Since we want to alter the value being passed into the square root function, we choose the middle down-arrow, choose the **Math** menu option, choose the addition operator (+), and choose **edge2** as its second operand, as shown in Figure 3-37.

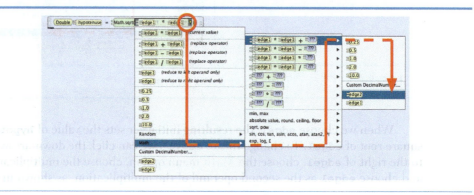

FIGURE 3-37   Computing the square root of $edge1^2 + edge^2$

To finish this off, we click the down-arrow next to **edge2**, choose the **Math** option, choose the multiplication operator (*), and choose **edge2** as the second operand, as shown in Figure 3-38.

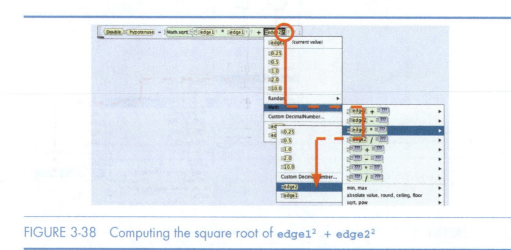

FIGURE 3-38   Computing the square root of $edge1^2 + edge2^2$

When we choose **edge2**, the initializer for variable **hypotenuse** should contain the correct formula.

Now that we have the **hypotenuse** calculated, how do we get **geo** to say it? We can easily get her to say **"The hypotenuse length is"**, but how do we get her to say the value of **hypotenuse** at the same time? The answer has to do with *types*. As you know, the type of **hypotenuse** is **Double**. The type of the value we send with the **say()** message must be a **String**, so we must somehow convert the value of **hypotenuse** into a **String**. Accomplishing this takes a few more steps.

The first step is to declare a new variable that will contain the value of **hypotenuse** converted to a **String**. We'll call it **hypotString**, make its type **String**, and set **"The hypotenuse length is"** as its initial value, as shown in Figure 3-39.

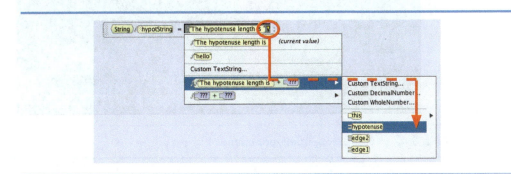

FIGURE 3-39   Initializing the hypotenuse string

The next step is to append the (**Double**) value of **hypotenuse** to the (**String**) value of **hypotString**. In programming, combining two strings **a** and **b** into a single string **ab** is called *concatenating* the strings, and for **String** values, the + symbol is called the *concatenation* operator. In a concatenation **a + b**, the order of **a** and **b** matters: **"en" + "list"** produces **"enlist"**, but **"list" + "en"** produces **"listen"**.

Alice makes it easy to concatenate: we just click the down-arrow at the end of the **hypotString** declaration, choose the first concatenation operator (+), and then choose **hypotenuse** as the value we wish to append to the string, as shown in Figure 3-40.

FIGURE 3-40   Concatenating the **hypotenuse** to a string

When the resulting statement is performed, Alice will convert the value of `hypotenuse` from a `Double` to a `String`, concatenate that `String` onto the end of `"The hypotenuse length is"`, and then use the resulting `String` to initialize our `hypotString` variable. Note that we must leave a space after the word "is" to separate it from the value of `hypotenuse`.

All that is left is to have `geo` speak our `hypotString`, which is easy, using the `say()` message. Figure 3-41 shows the final version of our method.

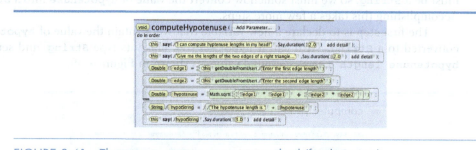

FIGURE 3-41   The `computeHypotenuse()` method (final version)

We then send `geo` the `computeHypotenuse()` message in `myFirstMethod()` to finish the program.

To test our work, we run our program and enter commonly known values. Figure 3-42 shows the result after we have entered edge lengths of 3 and 4 (the corresponding hypotenuse length is 5).

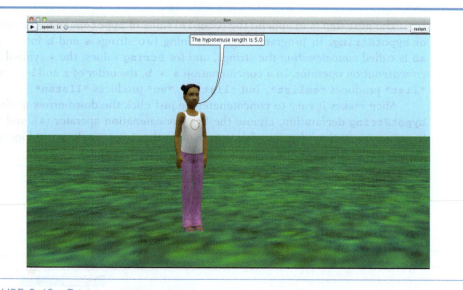

FIGURE 3-42   Testing `computeHypotenuse()`

Local variables thus provide a convenient means of storing values for use later on in a method.

3.2   Parameters

A value that we pass to an object via a message is called an **argument**. While this use of that word may be new to you, you have actually been using arguments ever since Chapter 1. For example, our very first program began with the code shown in Figure 3-43.

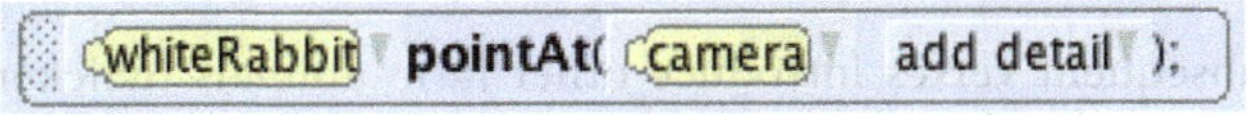

whiteRabbit **pointAt(** camera   add detail);

FIGURE 3-43   Two statements from our first program

In the first statement, we are sending **whiteRabbit** the **pointAt()** message, with **camera** as an argument—the *value* at which we want the White Rabbit to point. The statement in Figure 3-43 has one argument: **camera**.

Many of the Alice methods require two arguments. For example, the **move()** method requires both the *direction* the object is to move in and the *amount* it is to move. The **turn()** and **roll()** messages are similar.

When you send an object a message accompanied by an argument, that argument must be stored somewhere in order for the receiving object to access it.

> A **parameter** is a method variable that stores an argument, so that the receiver of the message can access that argument.

Thus, the **pointAt()** method has a single parameter, while the **move()**, **turn()**, and **roll()** methods have two parameters each. There is no limit to the number of parameters a method can have.

To make this a bit more concrete, let's work through some example problems that involve arguments and parameters.

3.2.1   Example 1: Old MacDonald Had a Farm

Suppose we have a user story containing a scene in which a pig is taking a bath and singing the song "Old MacDonald" one line at a time. Here are some of the lyrics to this song:

Verse 1:	*Verse 2:*
Old MacDonald had a farm, E-I-E-I-O.	*Old MacDonald had a farm, E-I-E-I-O.*
And on this farm he had a cow, E-I-E-I-O.	*And on this farm he had a duck, E-I-E-I-O.*
With a moo-moo here, and a moo-moo there,	*With a quack-quack here, and a quack-quack there,*
here a moo, there a moo, everywhere a moo-moo.	*here a quack, there a quack, everywhere a quack-quack.*
Old MacDonald had a farm, E-I-E-I-O.	*Old MacDonald had a farm, E-I-E-I-O.*

Verse 3: *Old MacDonald had a farm, E-I-E-I-O.* *And on this farm he had a horse, E-I-E-I-O.* *With a neigh-neigh here, and a neigh-neigh there,* *here a neigh, there a neigh, everywhere a neigh-neigh.* *Old MacDonald had a farm, E-I-E-I-O.*	*Verse 4:* *Old MacDonald had a farm, E-I-E-I-O.* *And on this farm he had a dog, E-I-E-I-O.* *With a ruff-ruff here, and a ruff-ruff there,* *here a ruff, there a ruff, everywhere a ruff-ruff.* *Old MacDonald had a farm, E-I-E-I-O.*

Subsequent verses introduce other farm animals (chicken, cat, etc.). For now, we will just have the character sing these four verses.

Clearly, we *could* use Divide and Conquer to have the pig sing four verses; in each verse, we send the pig five **say()** messages. For example, **singVerse1()** would contain statements like these:

```
say("Old MacDonald had a farm, E-I-E-I-O.");
say("And on this farm he had a cow, E-I-E-I-O.");
say("With a moo-moo here and a moo-moo there,");
say("here a moo, there a moo, everywhere a moo-moo.");
say("Old MacDonald had a farm, E-I-E-I-O.");
```

However, this approach has several disadvantages. One is that if we later want to add a fifth verse, then we must write a new method containing five more **say()** messages and add it to the program. With this approach, every new verse we want the scarecrow to sing will require a new method containing five more statements. This seems like a lot of repetitious work.

A related disadvantage of this approach is that each verse-method we write is identical, except for (1) the animal, and (2) the noise it makes.

Whenever you find yourself programming the same thing more than once, there is usually a better way to write the program.

In this case, the better way is to write a single "generic" **singVerse()** method, to which we can pass a given animal and its noise as arguments. That is, we want a message like this:

```
singVerse("cow", "moo");
```

to make the pig sing the first verse, a message like this:

```
singVerse("horse", "neigh");
```

to make it sing the second verse, and so on.

The trick to making this happen is to build a method with a generic *animal* parameter to store whatever animal we want to pass, as well as a generic *noise* parameter to store the noise that animal makes. The statements of this method then contain the lyrics that are common to each verse but use the *animal* parameter in place of the specific *cow*, *duck*, *horse*, or *dog* argument, and use the *noise* parameter in place of the specific *moo*, *quack*, *neigh*, or *ruff* argument.

We might begin by creating a world containing an instance of class **Pond** named **pond**, an instance of class **Pig** named **porkus**, and by positioning the pig in the pond. Since people might also sing this song, we next create a new **singVerse()** method in the **Biped** class. With this method open, we click the Add Parameter button that is between the method's parentheses. When we click it, this button generates an Add Parameter dialog box that is similar to the Insert Variable dialog box we saw in Figure 3-3. As before, we can specify the name of the parameter and its type. When we click this dialog box's OK button, it defines a new parameter, with the given name and type between the method's parentheses. In Figure 3-44, we have used this button to create two parameters, named **animal** and **noise**, both of type **String**.

FIGURE 3-44   String parameters for **animal** and **noise**

Now that the parameters have been defined, we can proceed to add statements to the method to make the pig sing a verse. Like a variable, a parameter's name appears in the menu of choices that appears when we drag and drop an appropriate statement into the method. Figure 3-45 shows one way we might define the **singVerse()** method.

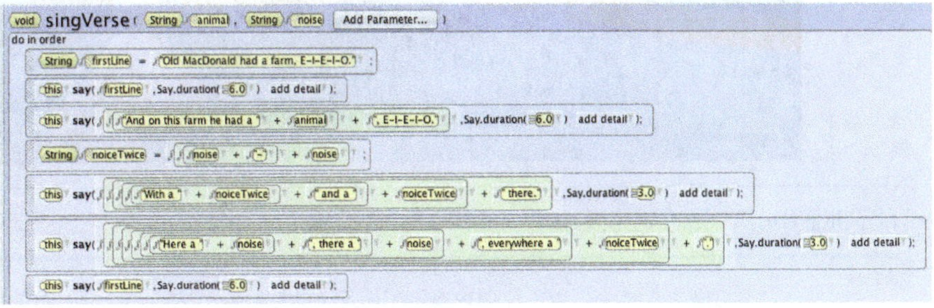

FIGURE 3-45   The **singVerse()** method

Since the first and last lines are the same, we defined a variable named **firstLine** to store those lines so that we need not type them twice. Also, seeing that a verse uses the string *noise-noise* three times, we defined a variable named **noiseTwice** and defined its value as **noise + "-" + noise**, using the string concatenation operator (+) we saw in the last section. In fact, we used the concatenation operator *14 times* in building this method, most often in the statements in which the scarecrow sings the third and fourth lines of the verse.

Given this method, we can now define a **singOldMacDonaldSong()** method in our **Biped** class, as shown in Figure 3-46.

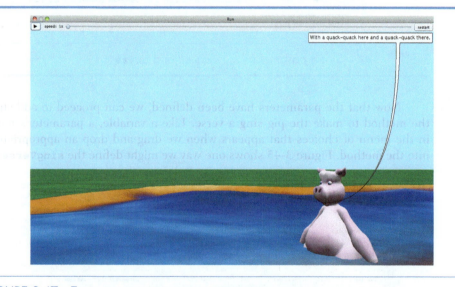

FIGURE 3-46   The **singOldMacDonaldSong()** method

Figure 3-47 shows the program running, partway through its third verse.

FIGURE 3-47   Testing **singOldMacDonaldSong()**

If we later decide to add a new verse, all we have to do is send **porkus** another **singVerse()** message, with the desired *animal* and *noise* arguments.

3.2.2   Example 2: Jumping Fish!

Suppose that after **porkus** sings "Old MacDonald," our user story has a fish jump out of the pond water, tracing a graceful arc through the air before re-entering the water. If we examine the various fish classes in the Alice **Gallery**, we notice that none of them offers a method providing this behavior. Choosing a golden **Carp** to contrast with the water and naming it **diem**, we will define a **jump()** method for it. Since it seems like this method could be useful for any of the subclasses of class **Swimmer**, we will define it there.

If we think about what kinds of arguments we might want to pass to a **jump()** message, one possibility is the *distance* we want the fish to jump. Another possibility is the *height* we want it to jump. (These are very different behaviors, as indicated by there being separate *high jump* and *long jump* events in track and field.) In this section, we will have the fish do the equivalent of the long jump, and we will pass to the method an argument indicating the *distance* we want the fish to jump.

If we think through the behavior this method should provide, we might sketch it as the sequence of steps shown in Figure 3-48.

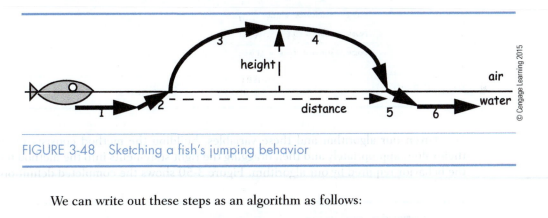

FIGURE 3-48   Sketching a fish's jumping behavior

We can write out these steps as an algorithm as follows:

1. Fish swims forward a starting distance (to get its speed up)
2. Fish angles upward
3. Fish moves upward the height and half the distance, angling upward
4. Fish moves downward the height and forward half the distance, angling downward
5. Fish levels off (since it is angled downward, it must angle upward)
6. Fish swims forward a stopping distance (coasting to a stop)

Consider how an animal jumps. When it jumps a short distance, it doesn't spring very high, but when it jumps a longer distance, it springs higher. The height and distance of an animal's jump are thus related. For the sake of simplicity, we will approximate the height as one third of the distance. (If this turns out to be too simplistic, we can always change it.) In the same way, if a fish is supposed to jump farther, it may need a longer starting distance to get its speed up, and the distance it glides before it stops will be greater. For simplicity's sake, we will assume that the starting and stopping distances are one fourth of the distance to be jumped.

Using our algorithm and our sketch, we might identify these objects: *fish, height, distance, half the distance, angle, starting distance,* and *stopping distance.* We have already selected the **Carp** class for the fish. Since we intend to pass the distance to be jumped as an argument, and since such a value is numeric, we will create a **Double** parameter named **distance** to store this value using the Add Parameter button. The remaining objects are all numeric values, so we will define a **Double** variable for each of them, using the variable… control. We will use the names **height**, **halfDist**, and **angle** for three of these variables. If we assume that the starting and stopping distances are the same, we can use one variable for both, which we will name **startStopDist**. Figure 3-49 shows these declarations with some initial values.

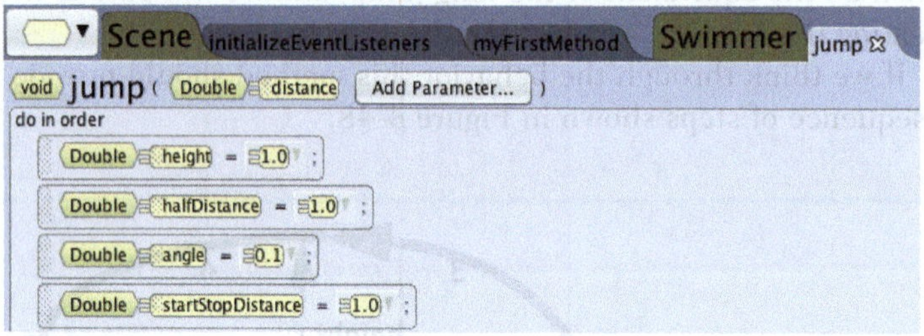

FIGURE 3-49   The jump() method's parameter and variables

Given our algorithm and these variables, building the method consists of setting their values appropriately and then dragging the right statements into the method to elicit the behavior required by our algorithm. Figure 3-50 shows the completed definition.

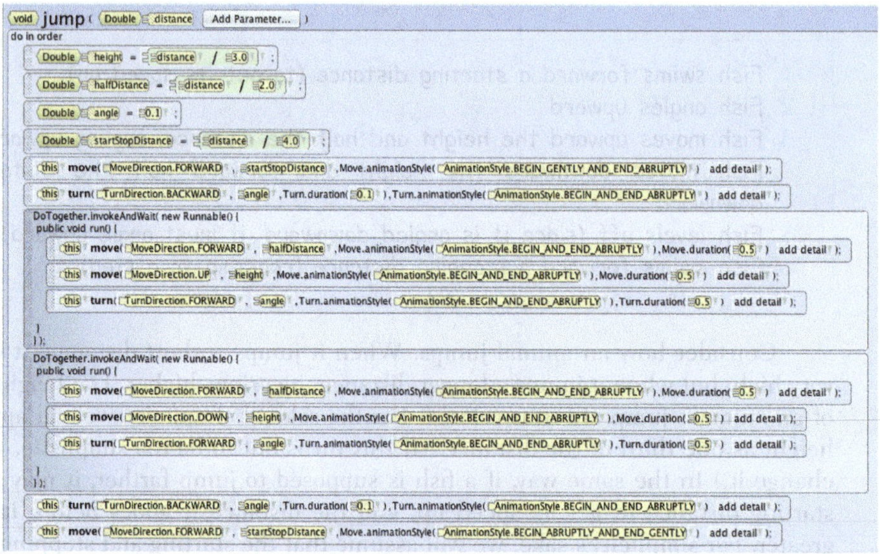

FIGURE 3-50   The jump() method (complete)

We can see that each variable's value is accessed multiple times. One of the benefits of using variables this way is that if we later decide to change a value (e.g., the height of the jump or its angle), we only have to change it in one place instead of in several places. This can be a big time saver when you are trying to find just the right value.

To test our program, we send **diem** the **jump()** message after **porkus** sings his song. To test **jump()** thoroughly, we can temporarily disable our song and pass **jump()** a variety of argument values (0.25, 0.5, 1, 2, ...) to check that its behavior is appropriate in each case. Figure 3-51 shows a test using one of these values.

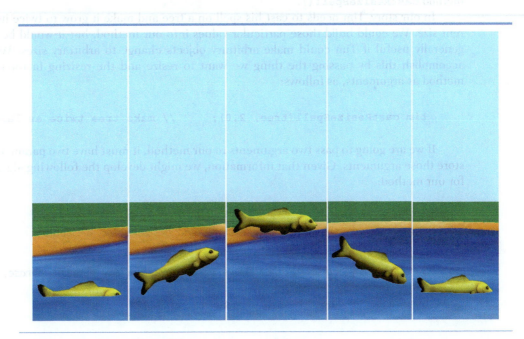

FIGURE 3-51   Testing the **jump()** method

Figure 3-52 is a montage of snapshots showing the behavior produced by the **jump()** method.

FIGURE 3-52   A jumping fish

Parameters are thus variables through which we can pass arguments to a method. By passing different arguments to the same method, that method can produce different (related) behaviors. For example, the `singVerse()` method allows any `Biped` to sing different verses of the same song, depending on what *animal* and *noise* values we pass it. Similarly, the `jump()` method lets us make any `Swimmer` jump different distances, depending on the numeric argument we pass to its *distance* parameter.

The key to using parameters well is to think carefully about how you will be invoking the method. If you can anticipate what values you will want to pass to the method as arguments, the need to store those argument values will determine (a) how many parameters you need to create and (b) what types those parameters should have. A well-written method with parameters is like a stone that (figuratively speaking) lets you kill multiple birds.

Before continuing, be sure to save this story for later use.

3.2.3   Example 3: Casting a Spell

Remember that in Scene 1 of our story about Tim the wizard, Tim notices that one of the trees in front of his castle is struggling. As a wizard, Tim should be able to give his tree a magical boost, but he has no predefined methods for casting any spells, much less one to make a tree grow.

Alice, however, allows us to create new methods, so if we can imagine Tim casting a spell to make a tree grow, we can build a method to make it happen. We will call this method `castResizeSpell()`.

In our story, Tim needs to cast his spell on a tree and make it grow to twice its current size. We could build those particular values into our method, but it would be more generally useful if Tim could make arbitrary objects change to arbitrary sizes. We can accomplish this by passing the thing we want to resize and the resizing factor to our method as arguments, as follows:

```
tim.castResizeSpell(tree, 2.0);      // make tree twice as large
```

If we are going to pass two arguments to our method, it must have two parameters to store those arguments. Given that information, we might develop the following algorithm for our method:

Parameters: *target*, the thing being resized; and *resizeFactor*, a Double

1. Have Tim turn to face the *target*.
2. Simultaneously: Raise both of Tim's arms, have him say a magic phrase, and resize *target* by *resizeFactor*.
3. Simultaneously: Lower both of Tim's arms.

Figure 3-53 shows one way to implement this algorithm, in which we have created `castResizeSpell()` as a method of class `AdultPerson`. If the story called for any person (or biped) to be able to cast a spell, then we would create `castResizeSpell()` as a method of those classes.

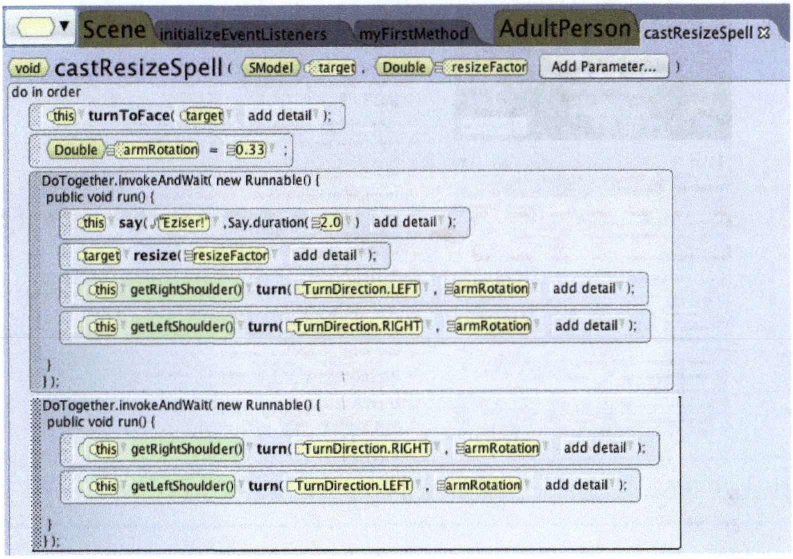

FIGURE 3-53   A `castResizeSpell()` method

Note that we have declared a local variable named **armRotation** to control how much Tim's arms raise as he casts his spell, because we must use this value four times within the method.

One subtle aspect of this method is the type we choose for our **target** parameter. Since Tim should presumably be able to resize any object he may encounter in our 3D world, we use the type **SModel** for our target parameter.[2] (When choosing the type of a variable or parameter, you will find this and other types under the Other Types menu option.) This allows us to pass any of the models in the Alice Gallery to this method. Appendix C provides a diagram that shows how all of these Other Types relate to one another.

The only other tricky thing in this method is sending the **resize()** message to our **target** parameter. To make this happen, we first dragged the **resize()** method into the editing area, giving us:

```
this.resize(resizeFactor);
```

We then clicked the down-arrow next to **this** and changed it to our parameter **target** in order to send the **resize()** message to **target** instead of Tim.

When we have finished this method, we can use it to fill in that part of our **doScene1()** method, as shown in Figure 3-54.

---

[2]The "S" in type names like **SModel** and **SThing** stands for *Story* and is used to distinguish classes to which the user cannot add methods or properties (such as **SBiped**) from classes to which the user can add methods or properties (such as **Biped**).

FIGURE 3-54   Having Tim resize the tree in `doScene1()`

With that change, Tim now resizes the stunted tree in Scene 1, as shown in Figure 3-55.

FIGURE 3-55   Tim resizing the tree

It is important to see that by designing `castResizeSpell()` to have `target` and `resizeFactor` parameters, we can use this "spell" method to make arbitrary 3D objects grow *or shrink* in our story. That is, the `target` parameter lets us choose the object whose size we wish to change, while the `resizeFactor` parameter lets us make the target grow by passing an argument greater than `1.0`, or shrink by passing an argument less than `1.0`. Parameters thus let us create methods that are more generally useful, rather than methods whose use is limited to a highly specialized purpose.

3.3   Property Variables

Now that we have discussed method variables and parameters, it is time to take a brief look at Alice's third kind of variable: **instance variables**, which are also known as **properties**. Whereas method variables and parameters are defined within a method, a property is defined within a class. A property can be defined using the **class** navigator, as we will see shortly.

A property allows an object to *remember* one of its characteristics. Each instance of the class (i.e., each object) has its own variable for the property, in which it can store a value distinct from any other object. This is why properties are also known as instance variables.

To clarify the use of properties, let's look at a concrete example. Back in our running example, suppose that the wizard Tim has an evil twin brother named Jim. People can generally remember their own names, and we can let the characters remember their names by defining a property named **myName** of type **String** in the **Person** class. One way to do so is to use the class navigator and select Person > Add Person Property..., as shown in Figure 3-56.

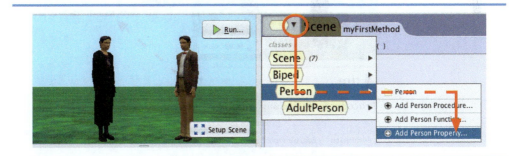

FIGURE 3-56   The **Add Property** menu choice

Clicking this button causes the Add Property dialog box to appear, which is almost identical to the Add Variable dialog box we saw back in Figure 3-3. In it, we enter **myName** for the name, select **String** as its type, and enter a space for its initializer. When we click the dialog box's OK button, Alice creates a new **String** variable named **myName** in the **Person** class, as shown in Figure 3-57.

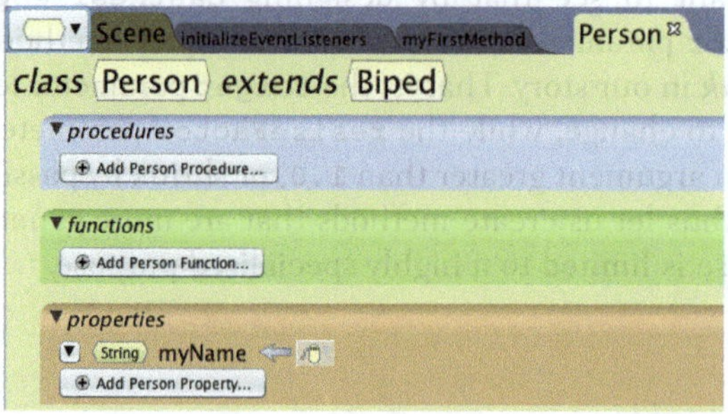

FIGURE 3-57   A new property variable

After we have added this variable to the **Person** class, each object that is created from that class or one of its subclasses (**AdultPerson** or **ChildPerson**) will have this property. Since Tim and Jim are both instances of **AdultPerson**, each now has a variable named **myName** in which we can store his name. To do so, we return to the details area where we select **tim** from the object selector and select the Procedures tab. There, we can see that Alice has created a new method named **setMyName()**. If we drag this method into our editing area, Alice displays a context menu for entering an argument for this method. If we choose Custom Textstring... from that menu, we can then enter **Tim** in the dialog box, producing the statement shown in Figure 3-58.

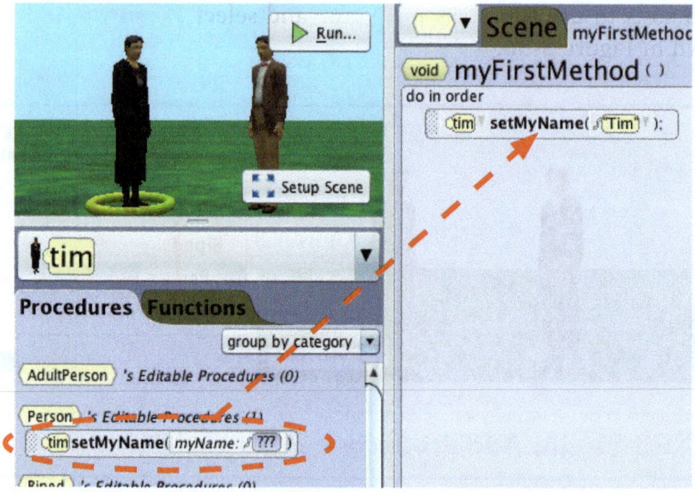

FIGURE 3-58   Setting Tim's **myName** property

We can use a similar approach to set Jim's name.

Once our twin-brothers' names are set, we can retrieve those names by returning to the details area and clicking on the Functions tab. There, we see that Alice has also created a new function named `getMyName()`. As you might guess, when we send this function-message to an object, it retrieves and returns the value of that object's `myName` property. In our scenario, we might use this to have each brother introduce himself, as shown in Figure 3-59.

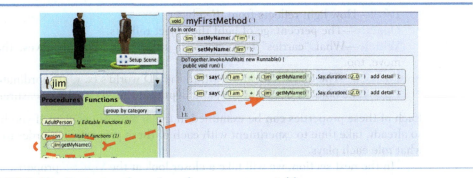

FIGURE 3-59   Retrieving the value of a property variable

Whenever we create a new property in a class, Alice creates two new methods in the class, related to that property:

1. A **procedure method** to *set* the value of that property
2. A **function method** to *get* the value of property

These methods are respectively known as **setters** and **getters**, because (a) their names begin with **set** or **get**, and (b) they allow a program to set or get the value of the property.

When we click Alice's Run button, we see that each wizard "knows" his own name, as shown in Figure 3-60.

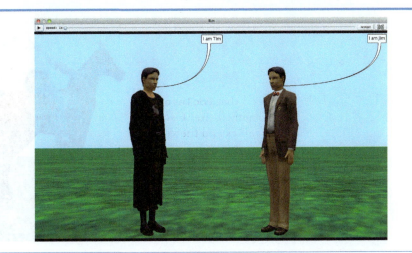

FIGURE 3-60   The twin wizards introduce themselves

A property variable thus provides a place for us to store an *attribute* of a class of objects, such as an object's name, its size, its weight, and anything else we want an object to remember about itself.

As we have seen, each Alice object has a number of predefined property variables. These variables store the following qualities of an object:

- Paint—How light reflects from the object.
- Opacity—The percentage of light the object reflects.
- Vehicle—What "carries" this object; if an object's vehicle moves, the object will move, too.
- Position—The object's location within the 3D world's (x, y, z) coordinate system.
- Size—The object's height, width, and depth, in the 3D world's measurement units.

Each of these properties can be examined in the scene editor view. If you have not done so already, take time to experiment with each of these properties in order to get a feel for what role each plays.

In the next section, we will take a closer look at the Vehicle property.

3.4   Alice Tip: Using the Vehicle Property

In some user stories, it may be desirable to link the movements of two objects, so that when one of the objects moves, the other moves with it. To illustrate, let us return to the example from Section 3.1. There, Scene 2 of a story had a girl named Annie approaching a horse. Suppose that Scene 4 of that story calls for her to ride the horse across the screen. We might set the scene as shown in Figure 3-61.

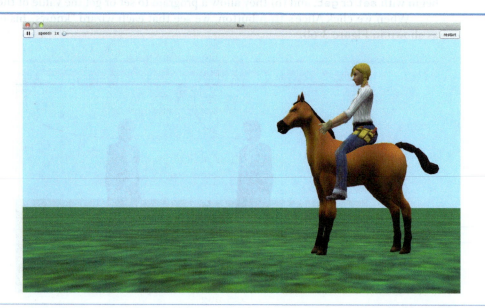

FIGURE 3-61   Annie on the horse

We can then use a **move()** message to move the horse across the screen, as shown in Figure 3-62.

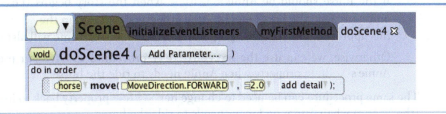

FIGURE 3-62   Moving the horse across the screen

However, as shown in Figure 3-63, when we do so, the horse moves, leaving Annie hanging suspended in mid-air!

FIGURE 3-63   Annie left hanging when horse moves

We could solve this problem using a **DoTogether** block, in which we make Annie and the horse move together. But doing so would force us to write twice as many statements as usual whenever we wanted her to ride the horse, and the additional statements to move Annie would be virtually identical to those we use to move the horse. It would be much better if we could somehow make her "ride" the horse, so that if the horse moves, Annie moves with it.

The way to achieve this better solution is by using the **Vehicle** property. As its name implies, an object's **Vehicle** is the thing on which it "rides," which is, by default, the

Scene or 3D world. If we want Annie to ride the horse, we need to change her Vehicle property to be the horse. There are two ways to do this:

1. If the horse should be Annie's Vehicle when the story begins (i.e., Annie should move any time the horse moves), this property can be set in the scene editor. Using this approach, any time our program moves the horse, Annie will also move.

2. Otherwise, we can use the `setVehicle()` procedure to have our program change Annie's Vehicle property when Annie needs to ride the horse.

The same procedure can be used to change her Vehicle property back to its original value (the Scene) when Annie no longer needs to ride the horse.

In Figure 3-64, we have used the `setVehicle()` approach at the beginning of the scene.

FIGURE 3-64   Changing Annie's `vehicle` property

After we make this change, playing the scene causes Annie to "ride" the horse across the screen, as shown in Figure 3-65.

FIGURE 3-65   Annie riding the horse across the screen

By setting Annie's Vehicle to the horse, any `move()` messages that we send to the horse will make her move as well, effectively linking her movements with those of the horse.

Note that if a later scene calls for Annie and the horse to move independently, we will need to reset her Vehicle to be the Scene. If we neglect to do this, then `move()` messages we send to the horse will make her move too, since their movements will still be linked.

The Vehicle property thus provides an easy and convenient way to **synchronize the movements** of two objects.

3.5   Functions

We have seen how to use a function to send an object a message in order to get information from it. We have also seen that Alice creates setter and getter methods whenever we create a new property. Suppose we wanted to be able to get information from an object, but there was no predefined function providing that information. In such circumstances, we can define our own function.

3.5.1   Functions and Parameters

Like methods, functions can have parameters to store arguments passed by the sender of the message. The arguments can then be accessed through the parameters. To illustrate, recall that in Section 3.2 we built a program in which a girl named Geo could compute hypotenuse lengths in her head. The method we wrote there inputs values for the two leg lengths, computes the hypotenuse, and then outputs the result. However, there might be situations where we just want to calculate the numerical hypotenuse length, without the input or output:

```
hypotenuse = geo.calculateHypotenuse(3.0, 4.0) ;
```

To define such a function for Geo, we can select her class in the class navigator and choose the Add New ChildPerson Function button. In the dialog box that appears, we enter the function's name (*calculateHypotenuse*) and select **Double** as the type of value it produces, as shown in Figure 3-66.

FIGURE 3-66   Creating a number-producing function

When we click the **OK** button, Alice adds `calculateHypotenuse` to `geo`'s Functions in the details area and opens the new function in the editing area, as shown in Figure 3-67.

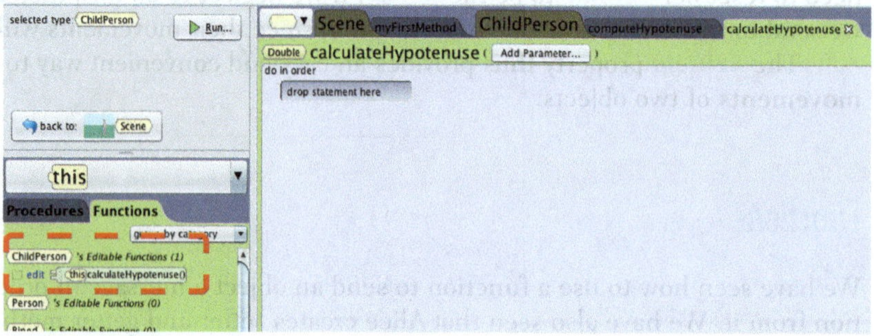

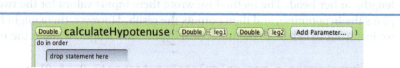

FIGURE 3-67   An empty number-returning function

To store the number arguments that the sender of this message passes for the two leg lengths, we need two numeric parameters, which we can make using the function's **Add Parameter** button. This displays a dialog box like the ones we have seen previously, in which we can enter a parameter's name and its type. Doing this for each of the two parameters gives us the function shown in Figure 3-68.

Double calculateHypotenuse (Double leg1 , Double leg2 Add Parameter...)
do in order
   drop statement here

FIGURE 3-68   A function with two parameters

To finish the function, we add a **return statement** by dragging the return control from the bottom of the window into the editing area and choosing a **placeholder** such as `1.0` for its return-value, as shown in Figure 3-69.

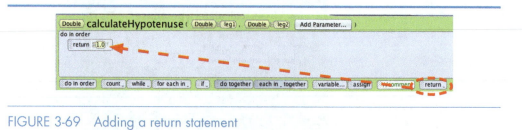

FIGURE 3-69   Adding a return statement

The **return** statement is a flow control statement. When flow reaches a **return** statement, its **return-value** is computed by evaluating whatever is to the right of the word **return**. The function then terminates, control flows back to the point at which the function-message was sent, and the return-value computed by the **return** statement is the value the function-message produces.

To complete our function, we can thus modify our **return** statement's return-value to make it compute the hypotenuse length using the function's parameters. Figure 3-70 shows one way to do so.

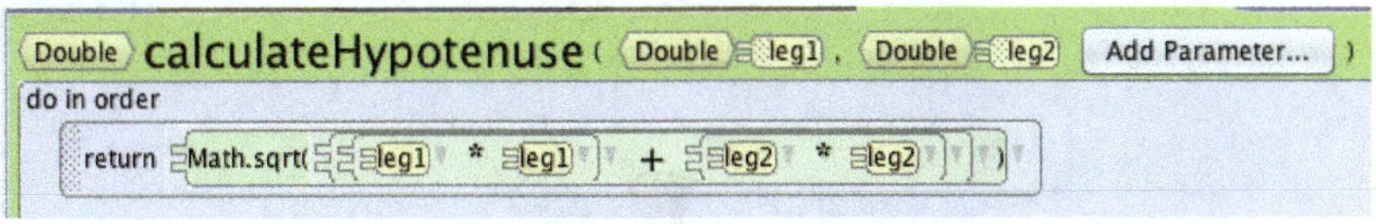

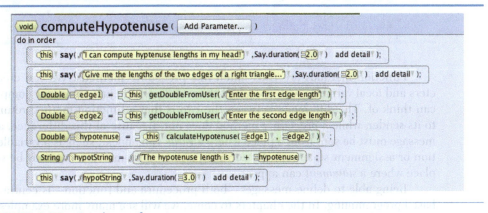

FIGURE 3-70   Calculating the hypotenuse

Given the lengths of the legs of a right triangle, our **calculateHypotenuse()** function thus applies the Pythagorean Theorem to compute and return the length of the hypotenuse.

Given this function, we can now send the **calculateHypotenuse()** message, pass arguments to it for the leg lengths, and expect its return-value to be the hypotenuse length. Figure 3-71 shows a revised version of the program in Figure 3-41, using our **calculateHypotenuse()** function.

FIGURE 3-71   Sending a function-message

Once we have built our function, dragging and dropping the **calculateHypotenuse()** message is a much easier way to compute the Pythagorean Theorem than encoding the formula by hand. Functions thus provide a way to use a "simple" name like **calculateHypotenuse(edge1, edge2)** to represent a complex formula like **Math.sqrt(edge1*edge1 + edge2*edge2)**. Computer scientists have a word for this idea of using a name to hide complexity; they call it **abstraction**. By hiding complexity, the wise use of abstraction produces programs that are easier to read.

When this program is run, Geo explains its purpose. The program then prompts the user to enter the lengths of the two triangle legs; Geo then "says" the corresponding hypotenuse length. For example, if the user enters **3** and **4** for the leg lengths, Geo reports the hypotenuse length as **5.0**, as shown in Figure 3-72.

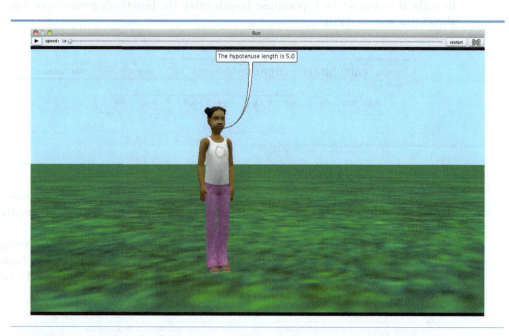

The hypotenuse length is 5.0

FIGURE 3-72   Testing the function

Function methods are thus much like procedure methods. We can create parameters and local variables within each of them and perform just about any computation we can think of. The difference between the two is that a function method returns a value to its sender, while a procedure method does not. Because of this difference, a function-message must be sent from a place where a *value* can appear, such as a variable initialization or assignment statement. By contrast, a procedure message can only be sent from a place where a *statement* can appear.

Being able to define messages—both procedure and function—is central to object-based programming. In the chapters to come, we will see many more examples of each.

3.6   Chapter Summary

❏ Method variables let us store computed and user-entered values for later use.

❏ Parameters let us store and access arguments passed by the sender of a message.

❏ Properties (object variables) let us store and retrieve an object's attributes.

❏ Alice's Vehicle property lets us synchronize the movements of two objects.

❏ A function lets us send a message to an object and get a value in response.

❏ A function must include a **return** statement, which returns a value to the message-sender.

3.6.1   Key Terms

abstraction	procedure method
argument	property
concatenation	**return** statement
define a variable	return-value
function method	setter
getter	synchronizing object movements
initializer	variable
instance variable	variable name
local variable	variable type
parameter	vehicle
placeholder	

Programming Projects

3.1   Following the approach used in Section 3.1.1, build a scene containing two people who walk toward each other from opposite sides of the screen. When they meet, they should turn and walk off together toward a building and then enter the building when they get there.

3.2   Using the horse we used in Section 3.4, build a **gallop()** method for the horse that makes its legs move realistically through the motions for one stride of a gallop. Then modify the **playScene4()** method so that the horse gallops across the screen. (For now, you may send the **gallop()** message multiple times.)

3.3   Using a **Person** from the Alice Gallery, define a method named **walkInSquare()** that has a parameter named **edgeLength**. When **walkInSquare(*dist*)** is sent to your person, he or she should move in a square with edges that are each *dist* units long. Make certain your person begins and ends at the same spot. When the person is done, have the person say the area and perimeter of the square.

3.4   Using the ideas in this chapter, build a world containing a person who can calculate Einstein's formula $e = mc^2$ in his or her head, where the user enters the *m* value (mass, in kilograms) and where *c* is the speed of light (299,792,458 meters per second). Define descriptive variables for each quantity, and use the function **Math.pow()** to compute c^2.

3.5   Choose a hopping animal from the Alice Gallery (e.g., a frog or a bunny). Write a **hop()** method that makes it hop in a realistic fashion, with a parameter that lets the sender of the message specify how far the animal should hop. Using your **hop()** method, have your animal hop around a building in four hops (with a **turn()** message in between each hop).

3.6 "The Farmer in the Dell" is an old folk song with the following lyrics. Create an Alice program containing a character who sings this song. Use a **singVerse()** method, parameters, and variables to write your program efficiently by using as few statements as possible.

Verse 1:	Verse 2:
The farmer in the dell.	The farmer takes a wife.
The farmer in the dell.	The farmer takes a wife.
Heigh-ho, the derry-o.	Heigh-ho, the derry-oh.
The farmer in the dell.	The farmer takes a wife.
Verse 3:	Verse 4:
The wife takes a child.	The child takes a nurse.
The wife takes a child.	The child takes a nurse.
Heigh-ho, the derry-oh.	Heigh-ho, the derry-oh.
The wife takes a child.	The child takes a nurse.
Verse 5:	Verse 6:
The nurse takes a cow.	The cow takes a dog.
The nurse takes a cow.	The cow takes a dog.
Heigh-ho, the derry-oh.	Heigh-ho, the derry-oh.
The nurse takes a cow.	The cow takes a dog.
Verse 7:	Verse 8:
The dog takes a cat.	The cat takes a rat.
The dog takes a cat.	The cat takes a rat.
Heigh-ho, the derry-oh.	Heigh-ho, the derry-oh.
The dog takes a cat.	The cat takes a rat.
Verse 9:	Verse 10:
The rat takes the cheese.	The cheese stands alone.
The rat takes the cheese.	The cheese stands alone.
Heigh-ho, the derry-oh.	Heigh-ho, the derry-oh.
The rat takes the cheese.	The cheese stands alone.

© Cengage Learning 2015

3.7 From the Alice Gallery, build male and female persons and add them to your world. Using your persons, build a program in which your people dance the waltz (or a similar dance in which the partners' movements are synchronized). Optional: Have your story play music while your people dance.

3.8 Create a story containing water, a **Person**, several **Fish**, and fishing props, including the **FishingBoat** and **FishingNet**. Create a **Person** method **pickup(obj)** that causes a person to bend over and pick up an object **obj**. Create a **Person** method **throw(obj, target)** that causes the person to throw an object **obj** at another object **target**. Then create a story in which your person is in the fishing boat and tries to catch the fish by throwing the fishnet at them. Create your own ending for the story.

3.9 Using the exercising characters from Section 3.1, add one or more additional exercise methods, such as **doCrunch()**, **doSitup()**, **doLegLift()**, and **doPushup()**. Then create an exercise video in which the characters lead the audience through a series of exercises.

3.10 Create a water scene, and add a **Shark** object from the Alice Gallery. Create a **swim(*distance*)** method that causes the shark or any other **Swimmer** to move its body parts as though swimming and move the distance passed to its **distance** parameter. Then add two persons to the scene appropriately dressed for swimming. Position them in the water as if they are swimming on the surface. Write a **swimOneStroke()** method that causes a person to move his or her arms and legs appropriately for a single stroke of swimming. Then create a scene using these methods in which your persons are swimming, the shark appears, and chases them. Create your own ending for the story.

Chapter 4
Flow Control

*C*ontrolling complexity is the essence of computer programming.

BRIAN KERNIGHAN

*W*hen you get to the fork in the road, take it.

YOGI BERRA

*I*f you build it, he will come.

THE VOICE (JAMES EARL JONES), IN *FIELD OF DREAMS*

*W*hile you're at it, why don't you give me a nice paper cut and pour some lemon juice on it?

MIRACLE MAX (BILLY CRYSTAL), IN *THE PRINCESS BRIDE*

Objectives

Upon completion of this chapter, you will be able to:

- ❏ Use the **Boolean** type and its basic operations
- ❏ Use the **if** statement to perform some statements while skipping others
- ❏ Use the **for** and **while** statements to perform (other) statements more than once
- ❏ Use **Boolean** variables and functions to control **if** and **while** statements
- ❏ Use the **wait()** message to temporarily suspend program execution

Screenshots from Alice 2 © 1999–2013, Alice 3 © 2008–2013, Carnegie Mellon University. All rights reserved. We gratefully acknowledge the financial support of Oracle, Electronic Arts, Sun Microsystems, DARPA, Intel, NSF, and ONR.

In Chapter 1, we saw that the *flow* of a program is the sequence of steps that the program follows in performing a story. From the perspective of an Alice program, we can think of a flow as the sequence of statements that are performed when we click the Run button.

Each of the methods we have written has used the **doInOrder** statement, which produces a sequential execution of the statements within it. However, we sometimes used a **DoTogether** statement, which produces a **parallel execution**. If we consider a group of N statements within a **doInOrder** statement compared to a **DoTogether** statement, we can visualize the difference in behavior of these two statements in a **flow diagram** like the one shown in Figure 4-1.

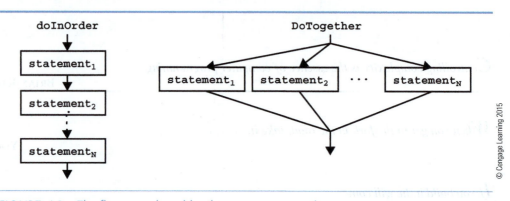

FIGURE 4-1   The flows produced by the **doInOrder** and **DoTogether** statements

The **doInOrder** and **DoTogether** are thus **flow control** statements, because their effect is to *control the flow* of the program through the statements within them. Computer scientists often describe flow control statements as **control structures**.

In this chapter, we will examine several of Alice's flow control statements, including:

- The **if** statement, which directs the flow through one group of statements and away from another group of statements
- The **for** statement, which directs the flow through a group of statements a fixed number of times
- The **while** statement, which directs the flow through a group of statements an arbitrary number of times

Before we examine these statements, let's briefly examine a related topic: the **Boolean** type.

4.1   The **Boolean** Type

You may recall from Chapter 3 that **Boolean** is one of Alice's basic types (for defining variables). The **Boolean** type is named after George Boole, a 19th-century English mathematician who studied *true/false* values and the kinds of operations that can be used with them.

Whereas a numeric variable (**Integer** or **Double**) can have many, many numeric values, a **Boolean** variable can have just one of two values: **true** or **false**. At first, this may seem pretty limiting: what good is a type that only provides two values? As we shall see, the **Boolean** type is extremely useful when we want a program to make decisions. Decision making depends on current circumstances or *conditions*, so a piece of a program that produces a **true** or **false** value is called a **Boolean expression** or **condition**.

4.1.1 **Boolean** Functions

The functions tab of Alice's details area provides questions that we can ask an object. For example, if we want to find out how tall an object is, we can send it the **getHeight()** message, which effectively asks the object, "How tall are you?" to which the object replies with a number.

When the answer to a question is **true** or **false**, the question is called a condition or **Boolean function**. Two of the questions we can ask an object produce a **Boolean** value for their answer, as shown in Figure 4-2.

Function	Value Produced
obj.isFacing(*obj2*)	**true**, if *obj* is facing *obj2*; **false**, otherwise.
obj.isCollidingWith(*obj2*)	**true**, if *obj* and *obj2*'s bounding boxes are touching; **false**, otherwise.

FIGURE 4-2   Boolean functions

© Cengage Learning 2015

For situations where it is useful to have the user of the program answer a true/false question, Alice also provides a **getBooleanFromUser(*prompt*)** function that, given a string value *prompt* that is a true/false question, displays a dialog box presenting that question, followed by buttons labeled True and False. The user answers the question by clicking one of the buttons; the function then returns the value of whichever button the user clicked.

Any of these functions can be used to set the value of a **Boolean** variable, or it can be used with an **if** or **while** statement to make a decision or otherwise control an object's behavior. We discuss these uses next.

4.1.2 **Boolean** Variables

Boolean functions are just one kind of condition. Another kind of condition is the **Boolean** variable or parameter. **Boolean** variables (or parameters) can be created by using the variable… control (or Add Parameter button) and then specifying **Boolean** as the type of the new variable (or parameter). Such variables can be used to store **true** or

false values until they are needed and can serve as a condition in an **if** or **while** statement, as we will see soon.

4.1.3 Relational Operators

Another kind of condition is produced by an *operator* that compares two values and produces a **true** or **false** value as its result. The six most common operators that produce **Boolean** values are called the **relational operators**; they are shown in Figure 4-3.

Relational Operator	Name	Value Produced
`val1 == val2`	equality	**true**, if *val1* and *val2* have the same value; **false**, otherwise
`val1 != val2`	inequality	**true**, if *val1* and *val2* have different values; **false**, otherwise
`val1 < val2`	less-than	**true**, if *val1* is less than *val2*; **false**, otherwise
`val1 <= val2`	less-than-or-equal	**true**, if *val1* is less than or equal to *val2*; **false**, otherwise
`val1 > val2`	greater-than	**true**, if *val1* is greater than *val2*; **false**, otherwise
`val1 >= val2`	greater-than-or-equal	**true**, if *val1* is greater than or equal to *val2*; **false**, otherwise

© Cengage Learning 2015

FIGURE 4-3   The relational operators

These six relational operators are most often used to compare numeric values. For example, suppose a person is to receive overtime pay when he or she works more than 40 hours in a week. If **hoursWorked** is a **Double** variable in which a person's weekly working hours are stored, then the condition:

```
hoursWorked > 40
```

will produce **true** if the person should receive overtime pay and **false** if he or she should not. Relational operators compare two values and produce an appropriate **true** or **false** value.

For string values, Alice provides several methods that can be used to compare the relationships of two strings, as shown in Figure 4-4.

String Function	Value Produced
`str.contentEquals(str2)`	**true**, if `str` and `str2` are identical strings; **false**, otherwise
`str.equalsIgnoreCase(str2)`	**true**, if `str` and `str2` contain the same letters (ignoring uppercase vs. lowercase differences); **false**, otherwise
`str.startsWith(str2)`	**true**, if `str2` and the beginning of `str` are the same; **false**, otherwise
`str.endsWith(str2)`	**true**, if `str2` and the end of `str` are the same; **false**, otherwise
`str.contains(str2)`	**true**, if `str2` appears as a substring within `str`; **false**, otherwise

© Cengage Learning 2015

FIGURE 4-4   The relational methods for strings

4.1.4 `Boolean` Operators

The final three conditional operators are used to combine or modify relational operations. These are called the **Boolean operators**; they are shown in Figure 4-5.[1]

Boolean Operation	Name	Value Produced
`val1 && val2`	AND	**true**, if `val1` and `val2` are both **true**; **false**, otherwise
`val1 || val2`	OR	**true**, if either `val1` or `val2` is **true**; **false**, otherwise
`!val`	NOT	**true**, if `val` is **false**; **false**, if `val` is **true**

© Cengage Learning 2015

FIGURE 4-5   The Boolean operators

---

[1]At the time of this writing, Alice is displaying the AND and OR operations using Alice syntax rather than Java syntax, even when Window > Preferences > Programming Language is set to Java. As a result, our examples that use these operators show the Alice syntax rather than the Java syntax. Hopefully, this will be fixed by the time you read this.

To illustrate the use of these operators, suppose we want to know if a person is a teen-ager and suppose his or her age is stored in an **Integer** variable named **age**. Then the condition

```
age > 12 && age < 20
```

will produce the value **true** if the person is a teenager; otherwise, it will produce the value **false**. Similarly, suppose that a valid test score is in the range 0 to 100 and that we want to guard against data-entry mistakes. If the score is stored in an **Integer** variable named **testScore**, then we can decide if it is invalid with the condition

```
testScore < 0 || testScore > 100
```

since the condition will produce **true** if either **testScore < 0** or **testScore > 100** is **true** but will produce **false** if neither of them is **true**.

Now that we have seen the various ways to build a condition, let's see how we can make use of conditions to control the flow of a program.

4.2   The if Statement

In Alice, the relational and the boolean operators reside in the drop-down menu that appears when we click the down-arrow next to any Alice condition. In this section, we will see how to use this mechanism to build useful conditions for Alice's **if** statement.

4.2.1   Introducing Selective Flow Control

In our story about Tim the wizard, the first part of the Shot 3e user story is as follows:

> Scene 3, Shot e: Tim approaches the dragon, not realizing that it is mute. He says, "Hello." The dragon just stares back at him. Tim asks it, "Can you understand me?" The dragon shakes its head up and down to indicate yes. Tim says, "Can you speak?" The dragon shakes its head sideways to indicate no. Tim says, "Can you only answer yes or no questions?" The dragon shakes its head yes. Tim says, "Are you a tame dragon?" The dragon shakes its head no.

The co-star of this shot is a mute dragon, who answers yes-or-no questions by shak-ing his head up and down for *yes* and by shaking it sideways for *no*. To animate these behaviors, we could write two separate **Dragon** methods, one named **shakeHeadYes()**

and another named **shakeHeadNo()**. Instead, let's kill two birds with one stone and write one **shakeHead()** method that provides both behaviors.

As we saw in Chapter 3, the key to making one method solve more than one problem is to pass arguments that make the method produce the different behaviors. In this case, we will pass the argument **yes** when we want the dragon to shake its head up and down, and we will pass the argument **no** when we want it to shake its head sideways. To store this argument, we will use a parameter whose type is **String**. For lack of a better name, we will name the parameter **yesOrNo**.

If we write out the behavior this method should produce, we might write the following:

Parameter: yesOrNo, a String.

If *yesOrNo* is equal to "yes", the dragon shakes its head up and down;

otherwise, the dragon shakes its head sideways.

The key idea here is that if the parameter has a certain value, we want a certain thing to happen; otherwise, we want something else to happen. The word *if* is the magic word. Any time we use the word *if* to describe a desired behavior, we can produce that behavior using Alice's **if statement**.

To build this method in Alice, we might start by opening our running example program, finding the **doShot3e()** method, and then setting up the shot: adding a dragon to the scene; moving Tim to the scene; positioning the camera so that we can see Tim and the dragon clearly; dropping markers for Tim, the dragon and the camera; and so on. With our scene arranged, we can create a **shakeHead()** method by selecting class **Dragon** in the class navigator; adding a new procedure named **shakeHead**; and then, within this method, creating a new parameter named **yesOrNo**, whose type is **String**. The result is shown in Figure 4-6.

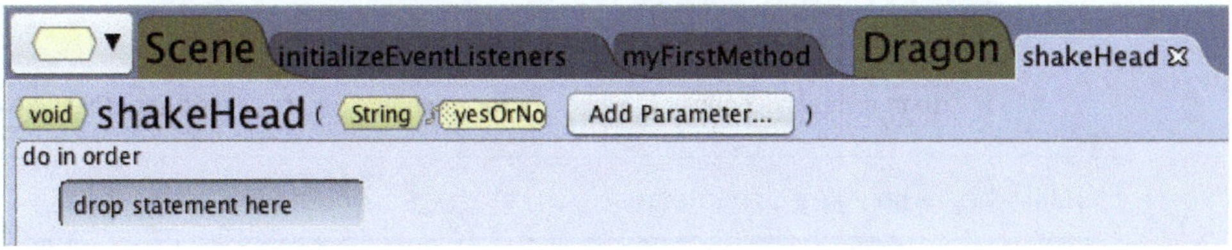

FIGURE 4-6   The empty **shakeHead()** method

Looking at the algorithm for this method, we see our magic word *if*. There is a control named **if** at the bottom of Alice's editing area, so we might begin by dragging it into the method. When we drop it, Alice produces a menu of possible conditions to use to control it. Since our method has no **Boolean** variables or parameters, this menu contains only the choices **true** or **false**, as shown in Figure 4-7.

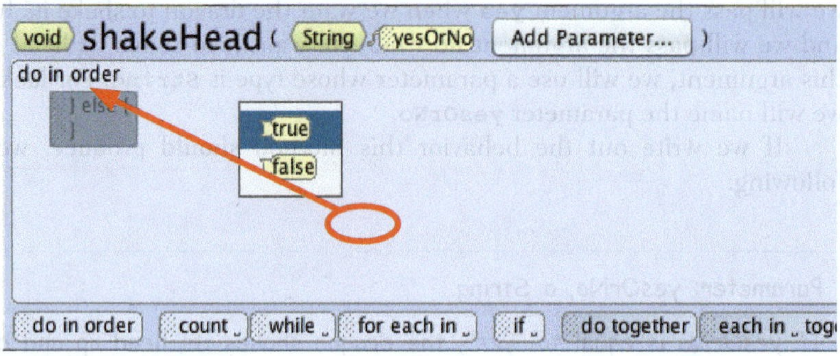

FIGURE 4-7   Dragging and dropping the **if** control

For the moment, we will just choose **true** as a temporary **placeholder** value. Alice then generates an **if** statement within our method, as shown in Figure 4-8.

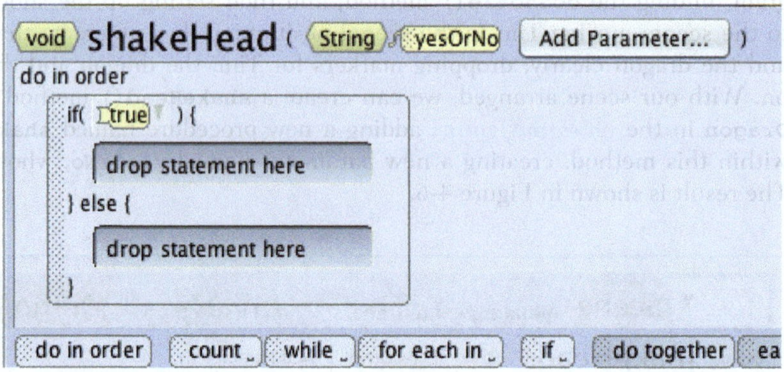

FIGURE 4-8   The Alice **if** statement

4.2.2   **if** Statement Mechanics

An **if** statement is a flow control statement that directs the program's flow according to the value of its condition. Alice's **if** statement has the structure

```
if ( Condition ) {
    Statements₁
} else {
    Statements₂
}
```

and we might visualize the **if** statement's flow-behavior as shown in Figure 4-9.

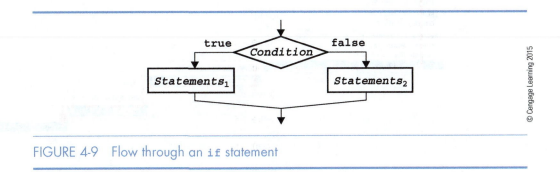

FIGURE 4-9   Flow through an **if** statement

Figure 4-9 indicates that when the flow reaches an **if** statement, it reaches a "fork" in its path. Depending on its *Condition*, the flow proceeds one way or the other, but not both. That is, when the flow first reaches an **if** statement, the **if** statement's *Condition* is evaluated. If the value of the *Condition* is **true**, then the flow is directed through the first group of statements (and the second group is ignored); if the *Condition*'s value is **false**, then the flow is directed through the second group of statements (ignoring the first group). Put differently, when the **if** statement's *Condition* is **true**, then the first group of statements is *selected* and the second group is skipped; otherwise, the second group of statements is *selected* and the first group is skipped. Because of this, the **if** statement's behavior is sometimes called **selective flow control**, or **selective execution**.

4.2.3   Building **if** Statement Conditions

Back in our user story, we want the dragon to shake its head up and down if **yesOrNo** is equal to **yes**; otherwise, it should shake its head sideways. In Figure 4-4, we saw that we can compare two string values using the **contentEquals()** or **equalsIgnoreCase()** methods. Since either the uppercase *YES* or lowercase *yes* or a mixed-case *Yes* would be acceptable in this situation, we will use the **equalsIgnoreCase()** method. To use it, we can click on the down-arrow next to the **true** placeholder in our **if** statement and then navigate down to TextString comparison > ???.equalsIgnoreCase(???) > yesOrNo > Custom TextString, as shown in Figure 4-10.

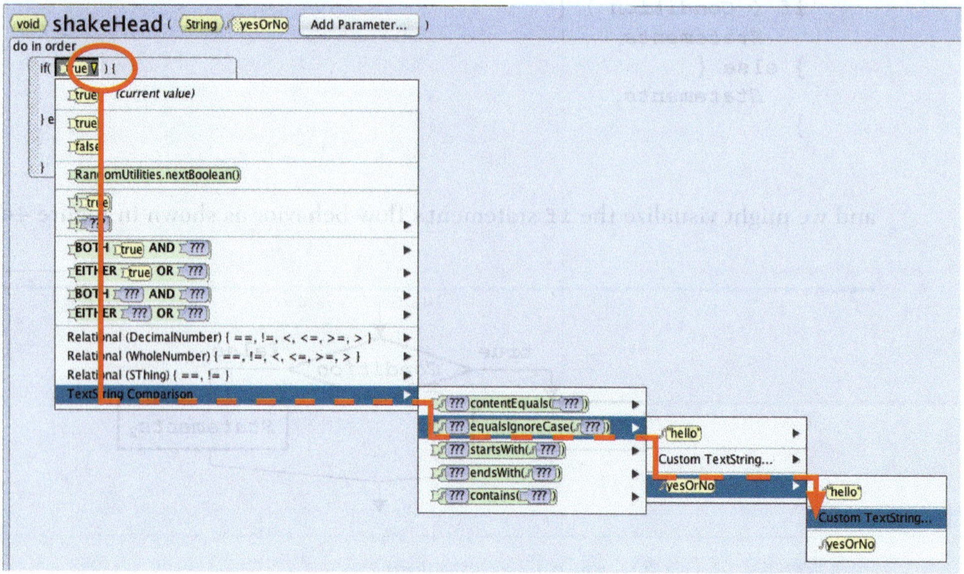

FIGURE 4-10   Choosing a parameter in an `if` statement's condition

This selects our parameter **yesOrNo** as the left operand of the **equalsIgnoreCase()** method; for the right operand, it will display a dialog box in which we can enter the string **yes** as the value to compare **yesOrNo** against. When we click its **Ok** button, Alice generates the condition shown in Figure 4-11.

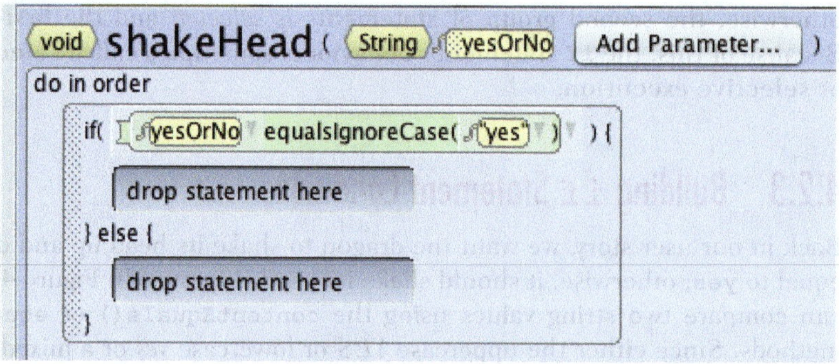

FIGURE 4-11   An `if` statement's condition using the **equalsIgnoreCase()** function

Before we continue, note that in Figure 4-10 the menu that appears when we click the down-arrow in the **if** statement's condition provides us with access to the Boolean operators and the numeric relational operators, as well as the string relational methods.

When the condition is in place, finishing the method consists of placing statements in the top drop statement here area to shake the dragon's head up and down, and then placing statements in the bottom drop statement here area to shake its head sideways. Figure 4-12 shows the finished method.

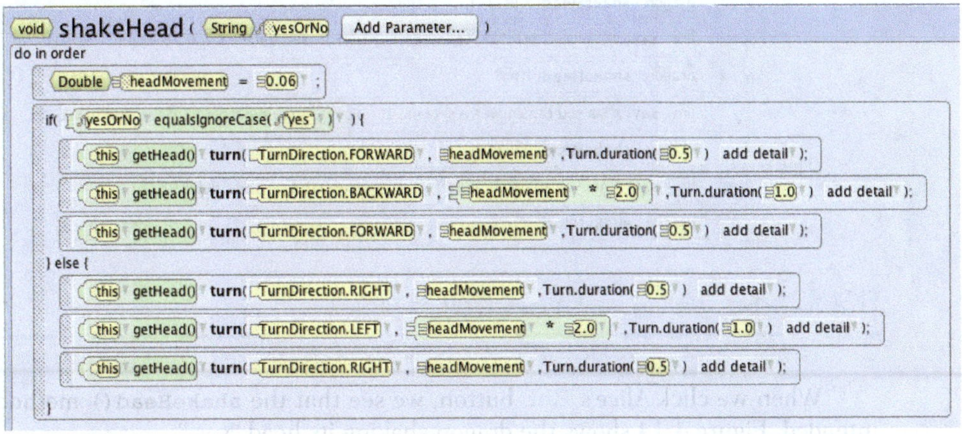

FIGURE 4-12   The **shakeHead()** method (final version)

In Figure 4-12, we have used a local **Double** variable named **headMovement** to store how far the dragon turns its head. By using that variable instead of actual numbers in each of the **turn()** messages, we simplify the task of finding the right amount by which the dragon should shake its head, since trying a given value requires just one change (to the variable) instead of six changes.

To test this **shakeHead()** method, we build the method for Shot 3e, the first part of which is shown in Figure 4-13.

```
void doShot3e ( Add Parameter... )
do in order
    camera  moveAndOrientTo( cameraShot3e  add detail );
    tim  turnToFace( dragon  add detail );
    tim  getHead() pointAt( dragon  add detail );
    tim  say( "Hello." ▼  add detail );
    this  delay( 3.0 );
    tim  say( "Can you understand me?" ,Say.duration( 2.0 )  add detail );
    dragon  shakeHead( "yes" );
    tim  say( "Can you speak?" ,Say.duration( 2.0 )  add detail );
    dragon  shakeHead( "no" );
    tim  say( "But you can answer yes-or-no questions?" ,Say.duration( 2.0 )  add detail );
    dragon  shakeHead( "yes" );
    tim  say( "Are you a tame dragon?" ,Say.duration( 2.0 )  add detail );
    dragon  shakeHead( "no" );
```

FIGURE 4-13   Testing `shakeHead()` in `doShot3e()`

When we click Alice's **Run** button, we see that the **shakeHead()** method works as intended. Figure 4-14 shows the dragon shaking its head "yes."

FIGURE 4-14   The dragon shakes its head "yes"

4.2.4 The `delay()` Statement

To make Tim wait between his first and second **say()** statements in Figure 4-13, we used another flow control statement named **delay()**, whose form is as follows:

```
this.delay(numSecs);
```

When the flow reaches this statement and the **delay()** message is sent to the scene, the scene then *pauses* the program's flow, sets an internal timer to **numSecs** seconds, and starts this timer counting down towards zero. When the timer reaches zero, the scene *resumes* the program's flow at whatever statement follows the **delay()** message.

4.2.5 Validating Parameter Values

In the previous example, we saw how the `if` statement can be used to direct the flow of a program through one group of statements while it bypasses another group, where each group of statements is equally valid. A different use of the `if` statement is to *guard* a group of statements and only allow the flow to enter them if "everything is ok."

Function `calculateHypotenuse()` Revisited

To illustrate this use of the `if` statement, let's revisit the `calculateHypotenuse()` function that we wrote in Figure 3-70. When two **Double** arguments are passed to its parameters `leg1` and `leg2`, the function uses the Pythagorean Theorem to calculate and return the length of a right triangle whose legs have those lengths. Something we did not discuss there was whether or not there are any restrictions or *preconditions* on the values of those arguments, but it should be evident that a triangle's leg lengths must be positive values or the problem makes no sense. This situation—where parameter values need to be checked for validity before we allow the flow to proceed—is called **validating a parameter**.

One way that we can validate our function's `leg1` and `leg2` parameters is to use an `if` statement and modify the function's logic as follows:

```
Double hypotenuse = 0.0

if either parameter is invalid:
    have Geo speak a descriptive error message
otherwise (both parameters are valid):
    assign hypotenuse the value: Math.sqrt(leg1*leg1 + leg2*leg2)

return hypotenuse
```

Figure 4-15 shows how we would encode this logic in Alice.

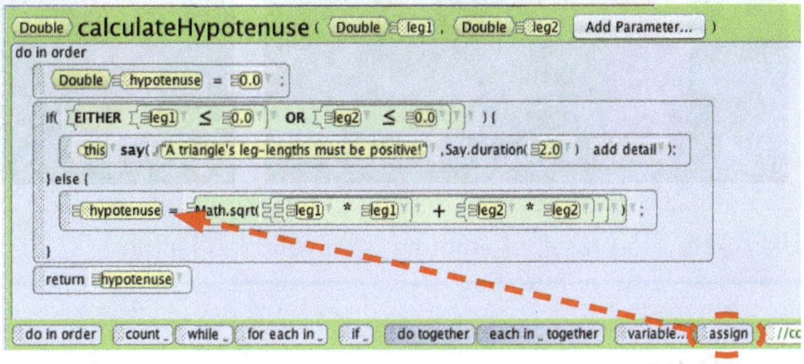

FIGURE 4-15 Validating parameter values

We first declare a local variable named **hypotenuse** to store the value that our function will return, and initialize it to zero. We then use an `if` statement to check whether **leg1** or **leg2** violates our function's precondition. If so, we have Geo speak a descriptive error message; otherwise, we apply the Pythagorean Theorem to **leg1** and **leg2** and store the result in **hypotenuse**. To change the value of variable **hypotenuse** from its initial value (0), we drag the assign control into the editing area, as indicated in Figure 4-15. When we drop it there, Alice displays a menu from which we can choose the option **hypotenuse =** with a placeholder value to the right of the = symbol. We can then replace that placeholder using the expression for the hypotenuse from the Pythagorean Theorem. Finally, we have our function return the value in **hypotenuse**. This will cause our function to return zero if either parameter was invalid but return the correct result if both parameters are valid. Figure 4-16 shows what happens if we enter the values 3 and −4 as the leg lengths.

FIGURE 4-16   The result of entering an invalid leg length

Assignment Statements

As can be seen in Figure 4-15, Alice's assign control lets us build **assignment statements**, which let us change the value that is stored in a variable. Assignment statements have the structure

```
variable = Expression;
```

When the flow of control reaches such a statement, the *Expression* to the right of the = symbol is performed first, producing a value. That value is then stored in (i.e., *assigned to*) the *variable* to the left of the = symbol. The = symbol is called the **assignment operator**.

Any time a program needs to change the value of a variable from its initial value, an assignment statement can be used.

The Jumping Fish Revisited

As another problem, let's return to our jumping fish example from Section 3.2. There, we built a method for the **Swimmer** class named **jump()**, with a parameter named **distance**, to which we could pass an argument indicating how far we wanted the fish to jump. If we assume that the fish can only jump forward, then a precondition for this method is that the argument passed to the parameter **distance** must be positive. We can check this with the condition **distance > 0**. Passing an argument that is 0 or less can be treated as an error.

There may also be an upper bound on how far a fish can jump, but identifying such a bound is more difficult. For small fish, 2 meters might be a reasonable upper bound. However, if a fish were bigger or super-strong, maybe it could jump farther, so we want to make this upper bound easy to change. We can do so by defining a variable named **MAX_DISTANCE**, and then using the condition **distance <= MAX_DISTANCE** to check that the argument passed to parameter **distance** is within this bound.

If a variable's value will not change and its purpose is to improve a program's readability, declare it as a *constant* and name it with all uppercase letters, to distinguish it from normal variables.

A *constant* can be declared by dragging and dropping the variable... control; when the Insert Variable dialog box appears, select the constant radio button.

We now have two conditions that need to be met in order for the argument passed to the parameter to be deemed valid: **distance > 0** and **distance <= MAX_DISTANCE**. Since *both* of these must be true in order for our argument to be acceptable, we use the Boolean AND operator (**&&**) to combine them: **distance > 0 && distance <= MAX_DISTANCE**.

We will use these ideas to revise the **jump()** method, as follows:

```
if (distance > 0 && distance <= MAX_DISTANCE) {
    // ... statements performed when distance is valid
    // (make the fish jump, as shown in Figure 3-50)
} else { // ... distance is invalid
    if (distance <= 0) {
        // ... statements performed when distance is too low
    } else {
        // ... statements performed when distance is too high
    }
}
```

Here, we are using an `if` statement with a second `if` statement nested within its `else` section. The first `if` is often called the **outer if**, and the second `if` is often called the **inner if**, or the **nested if**.

Figure 4-17 presents a revised version of the `jump()` method, using this approach to validate the parameter.

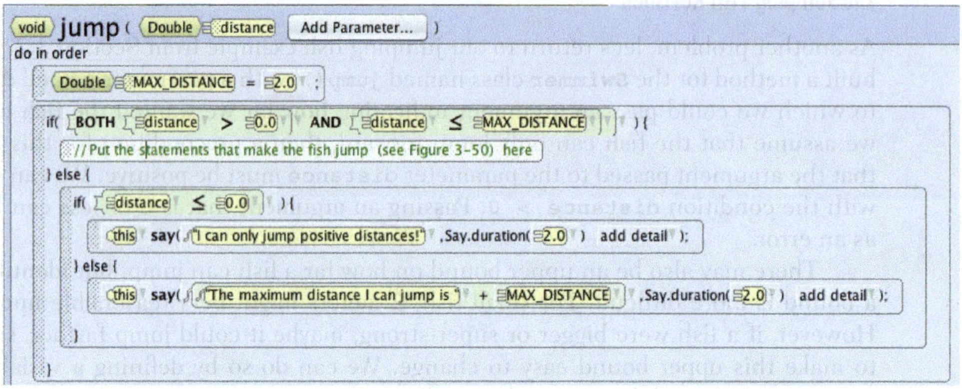

FIGURE 4-17   Validating a parameter's value with nested `if` statements

In order to let us focus on the `if` statements, we have omitted the statements that actually make the fish jump. These can be easily added, using the statements shown in Figure 3-50.

Let's take a moment to trace the program flow through the revised method:

- When **distance** is valid, the outer `if`'s condition will be **true**, so flow will proceed into the statements that make the fish jump and will skip the inner `if` statement.
- When **distance** is invalid, the first condition will be **false**, so flow will proceed into the **else** section of the outer `if`. The only statement in that section is the inner `if` statement, which determines *why* **distance** is invalid (was it too small or too large?):
  - If **distance** is zero or less, the flow proceeds to the statement in which we send the fish the first **say()** message.
  - Otherwise, **distance** must be greater than **MAX_DISTANCE**, so the flow proceeds to the **else** section, in which we send the fish the second **say()** message.

To illustrate, Figure 4-18 shows the fish's behavior when we send it the message `jump(-2)`.

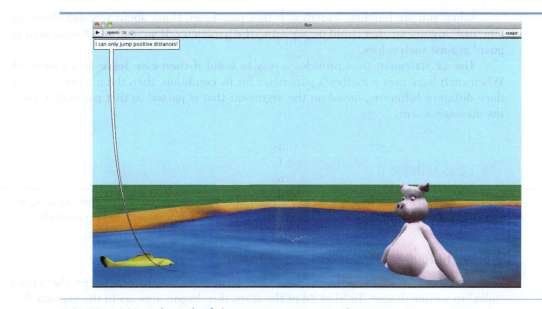

FIGURE 4-18   Asking the fish to jump a negative distance

Similarly, Figure 4-19 shows the fish's behavior when we send it the message `jump(3)`.

FIGURE 4-19   Asking the fish to jump too far

When you are building a method with a parameter, think about whether there are any "bad" arguments that could be passed to the parameter. If so, use an **if** statement to guard against such values.

The **if** statement thus provides a way to build **if-then-else logic** into a method. When such logic uses a method's parameter for its condition, then the method can produce different behaviors, based on the argument that is passed to that parameter when the message is sent.

4.3   The **for** Statement

The **if** statement provides a way to perform statements *selectively*. In this section, we examine the **for statement**, which provides a way to perform statements *repetitively*.

4.3.1   Introducing Repetition

In Section 4.2, we saw how to animate Shot 3e of our story, in which Tim the wizard "talks" to a mute dragon. In Shot 3d of the story, this dragon appears in the sky and flies around Tim's castle a few times before descending and settling on the castle gate. In order to fly, the dragon needs to flap its wings; unfortunately, the dragons in the Alice Gallery do not have such a method. However, we can build a method named **flapWings()** and pass it a numeric argument that specifies how many times the dragon should flap its wings. To store this argument, we will need a parameter, which we will name **numTimes**. It doesn't make sense for a dragon to flap its wings by a fractional amount, so we will make this parameter an **Integer**. We might describe the behavior we want this way:

> Parameter: *numTimes*, an Integer.
>
> Repeat the following action *numTimes* times:
>
>   The dragon flaps its wings once.

Using what we already know, we can figure out how to make the dragon flap its wings once. What we do not yet know is how to redirect the flow so as to *repeat* the wing-flapping behavior **numTimes** times.

We can start by creating a new method named **flapWings()** in the **Dragon** class with an **Integer** parameter named **numTimes**. We can then add statements to the method to make the dragon flap its wings once. Since the dragon's two wings are initially upright, making them flap once consists of four separate steps:

1. Move the dragon's wings from an upright position to the top of a flapping position.

2. Move the dragon's wings down (the wings' downbeat).

3. Move the dragon's wings up (the wings' upbeat).

4. Move the dragon's wings back to their original upright position.

Note that Steps 2 and 3 are those in which the dragon flaps its wings. Step 1 is merely setting up the flapping action, while Step 4 is returning the wings to their starting position. Steps 2 and 3 are thus those that we must repeat.

To make the dragon's wing-flapping more realistic, we adjust the **duration** values of the wing movements, so that downstrokes (i.e., beating against the air) take slightly longer than upstrokes (i.e., resetting for a downstroke). In the version below, we've made the downstroke take 0.6 seconds and the upstroke take 0.4 seconds, for a total time of 1 second per flap. With that completed, we are ready to add repetition.

To make the **flapWings()** method flap the dragon's wings more than once, we drag the count control from the bottom of the editing area into the method and drop it below the **DoTogether** block that performs the first step. When we drop it, Alice displays a menu from which we can choose our parameter **numTimes** as the number of repetitions we want, as shown in Figure 4-20.

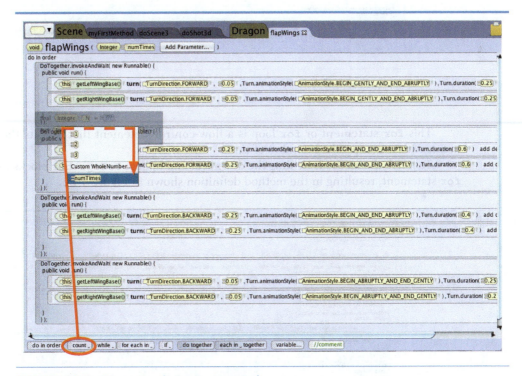

FIGURE 4-20   Dragging the **count** control

When we select **numTimes**, Alice inserts an empty **for** statement in the method, as shown in Figure 4-21.

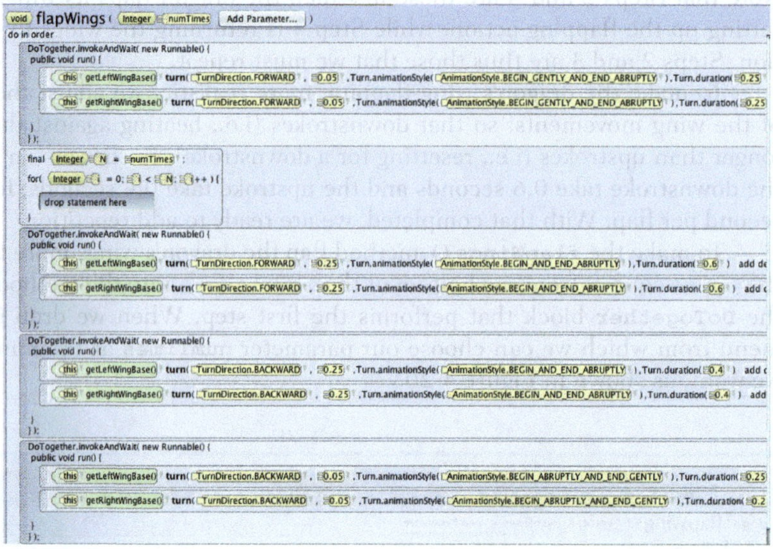

FIGURE 4-21   An empty `for` loop

This **for statement** or **for** loop is a flow-control statement that repeats the statements within it a specified number of times.

To finish the method, we drag the downbeat and upbeat **DoTogether** blocks into the **for** statement, resulting in the method definition shown in Figure 4-22.

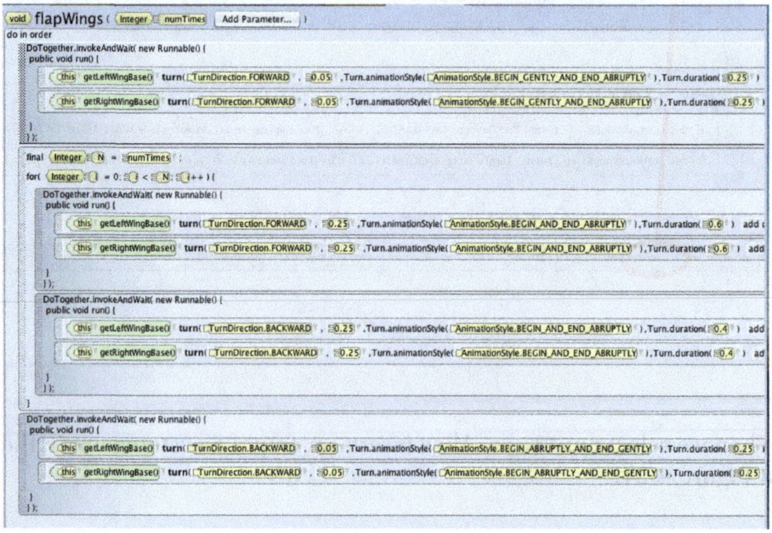

FIGURE 4-22   The final `flapWings()` method

With this method definition, if we send the **dragon** the message **flapWings(3)**, then it will flap its wings three times. If we send it the message **flapWings(8)**, it will flap its wings eight times. This will simplify the task of animating Shot 3d, in which the dragon flies into the scene, circles Tim's castle a few times, and then descends to the castle gate.

4.3.2 Mechanics of the **for** Statement

The **for** statement is a flow-control statement whose purpose is to repeatedly direct the program's flow through the statements within it while *counting* through a range of numbers. For this reason, it is sometimes called a **counting loop**. If we were to send the **dragon** the message **flapWings(3)**, then the **for** statement would count **0, 1, 2** (performing the statements within the loop once for each number), and then quit. If we were to send **dragon.flapWings(8);**, then the **for** statement would count **0, 1, 2, 3, 4, 5, 6, 7** (again, performing the statements within it once for each number), and then quit. More generally, the **for** statement in **flapWings()** will always count from **0** to **numTimes-1**.

How does it work? The **for** statement in Figure 4-22 has the following structure:

```
final Integer N = numTimes;
for (Integer i = 0; i < N; i++ ) {
    Statements
}
```

When the program's flow reaches this statement, the flow proceeds as shown in Figure 4-23.

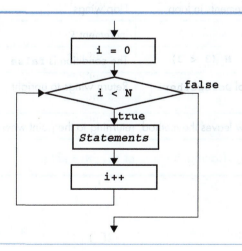

FIGURE 4-23   Flow through a **for** statement

If we follow the arrows in Figure 4-23, we see that the $i = 0$ in a **for** statement is performed just once, when the flow first reaches the statement. The **for** statement's condition $i < N$ is then checked. If the condition is **false**, then the flow is directed *around* the **Statements** within it to whatever statement follows the **for** statement. If the condition is **true**, then the **Statements** within the **for** statement are performed, followed by the i++ (++ is the **increment operator**, which adds 1 to its operand). The flow is then redirected *back* to the condition, restarting the cycle.

In Figure 4-24, we trace the behavior of the **for** statement in Figure 4-22 when we send **dragon** the message **flapWings(3)**.

Step	Flow is in...	Effect	Comment
0	First **DoTogether**	Reposition wings	Wings now ready for downbeat
1	$i = 0;$	Initialize i	i's value is 0
2	$i < N$ (0 < 3)	The condition is **true**	Flow is directed into the loop
3	Statements in loop	Flap wings	The first repetition
4	i++	Increment i	i's value changes from 0 to 1
5	$i < N$ (1 < 3)	The condition is **true**	Flow is directed into the loop
6	Statements in loop	Flap wings	The second repetition
7	i++	Increment i	i's value changes from 1 to 2
8	$i < N$ (2 < 3)	The condition is **true**	Flow is directed into the loop
9	Statements in loop	Flap wings	The third repetition
10	i++	Increment i	i's value changes from 2 to 3
11	$i < N$ (3 < 3)	The condition is **false**	Flow is directed *out of* the loop
12	Final **DoTogether**	Return wings to upright	Wings are back in original position
13	Flow leaves the method, returning to the point where it was invoked.		

FIGURE 4-24 Tracing the flow of **flapWings(3)**

As indicated above, Alice's **for** statement begins counting with **0**, uses **i < N** as the condition (for whatever value of **N** we specify), and uses the expression **i++** to increase the index. The **for** statement is thus useful in any situation where you need to repeat a group of statements a known number of times. For situations where repetition is needed but the number of repetitions is not known in advance, Alice provides the **while** statement (see Section 4.4).

4.3.3   Parallel Loops

The user story for Shot 3d is as follows:

> There is a rumble in the distance. Tim looks up and says, "Now what?" A dragon appears, flying toward the castle. When it gets close, it circles the castle twice and then descends, landing on the castle's gate.

Using Divide and Conquer, we might divide this shot into these steps:

1. There is a rumbling sound; Tim reacts.
2. A dragon appears, flying toward the castle.
3. When it gets close, it circles the castle two times.
4. It then descends, landing on the castle's gate.

We will see how to accomplish the first step in Chapter 5. There are different ways to accomplish the second step. Two of them are:

- Position the dragon off-screen, compute and store the distance from the dragon to the castle's gate in a variable, and then use a **move()** statement to move the dragon that distance.
- Position the dragon above the castle's gate (as we did in Section 4.2) and then work backwards:
  1. Move the dragon upwards from the top of the gate a given distance (e.g., 10 units).
  2. Drop a marker for the dragon at that spot.
  3. Move the dragon a long distance backward, so that it is off-screen.

Our program can then use the **moveAndOrientTo()** message to move the dragon to the marker above the gate.

Since we have already positioned the dragon above the castle gate in Section 4.2, we will use this second approach.

The third step can also be performed different ways. We will use a **for** statement to repeat a statement that makes the dragon circle above the castle, as shown in Figure 4-25.

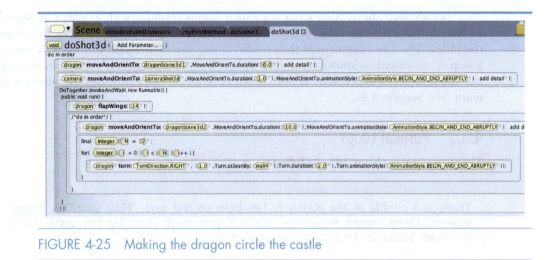

FIGURE 4-25   Making the dragon circle the castle

Our `doShot3d()` method begins by positioning the dragon to its off-screen marker and positioning the camera to its marker for this shot. Flow then enters a `DoTogether` statement that causes the dragon to simultaneously flap its wings, fly to its marker above the castle gate, and then fly around the castle (taking 2 seconds per circuit). As shown above, this behavior will repeat two times. If, after testing the method, we were to decide that more circuits around the castle tower would be preferable, all we would need to do is change the `for` statement's `N` value from `2` to the desired number.

The `asSeenBy` Attribute

One subtlety about Figure 4-25 is how the `turn()` message we send to the dragon causes it to circle the castle. Alice's `turn()` message has a special asSeenBy attribute. Normally, this attribute is unset, in which case `turn()` just causes its receiver to revolve about its LR axis or its FB axis. However, if we specify another object (like a part of our castle) as the value of the asSeenBy attribute, then the `turn()` message causes its receiver to *turn in a circle centered on that object*. Figure 4-25 uses this trick to make the dragon revolve around the castle once for each repetition of the `for` statement.

The `duration` Attribute

Because we are simultaneously flapping the dragon's wings and moving or turning the dragon, it takes a bit of trial and error to animate these actions smoothly. We began by setting the `move()` and `turn()` messages' style attributes to BEGIN_AND_END_ABRUPTLY. We also had to experiment with the number of wing flaps and the duration of the `turn()` message, resulting in the values seen in Figure 4-25. This produced a reasonably smooth animation for the first three steps of our shot; we will finish the fourth step of this shot by making the dragon descend to the gate in the next section.

Parallel Loops

A final subtlety about Figure 4-25 is that it contains two loops running simultaneously (i.e., in parallel). The obvious one is the **for** loop at the bottom of the method that makes the dragon circle the castle. The less obvious one is the **for** loop that is inside the **flapWings()** method. Since the **flapWings()** method and the **for** loop at the bottom of the method are both inside a **DoTogether** block, these two loops are running at the same time, which is necessary to make the dragon's flying seem realistic.

4.4   The `while` Statement

The **for** statement is a means of causing flow to repeatedly move through the same group of statements a fixed number of times. For this reason, the **for** statement is often called a counting statement or a counting loop. The program must "know" (or it must be able to compute) how many repetitions are needed when flow reaches the **for** statement, in order to set the value of the **N** variable that controls its repetitions.

This raises a question: What do we do when we encounter a situation for which we need repetitive flow-behavior, but we do not know in advance how many repetitions are required? For statements like this, Alice and other programming languages provide the **while** statement.

4.4.1   Introducing the `while` Statement

In the previous section, we built the first three steps of Shot 3d of our story about Tim the wizard, in which a dragon appears and circles the castle. In the fourth step of this shot, the dragon descends and lands on the castle gate.

Since we moved the dragon up 10 units above the castle gate, we could build the fourth step using a **for** loop that counts 10 times, moving the dragon down by 1 unit each repetition. A drawback to this approach is that if we later change the elevation of the dragon above the gate, we will have to also change the number of repetitions of the **for** loop.

To avoid this, we will perform the fourth step using a **while** statement instead of a **for** statement. The idea is to repeatedly move the dragon downwards 1 unit, so long as it is not touching the castle gate. To make this happen, we click the while control at the bottom of the editing area, drag it into the method, and drop it at the last position within the **doInOrder** statement. Alice will display a context menu from which we can choose **true** as a placeholder value for the loop's condition, as shown in Figure 4-26.

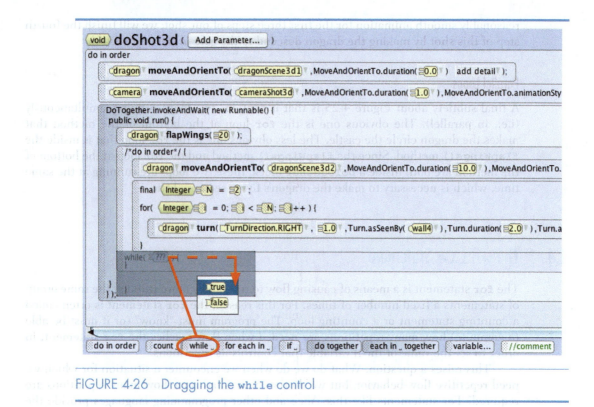

FIGURE 4-26   Dragging the **while** control

Alice then generates the empty **while** statement shown in Figure 4-27.

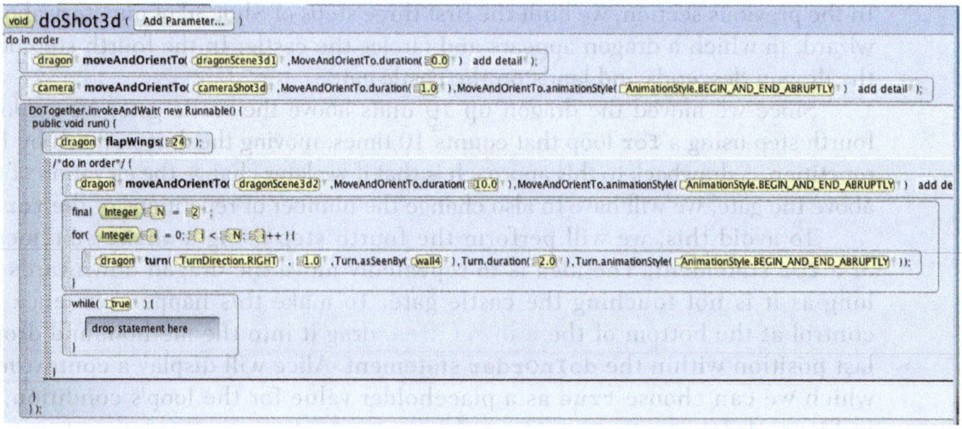

FIGURE 4-27   An empty **while** statement

For each repetition of the **while** statement, we want the dragon to flap its wings once and move downward 1 unit. We want this behavior to repeat as many times as necessary, so long as the dragon is not touching the castle gate. To build this condition, we start by clicking the down-arrow next to the **while** statement's placeholder condition and choose the NOT operator (!) from the menu, as shown in Figure 4-28.

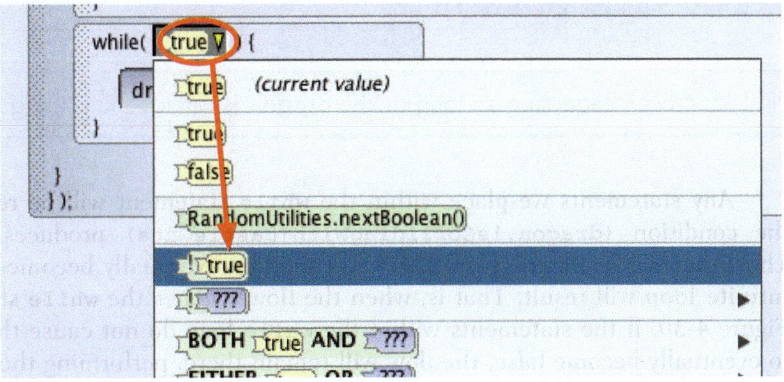

FIGURE 4-28   Choosing the NOT (!) operator

When we select this NOT operator, Alice modifies our **while** loop's condition accordingly, as shown in Figure 4-29.

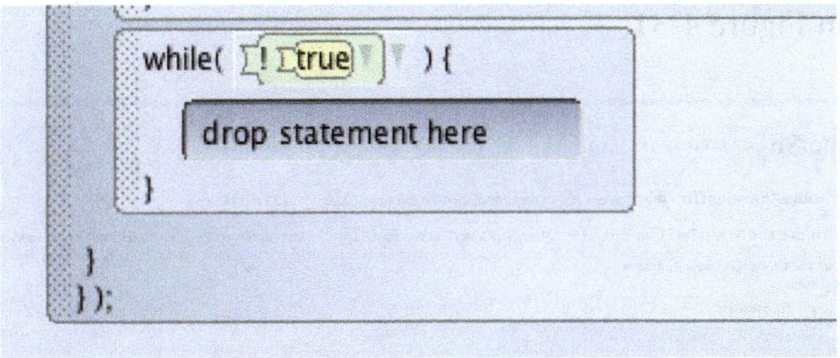

FIGURE 4-29   The **while** loop with a NOT (!) operator as its condition

We can then drag the **isCollidingWith()** function message from the Functions tab of the methods area onto our **true** placeholder and choose **castleGate** as its target, yielding the loop shown in Figure 4-30.

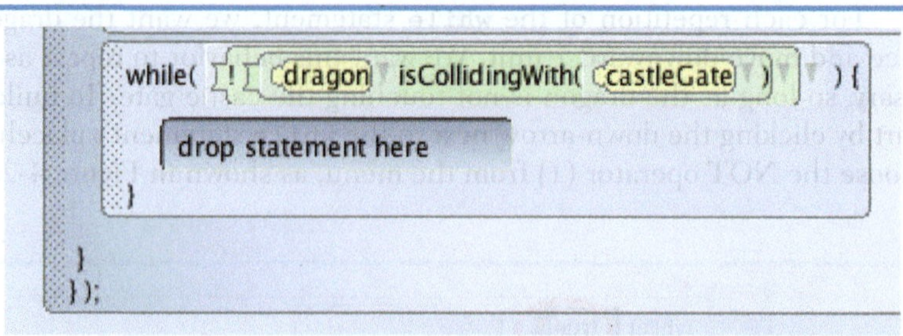

FIGURE 4-30   Repeating so long as the dragon is not touching the gate

Any statements we place within the **while** statement will be repeated so long as the condition **!dragon.isCollidingWith(castleGate)** produces the value **true**. Those statements must ensure that the condition eventually becomes **false** or else an **infinite loop** will result. That is, when the flow reaches the **while** statement shown in Figure 4-30, if the statements within the **while** loop do not cause the loop's condition to eventually become false, the flow will remain there, performing those statements and sending the dragon the **isCollidingWith(castleGate)** message over and over forever, or until we terminate the program, whichever comes first. Any time the flow reaches a **while** loop whose statements do not cause its condition to eventually become **false**, this infinite looping behavior will result.

To avoid an infinite loop, the loop's statements should move the dragon down a small distance, so that its bounding box eventually touches that of the gate. When that happens, the subexpression **dragon.isCollidingWith(castleGate)** will become **true**, which means the condition **!dragon.isCollidingWith(castleGate)** will become **false**, and the loop will terminate. We can use these ideas to complete the method, as shown in Figure 4-31.

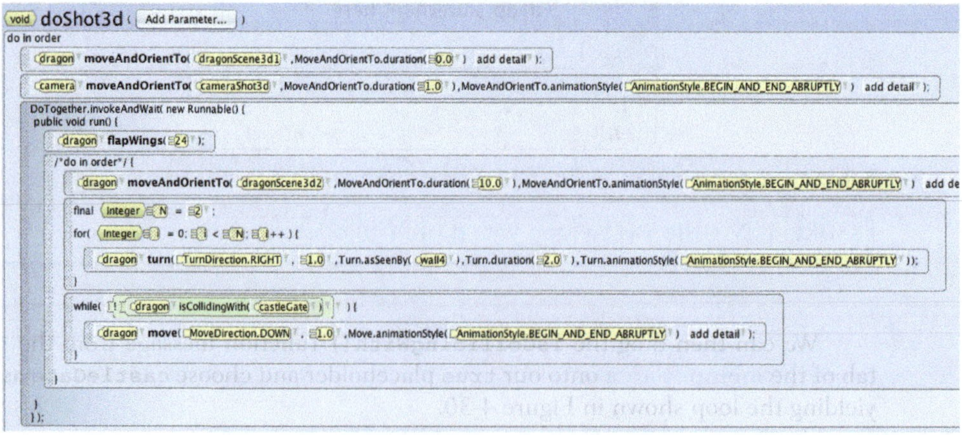

FIGURE 4-31   The **doShot3d()** method (final version)

Each repetition of the **move()** message inside the **while** statement in Figure 4-31 takes 1 second, during which the dragon simultaneously flaps its wings and moves down 1 meter. If we decide this descent is too slow, we can double its descent rate by changing the **1** to a **2**; or if it seems too fast, we can slow the descent by changing the **1** to a **0.5**. The key is to decide how fast the dragon should descend to produce a "realistic" animation and then adjust the number of wing-flaps accordingly.

That completes our work on this story for now. Save what you have done so we can return to it later.

4.4.2 **while** Statement Mechanics

Where the **for** statement is a counting loop, the **while** statement is a general, or **indefinite loop**, meaning the number of repetitions to be performed need not be known in advance. The structure of the Alice **while** statement is as follows:

```
while ( Condition ) {
    Statements
}
```

When flow reaches a **while** statement, it proceeds as shown in Figure 4-32.

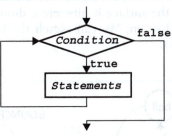

FIGURE 4-32   Flow through a **while** statement

© Cengage Learning 2015

In Figure 4-32, when flow first reaches a **while** statement, its **Condition** is evaluated. If it is **false**, then the flow leaves the **while** statement, bypassing its *Statements*. However, if it is **true**, then the *Statements* within the **while** statement are performed, after which the flow is redirected back to recheck its **Condition**, where the process begins again.

4.4.3 Comparing the **for** and **while** Statements

Alice's **for** and **while** statements both provide **repetitive flow control** or **repetitive execution** of the statements they control. If you compare Figure 4-32 to Figure 4-23, you will see that the **while** statement's behavior is actually much simpler than that of the **for** statement. This is because the **while** is the more general flow-control statement; whereas the **for** statement is useful in counting situations, the **while** statement can be used in *any* situation where repetition is required.

So when should you use each statement? Whenever you are working to produce a behavior that needs to be repeated, ask yourself this question: "Am I counting something?" If the answer is "yes," then a **for** statement should be your first choice; otherwise, use a **while** statement. For example, in Figures 4-22 and 4-25, we counted wing-flaps and castle-circlings, respectively. By contrast, in Figure 4-31, we were not counting anything, just making the dragon descend until it touched the castle gate.

Both the **while** and the **for** statements test their conditions *before* the statements inside the loop are performed. In both cases, if the condition is initially **false**, then statements within the loop will be bypassed (i.e., not performed). If you write a program containing a loop statement that seems to be having no effect, it is likely that the loop's condition is **false** when flow reaches it. To remedy this, either choose a different condition or ensure that its condition is **true** before flow reaches the loop.

4.4.4   A Second Example

As a second example of the **while** statement, suppose that Scene 1 of a story has a girl named Jane dropping a soccer ball (called a football in most countries). Jane lets it bounce until it stops on its own. Our problem is to get it to bounce realistically.

When it is dropped, a ball falls until it strikes a surface beneath it. Then it rebounds upwards some distance (depending on some bounce factor that combines its elasticity, the hardness of the surface it hits, etc.), drops again, rebounds again, drops again, rebounds again, and so on. We can sketch the behavior as being something like that shown in Figure 4-33.

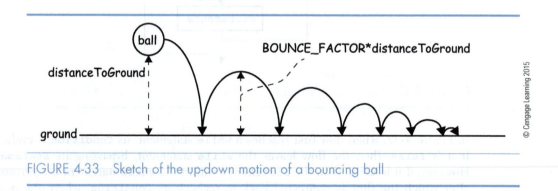

© Cengage Learning 2015

FIGURE 4-33   Sketch of the up-down motion of a bouncing ball

For simplicity, we will just have the soccer ball bounce straight up and down.

Using the **Child** and **SoccerBall** classes from Alice's Gallery, we might start by building a scene like the one shown in Figure 4-34.

FIGURE 4-34 Jane with the soccer ball

To produce the desired bouncing behavior, we might write a **dropAndBounce()** method for the **SoccerBall** class, which is shown in Figure 4-35.

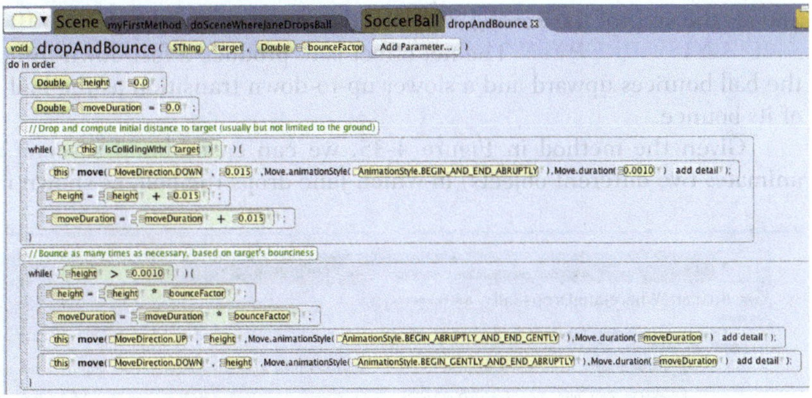

FIGURE 4-35 Method **dropAndBounce()**

There are a few subtleties in this method that are worth discussing:

- Since this is a **SoccerBall** method, the **ground** is not visible within the method. Moreover, a programmer might want to drop the ball onto a surface other than the **ground**, so we will pass the **ground** to the method as an argument. To store this argument, we declare a parameter named **target**. When we create this parameter, we give it the type **SThing** that can store an Alice object such as the **ground**.

- Since different surfaces have differing hardnesses, we might want to pass a second argument that indicates how "bouncy" the first argument is. To store this argument, we declare a second parameter named **bounceFactor** to store the percentage of its original height an object will bounce. Through trial and error, we determined that **0.55** seems to work well for this argument.

- When Jane drops the ball, we do not know in advance how high it is above the ground,[2] so we use one **while** loop to move the ball down by small (**0.015**) increments, so long as it has not collided with the ground. In the same loop, we use an assignment statement to sum those increments, storing them in a variable named **height**. We also use a different assignment statement to sum the durations, storing them in a variable named **moveDuration**. Since we are adding to them each iteration of the loop, both of these variables must be initialized to zero.

- After the first **while** loop completes and we have accumulated the distance the ball drops in variable **height**, we use a second **while** loop to repeatedly make the ball bounce so long as the height it rebounds exceeds a very small number (e.g., **0.001**). The body of this loop calculates the next bounce's **height** (and **moveDuration**) by multiplying the old **height** (and **moveDuration**) by the **bounceFactor** parameter and then uses two **move()** messages to move the ball up and down by that distance (and duration). To set the duration of the **move()** messages, we had to first set the duration to a placeholder value and then drag the **moveDuration** variable onto that placeholder. Thanks to this, each successive bounce-movement occurs faster as the distance to the ground gets smaller.

Another refinement that increases realism was to set the style of the **move()** message that causes the ball's bounce upward to BEGIN_ABRUPTLY_AND_END_GENTLY and set the style of the **move()** message that causes the ball's drop to BEGIN_GENTLY_AND_END_ABRUPTLY. The net effect is to produce a fast down-to-up transition when the ball bounces upward and a slower up-to-down transition as the ball reaches the peak of its bounce.

Given the method in Figure 4-35, we can easily build a scene method (since it animates two different objects) in which Jane drops the ball, as shown in Figure 4-36.

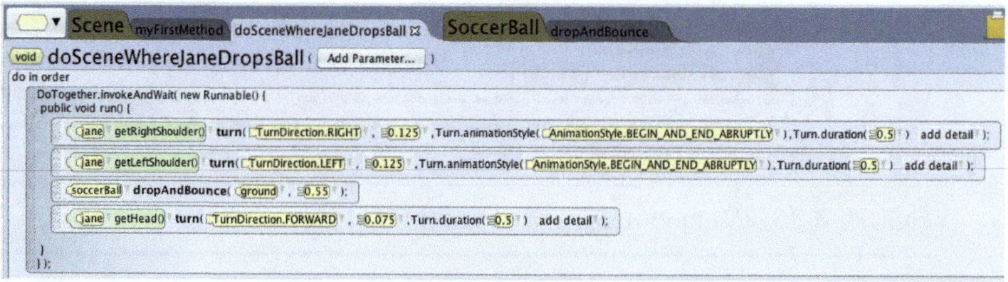

FIGURE 4-36   Method doSceneWhereJaneDropsBall()

---

[2]When this chapter was written, Alice did not provide a **distanceAbove()** function that would let us compute the distance above the ground. As a result, we use a **while** loop to compute that distance. By the time you read this, Alice will hopefully provide a **distanceAbove()** function that you can use to compute the ball's height.

Try this yourself, and experiment with the statements and settings shown in Figures 4-35 and 4-36, to see how each one affects the ball's behavior. (There's always the **Undo** button!)

4.5   Flow-Control in Functions

At the end of Chapter 3, we saw that if we want to ask an object a question for which there is not already a function, we can define our own function to provide the answer. The functions we wrote there used sequential flow and were fairly simple. The flow-control statements we have seen in this chapter allow us to build functions that answer more complex questions.

4.5.1   Spirals and the Fibonacci Function

Suppose that we have a story in which a girl named Frita finds an old book, which tells her that there is a treasure hidden near a certain palm tree in the middle of the desert. The book contains a map showing how to find the tree, plus instructions for locating the treasure from the tree. Suppose that Scene 1 of the story has Frita finding the old book and reading its contents. In Scene 2, she uses the map to locate the palm tree. In Scene 3 she follows the instructions:

> Scene 3: Frita is facing the palm tree, her back to the camera. She says, "Now that I am at the tree, I turn to face north." She turns to her right and says, "Then I walk in a spiral of six quarter turns to my left, and then shout the magic words." She walks in a spiral of six quarter turns to her left, shouts the magic words, and an opening appears in the ground at her feet.

The main challenge in building this user story is getting Frita to move in a spiral pattern. Mathematicians have discovered that many of the spirals that occur in nature—for example, the spiraling chambers inside a nautilus shell, the spiral of petals in a rose, and the spiraling seeds in sunflowers and pinecones—all use a pattern given in the following numbers:

> 1, 1, 2, 3, 5, 8, 13, 21, 34, 55, 89, 144, ...

Can you see the pattern? The first known mention of these numbers was by the Indian scholar Gospala sometime before 1135 AD. The first European to discover them was Leonardo Pisano, a 13th-century mathematician who found that they predict the growth of rabbit populations. Leonardo was the son of Guglielmo Bonaccio and often called himself Fibonacci (short for "son of Bonaccio"). Today, these numbers are called the **Fibonacci series**.

To draw a spiral from the series, we draw a series of squares whose lengths and widths are the Fibonacci numbers. Starting with the smallest square, we draw a series of quarter turn arcs, crossing from one corner of the square to the opposite corner, as shown in Figure 4-37.

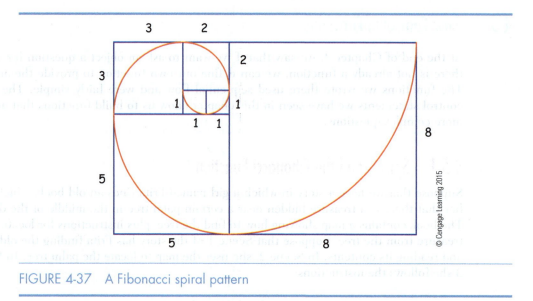

FIGURE 4-37   A Fibonacci spiral pattern

If you examine the various squares in Figure 4-37, it should be evident that the spiral's path through each square is an arc through a quarter of a circle, and that the radius of that circle is the edge-length of that square. If we do a quick Internet search for *arc distance formula*, we can find that for a circle, the distance of a quarter-circle arc is given by the following formula:

quarterCircleArcDistance = radius * Π/2

Since π is a constant, so is π / 2, so we will declare a constant named **HALF_PI** and give it the value **1.570796**, as our representation of π / 2.

We can use this information to move Frita in a spiral pattern. More precisely, we can move her in a close approximation of the Fibonacci spiral as follows:

1. Move her forward **1 * HALF_PI** meters while turning left 1/4 revolution
2. Move her forward **1 * HALF_PI** meters while turning left 1/4 revolution
3. Move her forward **2 * HALF_PI** meters while turning left 1/4 revolution
4. Move her forward **3 * HALF_PI** meters while turning left 1/4 revolution
5. Move her forward **5 * HALF_PI** meters while turning left 1/4 revolution
6. Move her forward **8 * HALF_PI** meters while turning left 1/4 revolution

We could accomplish this using six separate `move()` messages, but a better approach is to use a single `move()` message inside a loop that iterates six times. Each iteration needs to move Frita a distance equal to the corresponding Fibonacci number * `HALF_PI` while turning her left 1/4 revolution.

To use this approach, we need a function that, given a positive number *i*, computes the *i*th Fibonacci number. Given such a function, we can write the `doScene3()` method by using a loop to count from 1 to 6. Since this is a counting problem, we can use a `for` loop that counts from 0 to 5 and add 1 to the counting variable `i`, as shown in Figure 4-38.

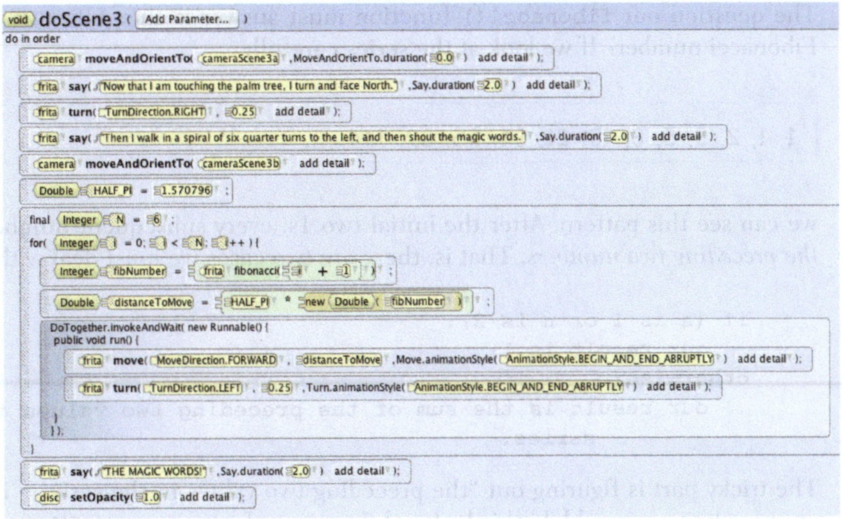

FIGURE 4-38   The `doScene3()` Method

In the next subsection, we will build the `fibonacci()` function used in Figure 4-38.

For clarity, we have used an `Integer` variable named `fibNumber` to store the current Fibonacci number, a separate `Double` variable named `distanceToMove` to store the length of the arc we want Frita to move, and a `Double` constant named `HALF_PI` to store π / 2. One subtlety is that in order to calculate `distanceToMove` by multiplying `HALF_PI` and `fibNumber` together, we must convert `fibNumber` from an `Integer` to a `Double`. To accomplish this, we can use the menu choice Whole to Decimal Number > new Double(???) > fibNumber to choose the operand by which we multiply `HALF_PI`.

Note also that in addition to a `CoconutPalm` tree, our scene uses an instance of the `Disc` class from the Shapes section of the Alice Gallery as the hole that appears in the ground at Frita's feet after she shouts the magic words.

4.5.2   The Fibonacci Function

The `fibonacci()` function that is invoked in Figure 4-38 seems like the kind of thing that only a person might need to calculate, so we click Person in the class navigator and then choose Add Person Function from the resulting menu. Alice prompts us for the name of the function, and we enter **fibonacci**. In the same dialog, we must indicate the type of value this function will return; since Fibonacci numbers are whole numbers, we choose the **Integer** type.

To invoke this function, we must pass it a positive number argument indicating which Fibonacci number we want it to return. To store this argument, we will give our function an **Integer** parameter named **n**.

Design

The question our **fibonacci()** function must answer is this: Given *n*, what is the *n*th Fibonacci number? If we look at the series carefully

> 1, 1, 2, 3, 5, 8, 13, 21, 34, 55, 89, 144, ...

we can see this pattern: After the initial two 1s, every subsequent number is the *sum of the preceding two numbers*. That is, there are two cases we must deal with:

```
if (n is 1 or n is 2):
    our result is 1;
otherwise:
    our result is the sum of the preceding two values in the
            series.
```

The tricky part is figuring out "the preceding two values in the series." To see how, let's examine how we would do this by hand. For example, to compute **fibonacci(9)**:

Since we are doing the same thing over and over, we can do this using a loop. To accomplish this, we store each value used per iteration in a variable: one for the next-to-last term, one for the last term, one for the result, and one for the count; we can then use a loop to count from 3 to **n**. When **n** is 9:

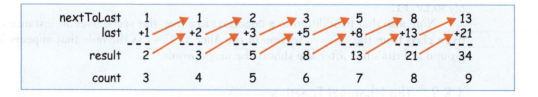

The only remaining question is what kind of loop to use. This is clearly a counting problem, and so a **for** loop seems like the logical choice. While this can be done with a for loop, Alice's **for** loop only counts from **0** to **N-1**, while our loop needs to count from **3** to **n**. This makes a solution using an Alice **for** loop somewhat less intuitive and readable, so we will use a **while** loop instead.

Putting all of this together yields the following algorithm for our function:

```
Parameter: n, a Integer.
Integer result = 0;
if (n == 1 or n == 2) {
    result = 1;
} else {
    Integer nextToLast = 1; Integer last = 1; Integer count = 3;
    while (count <= n) {
        result = last + nextToLast;
        nextToLast = last;
        last = result;
        count = count + 1;
    }
}
return result;
```

Coding in Alice

We can encode the algorithm in Alice as shown in Figure 4-39.

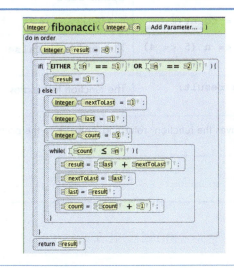

FIGURE 4-39   One way to build the **fibonacci()** function

As discussed previously, this function uses the **while** loop to count from **3..n**. As a more general kind of loop, a **while** loop can do anything a **for** loop can do and more, but *we* must initialize the **count** variable (to **3**) before entering the loop, *we* must build the loop's condition (**count <= n**) explicitly, and *we* must increment the **count** variable (**count = count + 1**) inside the loop or an infinite loop will occur. Because it does these things for us, the **for** loop is often more convenient in situations where it can be used.

Figure 4-40 traces the execution of our function when **4** is passed to **n**.

Step	Flow is in...	Effect	Comment
1	if *Condition*	*Condition* is **false**	Control flows to the **if**'s **else** branch
2	count = 3	Counter is initialized	**count** is 3
3	count <= n (3 <= 4)	The condition is **true**	Flow is directed into the loop
4	result = ...	Compute fibonacci(3)	**result** is 2
5	nextToLast = last	Update **nextToLast**	**nextToLast** is 1
6	last = result	Update **last**	**last** is 2
7	count = count+1	Increment **count**	**count** is 4
8	count <= n (4 <= 4)	The condition is **true**	Flow is directed into the loop
9	result = ...	Compute fibonacci(4)	**result** is 3
10	nextToLast = last	Update **nextToLast**	**nextToLast** is 2
11	last = result	Update **last**	**last** is 3
12	count = count+1	Increment **count**	**count** is 5
13	count <= n (5 <= 4)	The condition is **false**	Flow is directed out of the loop
14	return result;	The function terminates	**result** is 3, the 4th Fibonacci number
15	Flow leaves the function, returning **result** to the point where the function was invoked.		

FIGURE 4-40   Tracing the **fibonacci()** function

Note that we initialize **result** to zero. If the user passes an invalid argument (e.g., zero or a negative number), then the function returns this zero. The reason is that if **n** is negative or zero, then **n** is not 1 or 2, so our **if** statement's condition is **false** and flow proceeds to its **else** branch. There, **count** gets set to 3, and when the **while** loop tests its condition (**count <= n**), that condition is **false**, so the flow skips over the body of the **while** loop, leaving the variable **result** unchanged. From there, flow proceeds to the **return** statement at the end of the function, and since **result**'s initial value of zero has not been changed, the function returns **0**.

Using this function, the **while** loop in Figure 4-39 will cause Frita to move in a spiral pattern, after which she shouts the magic words and a dark opening appears in the ground at her feet. What happens next? It's up to you!

4.6   Putting It All Together: A `walk()` Method

To review and apply what we have learned in this chapter, let's put it all to use in a final example. Back in Chapter 2, the first scene of our story about Tim the wizard called for Ann to walk on screen, talk to Tim, and then walk away. At the time, we did not know how to build a method to make Ann walk, so we simply moved her on and off the screen. Now that we know about methods, parameters, **if** statements and loops, we have all the tools we need to build a reasonable **walk()** method, so let's do it!

Take a moment and walk a few steps. If you consider everything in your body that is moving as you walk, it should be evident that this is a pretty complicated behavior. Let's take it one step at a time (ha, ha, get it—one *step* at a time?) but keep it fairly simple.

Let's begin by considering what information we might want to pass to a **walk()** method via arguments. One approach is to pass the number of steps we want the person to walk. To keep things simple, let's ignore fractional steps and give our **walk()** method an **Integer** parameter named **numSteps**.

If you think carefully about the act of walking, we might identify two basic cases: one in which we take an even number of steps and the other in which we take an odd number of steps. Again to keep things simple, let's assume we start with our left foot. If we take an *even* number of steps, we move our left foot and then move our right foot and repeat this pair of movements **numSteps / 2** times. If we take an *odd* number of steps, we can do the same thing we do for an even number of steps and then take one more step to make it odd. We might build an algorithm for this approach as follows:

```
Parameter: numSteps, an Integer.

for (Integer i = 0; i < (numSteps / 2); i++) {
    step with the left foot
    step with the right foot
}
if (numSteps is odd) {
    step with the left foot
} else {
    do nothing
}
```

Note that in the expression **numSteps** / 2, we are performing *integer division*—the kind of division we learned in grade school before we studied decimal points and real numbers:

 1 / 2 is 0 with a remainder of 1;
 2 / 2 is 1 with a remainder of 0;
 3 / 2 is 1 with a remainder of 1;
 4 / 2 is 2 with a remainder of 0;
 5 / 2 is 2 with a remainder of 1;
 and so on.

To illustrate why this is important:

- When **numSteps** is 1, the statements inside our algorithm's **for** loop will not be performed because **i** equals 0 and **numSteps** / 2 equals 0, so the loop's condition **i < numSteps / 2** is false. However, the statement in the true branch of the **if** statement will be performed because **numSteps** is odd.
- When **numSteps** is 2, **numSteps** / 2 equals 1, so the expression **i < numSteps / 2** is true, and the statements inside the **for** loop will be performed once; but since **numSteps** is even, the statement in the true section of the **if** will not be performed.
- When **numSteps** is 3, the statements inside the **for** loop will be performed once and the statement in the true section of the **if** will be performed.
- When **numSteps** is 4, the statements inside the **for** loop will be performed twice, but the statement in the true section of the **if** will not be performed.

The preceding algorithm includes actions like "step with the left foot" and "step with the right foot." To perform these actions, we can build a method named **step()** and pass it an argument indicating the foot with which we wish to step. Stepping with just one foot involves (minimally) leaning forward slightly, rolling your pelvis, rolling your shoulders, bending your hip, bending your knee, swinging your arm, and moving forward slightly. Because this is such a complex behavior, we cannot fit it all in a single figure, but Figure 4-41 shows a simplistic way to build the behavior of stepping with the left foot.

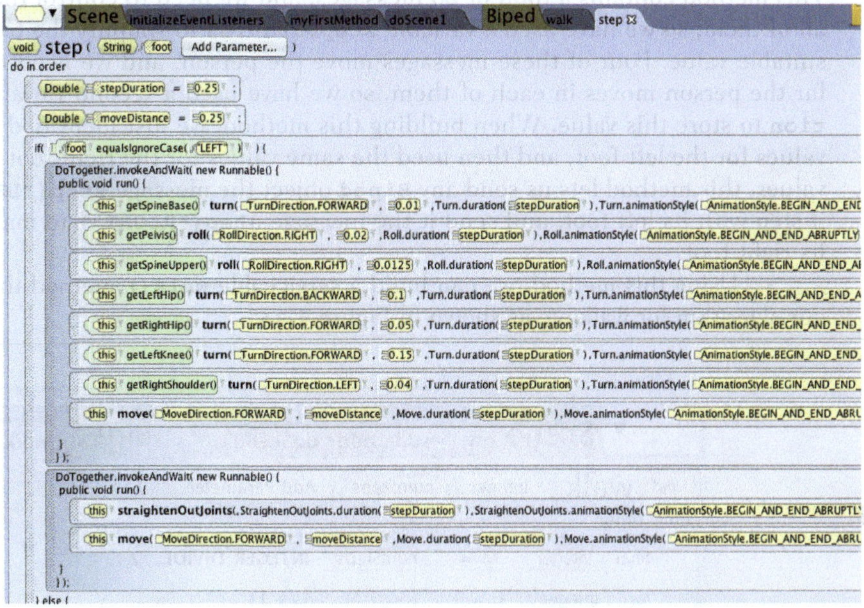

FIGURE 4-41 Stepping with the left foot

Figure 4-42 shows the rest of the method, which uses similar logic for stepping with the right foot.

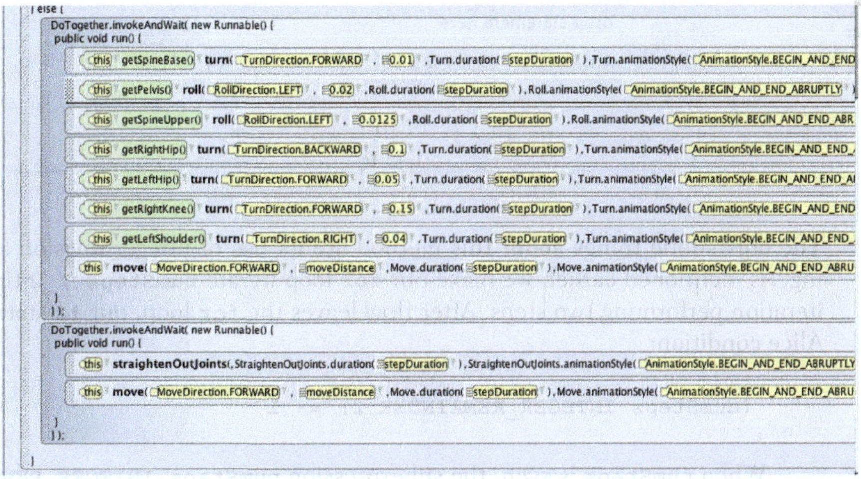

FIGURE 4-42 Stepping with the right foot

This method contains a total of 20 messages, and we need to control the **duration** in all of them, so we have used a variable **stepDuration** to simplify the task of finding a suitable value. Four of these messages move the person, and we need to control how far the person moves in each of them, so we have used a second variable **moveDuration** to store this value. When building this method, we just identified the remaining values for the left foot, and then used the same values for the right foot. With suitable values, this method lets us send any **Biped** object the message **step("LEFT")** to make it step with its left foot, and send it the message **step("RIGHT")** to make it step with its right foot.

Using this method, we can build a serviceable **walk()** method that implements our algorithm for walking, as shown in Figure 4-43.

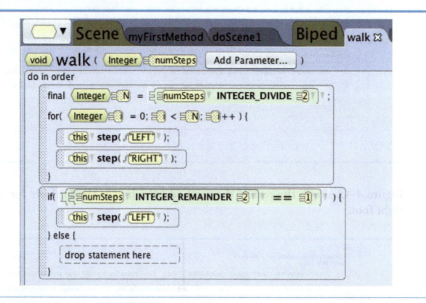

FIGURE 4-43   A **walk()** method

The only subtle things about this method are its use of integer division and remaindering. As mentioned earlier, we make our **for** loop iterate **numSteps / 2** times, with each iteration performing two steps. After flow leaves the **for** loop, our **if** statement uses the Alice condition:

```
(numSteps INTEGER_REMAINDER 2) == 1
```

When **numSteps** is even, the subexpression **numSteps INTEGER_REMAINDER 2** produces 0, because any even number divided by 2 produces no remainder. When this is the case, the condition becomes **0 == 1**, which is false, so the condition produces **false** when **numSteps** is even.

Likewise, when **numSteps** is odd, the subexpression **numSteps INTEGER_REMAINDER 2** produces 1, because any odd number divided by 2 produces a remainder of 1. When this is the case, the condition becomes **1 == 1**, which is true, so the condition produces **true** when **numSteps** is odd. This use of remainders is a common method of determining whether an integer is even or odd.

When we are finished building our **walk()** method, we can return to our **doScene1()** method and send Ann **walk()** messages to make her enter and exit the scene, as shown in Figure 4-44.

```
void doScene1 ( Add Parameter... )
    ann moveAndOrientTo( annScene1 , MoveAndOrientTo.duration( 0.0 ) add detail );
    camera moveAndOrientTo( cameraScene1a , MoveAndOrientTo.duration( 0.0 ) add detail );
    this delay( 1.0 );
    camera moveAndOrientTo( cameraScene1b , MoveAndOrientTo.duration( 2.0 ) add detail );
    DoTogether.invokeAndWait( new Runnable() {
    public void run() {
        /*do in order*/ {
            tim think( "Hmmmm. I planted these trees at the same time, but this one hasn't grown much. It sure needs some help." ,Think.duration( 5.0 ) add
            ann say( "Hi Tim. What's my favorite neighbor up to today?" ,Say.duration( 5.0 ) add detail );
        }
        ann walk( 10 );
    }
    });
    tim say( "Hi Ann. Nothing special. I was just looking at my trees and noticed this one could use a boost." ,Say.duration( 4.0 ) add detail );
    tim castGrowSpell( leftTree , 2.0 );
    ann say( "Wow! That is so handy!" ,Say.duration( 2.0 ) add detail );
    tim say( "That's my exciting life as a wizard: helping trees grow." ,Say.duration( 2.0 ) add detail );
    ann say( "Speaking of excitement, I came over to tell you that I heard the ogres beating their drums last night." ,Say.duration( 4.0 ) add detail );
    tim say( "Hmmm. I wonder what has them riled up?" ,Say.duration( 2.0 ) add detail );
    ann say( "I don't know, but watch out for them. They can be nasty sometimes." ,Say.duration( 4.0 ) add detail );
    tim say( "Thanks for the warning." ,Say.duration( 2.0 ) add detail );
    ann say( "You're welcome. Bye-bye." ,Say.duration( 2.0 ) add detail );
    ann turn( TurnDirection.RIGHT , 0.5 add detail );
    ann walk( 5 );
```

FIGURE 4-44 The completed **doScene1()** method

Alice's flow-control statements thus provide us with tools that allow us to produce complex animations.

4.7   Chapter Summary

- ❏ **Boolean** operators allow us to build *conditions*.
- ❏ The **if** statement uses a condition to direct program flow *selectively* through one group of statements while bypassing others.
- ❏ The **for** statement uses a condition to direct program flow through a group of statements *repeatedly*, a fixed number of times.
- ❏ The **while** statement uses a condition to direct program flow through a group of statements *repeatedly*, where the number of repetitions is not known in advance or where Alice's **for** statement is too restrictive. A **while** statement can do anything a **for** statement can do, and more.
- ❏ The *assignment* statement lets us change the value of a variable.
- ❏ The **delay()** message lets us suspend a program's flow for a fixed length of time.
- ❏ The **asSeenBy** attribute alters the behavior of the **turn()** message.

4.7.1   Key Terms

assignment operator
assignment statement
Boolean expression
Boolean operators (&&, ||, !)
boolean type
condition
control structure
counting loop
flow control
flow diagram
for statement
general loop
if-then-else logic **if** statement

indefinite loop
infinite loop
nested **if** (inner **if**, outer **if**)
placeholder
relational operators (==, !=, <, >, <=, >=)
repetitive execution
repetitive flow control
selective execution
selective flow control
validating parameter values
wait() statement
while statement

Programming Projects

4.1   Choose an animal that hops from the Alice **Gallery** (e.g., a frog or a bunny). Write a **hop()** method that makes it hop in a realistic fashion, with a (validated) parameter that lets the sender of the message specify how far the animal should hop. Then build a method containing just one **hop()** message that causes your animal to hop around a building.

4.2   *Johnny Hammers* is a traditional song with the following lyrics. Create an Alice program containing a character who sings this song. Write your program using as few statements as possible.

Verse 1: Johnny hammers with 1 hammer, 1 hammer, 1 hammer. Johnny hammers with 1 hammer, all day long.	Verse 2: Johnny hammers with 2 hammers, 2 hammers, 2 hammers. Johnny hammers with 2 hammers, all day long.
Verse 3: Johnny hammers with 3 hammers, 3 hammers, 3 hammers. Johnny hammers with 3 hammers, all day long.	Verse 4: Johnny hammers with 4 hammers, 4 hammers, 4 hammers. Johnny hammers with 4 hammers, all day long.
Verse 5: Johnny hammers with 5 hammers, 5 hammers, 5 hammers. Johnny hammers with 5 hammers, all day long.	Verse 6: Johnny's very tired now, tired now, tired now. Johnny's very tired now, so he goes to sleep.

© Cengage Learning 2015

4.3 Using the horse we used in Section 3.4, build a `gallop()` method for the horse that makes its legs move realistically through the motions of a gallop, with a (validated) parameter that specifies the number of strides (or alternatively, the distance to gallop). Then create a story containing a scene that uses your method to make the horse gallop across the screen.

4.4 *The Song That Never Ends* is a silly song with the following lyrics. Create an Alice program containing a character who sings this song, using as few statements as possible. (If you do not know the tune, search for and listen to the song on the World Wide Web.)

Verse 1: This is the song that never ends, and it goes on and on my friends. Some people started singing it not knowing what it was, and now they'll keep on singing it forever just because.	Verse 2: This is the song that never ends, and it goes on and on my friends. Some people started singing it not knowing what it was, and now they'll keep on singing it forever just because.
Verse 3: This is the song that never ends, and it goes on and on my friends. Some people started singing it not knowing what it was, and now they'll keep on singing it forever just because.	. . . (ad infinitum, ad annoyum, ad nauseam)

© Cengage Learning 2015

4.5 Build a world containing a person who can calculate the average of a sequence of numbers in his or her head. Have the person ask the user how many numbers are in the sequence, and then use the `getDoubleFromUser()` function that many times to get the numbers from the user. When all the numbers have been entered, have your person "say" the average of those numbers.

4.6 Proceed as in Project 4.5, but instead of having your person ask the user in advance how many numbers are in the sequence, have your person (and each `getDoubleFromUser()` function) tell the user to enter a special value (e.g., –999) after the last value in the sequence.

4.7 *99 Bottles of Pop* is a silly song with the following lyrics. Create an Alice program in which a character sings this song. Use as few statements as possible. (Hint: Think carefully. Can you use a **for** statement to solve this problem? Why or why not?)

Verse 1: 99 bottles of pop on the wall, 99 bottles of pop, take one down, pass it around, 98 bottles of pop on the wall.	Verse 2: 98 bottles of pop on the wall, 98 bottles of pop, take one down, pass it around, 97 bottles of pop on the wall.
(96 verses omitted) . . .	Verse 99: 1 bottle of pop on the wall, 1 bottle of pop, take one down, pass it around 0 bottles of pop on the wall.

© Cengage Learning 2015

4.8 Modify the exercise methods we built in Section 3.1 so that each method accepts a positive integer argument and then causes the characters to perform the exercise that many times. Be sure to validate the integer; have the characters speak an error message if a non-positive argument is passed. Then build an aerobic exercise video in which the characters lead the user through an exercise routine. Using repetition statements, your characters should do each exercise a fixed number of times.

4.9 Proceed as in Project 4.8, but at the beginning of the program, ask the user to specify the difficulty level of the workout (1, 2, 3, 4, or 5). If the user specifies difficulty level 1, have your characters do each exercise 10 times; if the user specifies difficulty level 2, then 20 times; if level 3, then 40 times; if level 4, then 80 times; if level 5, then 100 times.

4.10 From the Alice Gallery, choose a clock class that has subparts for the minute and hour hands, such as class **PocketWatch**.

   a. Build a class method named **run()** that moves the minute and hour hands realistically (i.e., each time the minute hand completes a rotation, the hour hand should advance 1 hour). Define a parameter named **speedUp** that controls the **duration**s of the hand movements, such that **run(1)** will make the clock run at normal speed, **run(60)** will make the clock run at 60 times its normal speed, **run(3600)** will make the clock run at 3,600 times its normal speed, and so on.

   b. Build a clock method **setTime(h, m)** that sets the clock's time to **h:m** (**m** minutes after hour **h**).

    c. Build three functions for your clock: one that returns its current time (as a **String**), one that returns its current hours value (as an **Integer**), and one that returns its current minutes value (as an **Integer**).

    d. Build a clock method **setAlarm(h, m)** that lets you set the clock's alarm to **h:m**. Then modify your **run()** method so that when the clock's current time is equal to **m** minutes after hour **h**, the clock plays a sound (e.g., a royalty-free sound from *www.pacdv.com*).

4.11 Using appropriately colored **Shapes** from the Alice Gallery, build a chessboard. Then choose objects from the Gallery to serve as chess pieces. Build a class-level method named **chessMove()** for each piece that makes it move appropriately (e.g., a bishop should move diagonally). For pieces that can move varying distances, the definition of **chessMove()** should have a (validated) parameter indicating the distance (in squares) of the move, plus any other parameters necessary. When your "pieces" are finished, build a program that, using your board and pieces, animates the opening moves of a game of chess, such as a Fool's Checkmate.

4.12 Design an original 3–5-minute story that uses each of the statements presented in this chapter at least once.

Chapter 5
Arrays

When a cat is dropped, it always lands on its feet, and when toast is dropped, it always lands with the buttered side down. I propose to strap buttered toast to the back of a cat; the two will hover, inches above the ground. With a giant buttered-toast-cat array, a high-speed monorail could easily link New York with Chicago.

JOHN FRAZEE

For seven men she gave her life. For one good man she was his wife. Beneath the ice by Snow White Falls, there lies the fairest of them all.

VIRGINIA (KIMBERLY WILLIAMS), IN *THE 10TH KINGDOM*

The generation of random numbers is too important to be left to chance.

ROBERT R. COVEYOU

Objectives

When you complete this chapter, you will be able to:

❑ Use an array to store multiple items

❑ Use Alice's for each in array loop, each in array together loop, and **for** loop to process an array's items

❑ Use random numbers to vary the behavior of a program

Screenshots from Alice 2 © 1999–2013, Alice 3 © 2008–2013, Carnegie Mellon University. All rights reserved. We gratefully acknowledge the financial support of Oracle, Electronic Arts, Sun Microsystems, DARPA, Intel, NSF, and ONR.

In the preceding chapters, we have often used variables to store values for later use. Each variable we have seen so far has stored a *single* value, which might be a **Double**, a **Boolean**, a **String**, an **SThing**, or any of the other types that Alice supports. For example, if we have three variable definitions like this in our program:

```
Double result = 0.0;
Boolean done = false;
String name = "Jo";
```

then we might (simplistically) visualize these three variables as shown in Figure 5-1.

FIGURE 5-1   Storing three values in three variables

Each variable stores a single value (of a given type) that can be changed by the program.

It is sometimes convenient to be able to define a variable that can store *multiple* values. For example, suppose we have 12 songs (call them $s_0 \ldots s_{11}$) in our music player that we want to represent in a program as a playlist. We could represent this playlist using 12 single-value variables (e.g., $song_0$, $song_1$, $song_2$, ..., $song_{10}$, $song_{11}$), but it would be more convenient if we could define one "playlist" variable capable of storing all 12 songs, as shown in Figure 5-2.

FIGURE 5-2   Storing 12 values in one variable

One advantage of this approach is that if we need to pass our playlist to a method, we only have to pass 1 argument (**playList**) instead of 12. Likewise, our method needs only 1 parameter instead of 12.

A variable like this is called a **data structure**—a structure for storing a group of data **items**. In this chapter, we will examine Alice's **array** data structure. An array is a single variable with room to store a group of items, like the **playList** variable in Figure 5-2.

5.1   Alice Arrays

In the preceding chapters, we have declared numerous variables, using Alice's variable... control. In this section, we will see how to use this mechanism to create *array variables*.

5.1.1 Example 1: Flight of the Pixies

Scene 4 of our story about Tim the wizard has the pixie queen delivering a speech to a squad of pixies, after which the squad members take off one at a time to go and capture Tim. We might begin by building the scene, which involves moving our camera to some remote part of our 3D world, adding a marker for it, and setting up the scene with our pixie queen and her 12 squad members. Figure 5-3 shows one possibility. (We will add a forest to the background later.)

FIGURE 5-3   The pixie queen and her squad

To animate the scene and make the pixies take off one at a time, we could use 12 separate **move()** statements:

```
pixie01.move(UP, verticalDistance);
pixie02.move(UP, verticalDistance);
...
pixie12.move(UP, verticalDistance);
```

Note, however, that although the pixie to which we are sending the **move()** message changes, each statement is otherwise identical. Remember: *Any time you find yourself programming the same thing over and over, there is usually a better way.* In this case, the better way is to create an array variable named **squad** that stores references to the 12 pixies, and then use a loop to visit each pixie in the array, sending the **move()** message to each one. This act of using a loop to process the items in an array is called **iterating** through the array. We might visualize this array as shown in Figure 5-4.

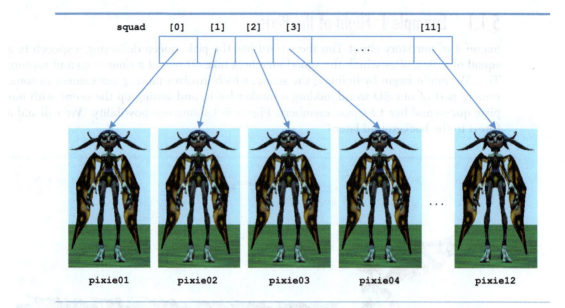

FIGURE 5-4   Visualizing an array of 12 pixies

As indicated in Figure 5-4, this single variable can store 12 references—one for each of the pixies in our squad. More generally, an Alice array can store an arbitrary number of references to any Alice type (e.g., **Double**, **Boolean**, **Object**, **String**, **Color**, **STurnable**, etc.).

Note that we have named the pixies in our squad **pixie01**, **pixie02**, ..., and **pixie12**. However, after we store them in the array variable named **squad**, we can use the following notations:

```
squad[0] refers to pixie01
squad[1] refers to pixie02
squad[2] refers to pixie03
...
squad[11] refers to pixie12
```

The numbers inside the square brackets are called subscript or **index** numbers. In Alice, the index of the first item in an array is always zero and the square brackets ([and]) that surround an index are called the **subscript operator**.

Given this array variable named **squad**, we can use Alice's **for** statement to send each pixie in the array the message **move(UP, verticalDistance)**:

```
for (Pixie pixie : squad) {
    pixie.move(UP, verticalDistance);
}
```

We next examine how to make all of this happen in Alice.

Defining an Array Variable

To animate the scene, we open the **doScene4()** method in our project and then define a local array variable named **squad** within the scene to store our squad of pixies. To create a variable that is an array, we drag the variable… control into the editing area, as usual. Since the items we want to store in the array are pixies, we select **Pixie** as the variable's type in the dialog box that appears. We then (1) click the checkbox labeled is array and (2) initialize this variable by choosing Custom Array…, as shown in Figure 5-5.

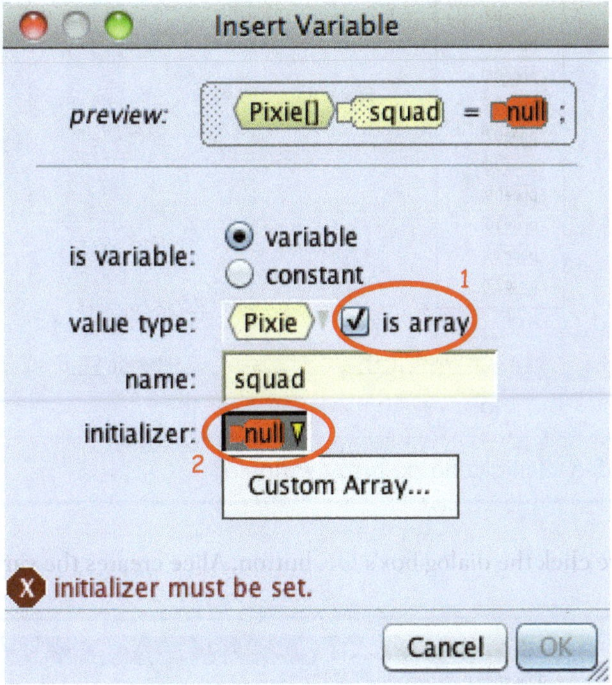

FIGURE 5-5   Creating an array variable

This opens a Custom Array dialog box that we can use to add our pixies to the array. In Figure 5-6a, we are adding the first pixie, **pixie01**. It and its index number then appear in the value: area of the dialog box, as shown in Figure 5-6b. We can then add the remaining pixies the same way. Figure 5-6c shows the dialog box after we have added all of the pixies.

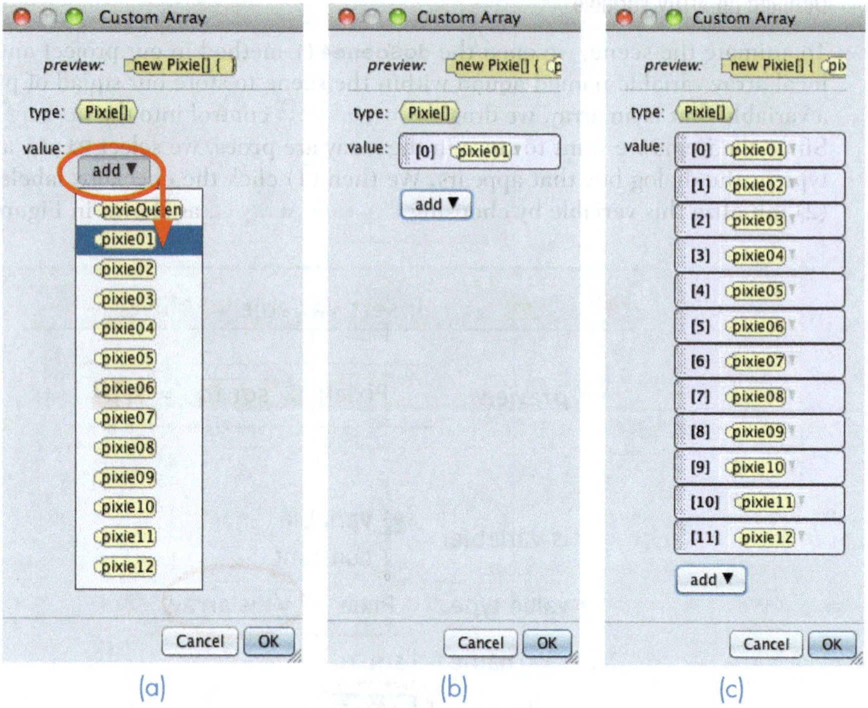

FIGURE 5-6   Initializing an array variable

When we click the dialog box's **OK** button, Alice creates the variable shown in Figure 5-7.

FIGURE 5-7   An array variable definition

The form of this definition is:

```
Pixie[] squad = new Pixie[] {pixie01, pixie02, ..., pixie12};
```

Alice uses square brackets (**[** and **]**) to distinguish array variables from "normal" variables, and it uses curly braces (**{** and **}**) to wrap the values used to initialize an array.

Processing Array Entries

Now that we have defined an array variable, the next step is to use a new Alice control—the **for each in _** control—to iterate through the array, sending the **move()** message to each pixie. To do so, we drag the for each in _ control from the bottom of the editing area into our **doScene4()** method. When we drop it, Alice displays an Insert For Each In Array Loop dialog box in which we can (1) specify the type of values we have in our array (**Pixie**), (2) specify a generic variable name for one of the items in the array (**pixie**), and (3) specify the array through which we want to iterate (**squad**), as shown in Figure 5-8.

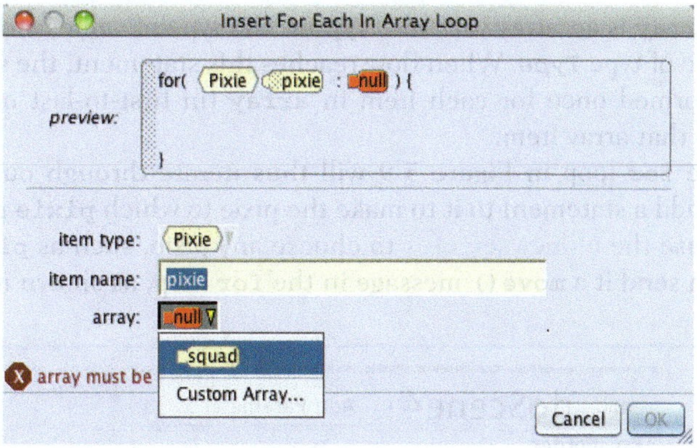

FIGURE 5-8   The **Insert For Each In Array Loop** dialog box

After we have specified all of these values and then click the OK button, Alice generates a new kind of **for** statement, as shown in Figure 5-9.

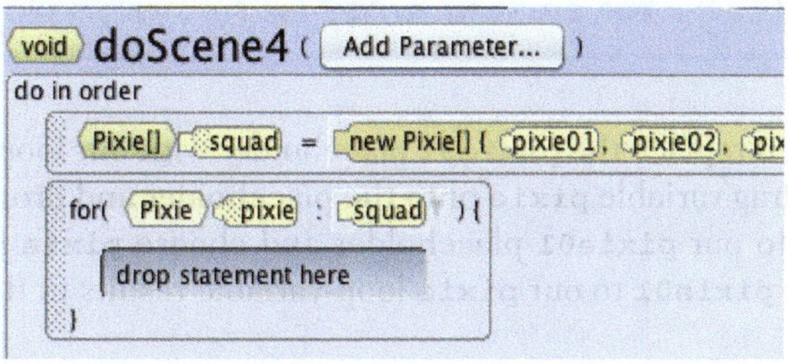

FIGURE 5-9   The **for each in array** loop

Unlike the version of the **for** statement we learned about in Chapter 4, this for each in array **statement** is designed specifically for processing each of the items in an array. When the flow reaches this statement, the following actions will take place:

- The variable **pixie** is set to the first item in **squad**; then *Statements* are performed.
- The variable **pixie** is set to the second item in **squad**; then *Statements* are performed.
- The variable **pixie** is set to the third item in **squad**; then *Statements* are performed.
- ...
- The variable **pixie** is set to the final item in **squad**; then *Statements* are performed.

Alice calls this kind of **for** loop a for each in array statement, and they have this general form:

```
for ( Type item : array ) {
    Statements
}
```

where **array** is an array variable, **Type** is the type of values stored in **array**, and **item** is a variable of type **Type**. When flow reaches this statement, the statements in **Statements** are performed once for each item in **array** (in first-to-last order), during which **item** refers to that array item.

The **for** loop in Figure 5-9 will thus iterate through our squad of pixies; we just need to add a statement to it to make the pixie to which **pixie** refers move up. To do this, we can use the object selector to choose any pixie, such as **pixie01** (as a placeholder), and then send it a **move()** message in the **for** loop, as shown in Figure 5-10.

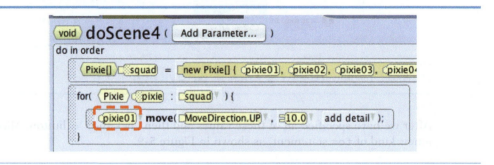

FIGURE 5-10   The **for each in array** loop moving a placeholder pixie

We then replace the **pixie01** placeholder with our loop-variable **pixie**. To do so, we can either drag variable **pixie** onto the placeholder and drop it, or we can click the down-arrow next to our **pixie01** placeholder and choose **pixie** from its menu. Changing the placeholder **pixie01** to our **pixie** loop-variable results in the loop shown in Figure 5-11.

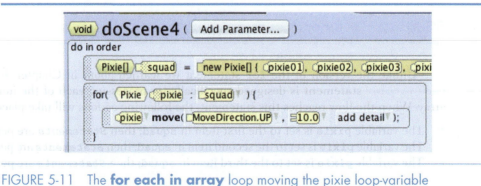

FIGURE 5-11   The **for each in array** loop moving the pixie loop-variable

The resulting loop will send the **move()** message to each pixie in the array, one at a time, causing them to "take off." To finish our scene, we can add statements to make the pixie queen give her speech, and also have her turn to face each pixie and order it to take off before we move it upwards. Figure 5-12 shows the completed scene method.

```
void  doScene4 ( Add Parameter... )
do in order
    Pixie[]  squad  =  new Pixie[] { pixie01, pixie02, pixie03, pixie04, pixie05, pixie06, pixie07, pixie08, pixie09, pixie10, pixie11, pixie12 } ;

    pixieQueen  say( "BELOVED PIXIES, TODAY IS THE DAY WE HAVE LONG AWAITED!" ,Say.duration( 5.0 )  add detail );

    pixieQueen  say( "TODAY IS THE DAY WE GET OUR REVENGE ON TIM THE WIZARD!!" ,Say.duration( 5.0 )  add detail );

    pixieQueen  say( "ON MY COMMAND, I WANT YOU TO FLY TO HIS CASTLE," ,Say.duration( 5.0 )  add detail );

    pixieQueen  say( "AND BRING HIM BACK HERE ALIVE!!" ,Say.duration( 4.0 )  add detail );

    for( Pixie  pixie  : squad ){
        pixieQueen  turnToFace( pixie ,TurnToFace.duration( 0.5 )  add detail );

        pixieQueen  say( "GO!" ,Say.duration( 0.5 )  add detail );

        pixie  move( MoveDirection.UP , 10.0 )  add detail );
    }
```

FIGURE 5-12   The **doScene4()** method

We can trace the flow through this loop in Figure 5-12 as follows:

- In the first iteration of this loop, the **pixieQueen** faces **pixie01** and shouts **GO!**; then **pixie01** moves up 10 meters, because loop-variable **pixie** refers to **pixie01**.
- In the second iteration of the loop, the **pixieQueen** faces **pixie02** and shouts **GO!**; then **pixie02** moves up 10 meters, because loop-variable **pixie** refers to **pixie02**.
- In the third iteration of the loop, the **pixieQueen** faces **pixie03** and shouts **GO!**; then **pixie03** moves up 10 meters, because loop-variable **pixie** refers to **pixie03**.
- This process repeats for pixies **pixie04** through **pixie11**.
- In the 12th (and final) iteration of the loop, the **pixieQueen** faces **pixie12** and shouts **GO!**; then **pixie12** moves up 10 meters, because loop-variable **pixie** refers to **pixie12**.

Figure 5-13 shows the scene during the loop's first, third, and last repetitions.

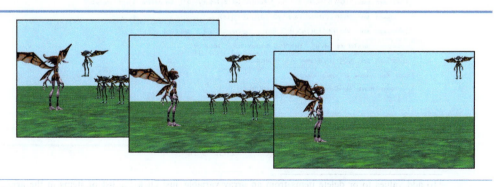

FIGURE 5-13   Repetitions 1, 3, and 12 of the loop

The **for** loop shown in Figure 5-12 thus achieves the effect of 12 **turnToFace()** messages, 12 **say()** messages, and 12 **move()** messages. However, it does so using only one **turnToFace()** statement, one **say()** message, one **move()** message, a **for** loop, and an array!

Moreover, suppose we decide later that, to be more convincing, the scene needs more pixies taking off (e.g., positioned behind those already in the scene). All we have to do is (1) add the new pixies to the world, and (2) add them to our **squad** array.[1] We do not need to add any new **turnToFace()**, **say()**, or **move()** statements to our **doScene4()** method!

In any situation for which you need to do the same thing to multiple items, an array and a for each in array loop may save you a lot of work!

5.1.2   The Each In Array Together Loop

The preceding example illustrates how the for each in array loop can be used to process each of the items in an array in turn. It provides a very simple way to iterate through the items in the array, doing the same thing to each item.

You may have noticed that there is also an each in ... together control at the bottom of the editing area. This can be used to create what Alice calls each in array together statements. Like the for each in array loop, the each in array together statement operates on an array. However, where the for each in array loop performs the statements within it once for each item in the array *sequentially*, the each in array together statement performs the statements within it for each item in the list *simultaneously* (i.e., in parallel).

To illustrate, suppose that after testing our **doScene4()** method, we decide that having the pixies take off one at a time is too slow. If we want all of the pixies to take off at the same time instead of one at a time, we could revise the **doScene4()** method using the each in array together statement, as shown in Figure 5-14.

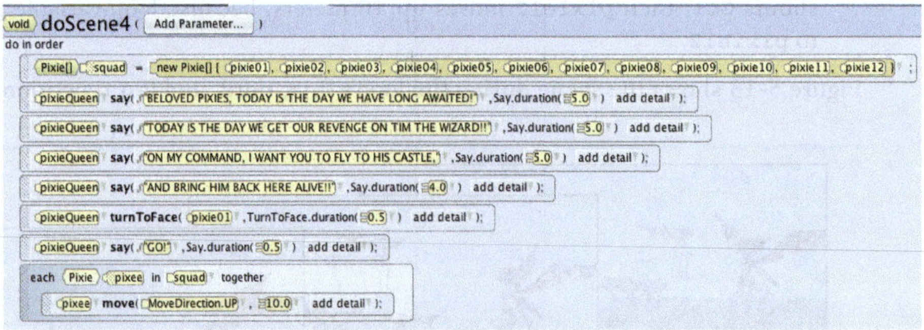

FIGURE 5-14   Making the pixies take off together

---

[1]To add values to or delete items from an array variable, just click the list of items in the array's definition ({**pixie01, pixie02, ..., pixie12**}), choose Custom Array, and use the dialog box that appears to add or delete the items.

Note that in this version, we have moved the **turnToFace()** and **say()** messages outside of the each in array together statement. If we place these statements within the each in array together statement, the **pixieQueen** will shout **"GO!"** 12 times simultaneously, which is kind of funny (try it!) but not really the effect we want.

Using this version of **doScene4()**, all of the pixies in the squad take off at the same time, as shown in Figure 5-15.

FIGURE 5-15   The pixies taking off together

The for each in array and the each in array together loops thus make it easy to animate each of the objects in an array, either one at a time or simultaneously.

5.1.3   Example 2: Penguin Party!

Suppose that Scene 3 of a story has a line of penguins waiting for their turn to jump into water through a hole in the ice. After the first penguin jumps in the water, the remaining penguins in the line should then move forward, so that the penguin who was second in line is the new first in line, the penguin who was third is now second, and so on. We might begin by building the scene shown in Figure 5-16.

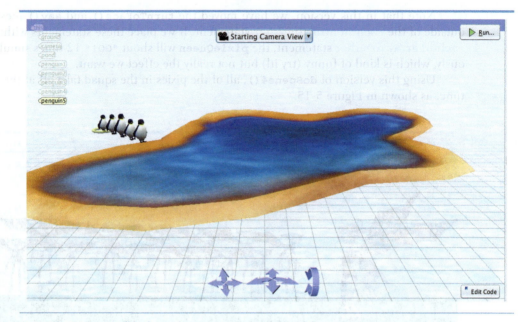

FIGURE 5-16 Well-behaved penguins waiting in a line

Alice makes it fairly easy to animate such a scene, using an array and some for each in array loops. The basic idea is to represent the line of penguins with an array containing each of the penguins in the scene. Then we can move the penguins by using a loop to process the array, using an algorithm like this:

```
penguins = {penguin1, penguin2, penguin3, penguin4, penguin5};
for each penguin in penguins {
    move penguin to the edge of the pool
    make penguin simultaneously:
        jump in the pool and yell, "COWABUNGA!"
    advance the line, moving each penguin forward
}
```

The only semi-tricky part here is the final step of advancing the line, to move each penguin forward. For this, we can use a second for each in array loop, nested inside the first. Figure 5-17 shows the completed scene method.

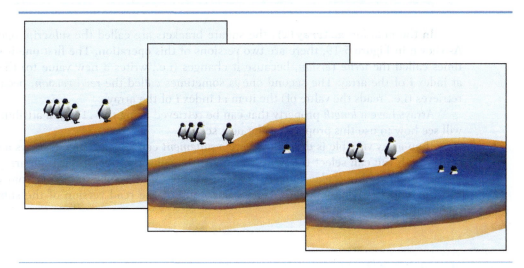

```
Scene   initializeEventListeners   myFirstMethod   doScene3

void doScene3 ( Add Parameter... )
do in order
  Penguin[] penguins = new Penguin[] { penguin1, penguin2, penguin3, penguin4, penguin5 } ;

  for( Penguin penguin : penguins ) {
    // hop up on bank
    DoTogether.invokeAndWait( new Runnable() {
      public void run() {
        penguin move( MoveDirection.FORWARD , 1.0 ),Move.duration( 0.5 ) ),Move.animationStyle( AnimationStyle.BEGIN_GENTLY_AND_END_ABRUPTLY ) add detail );
        penguin move( MoveDirection.UP , 0.25 ),Move.duration( 0.5 ) ),Move.animationStyle( AnimationStyle.BEGIN_GENTLY_AND_END_ABRUPTLY ) add detail );
      }
    });
    // jump into pool
    DoTogether.invokeAndWait( new Runnable() {
      public void run() {
        penguin say( "COWABUNGA!" ),Say.duration( 0.5 ) add detail );
        penguin move( MoveDirection.FORWARD , 2.0 ),Move.duration( 0.25 ) ),Move.animationStyle( AnimationStyle.BEGIN_AND_END_ABRUPTLY ) add detail );
        penguin move( MoveDirection.DOWN , 0.6 ),Move.duration( 0.25 ) ),Move.animationStyle( AnimationStyle.BEGIN_AND_END_ABRUPTLY ) add detail );
      }
    });
    // advance the line
    for( Penguin penguin1 : penguins ) {
      penguin1 move( MoveDirection.FORWARD , 0.5 ),Move.duration( 0.5 ) add detail );
    }
  }
}
```

FIGURE 5-17   Animating a line of penguins

Figure 5-18 shows three screenshots of **doScene3()**, taken when the first, second, and third penguins have hopped up on the bank and are preparing to jump in the pool.

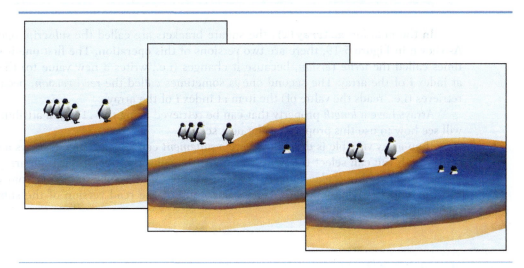

FIGURE 5-18   Screen captures from **doScene3()**

If you examine Figure 5-18 closely, you can see how the penguins are moving by noting how their positions change between screen captures. Our **penguins** array plus the for each in array loops have made it relatively easy to animate this scene.

5.1.4   Other Array Operations

We have seen that Alice provides the for each in array and the each in array together loops to simplify the task of processing all items in an array. We have also seen that arrays are **indexed variables**, meaning each item is stored within the array at a **position** called the item's *index*. The item at a specific position within an array can be accessed using the name of the array, the item's index and the *subscript operator*. Figure 5-19 lists the additional operations that can be performed with Alice arrays.

Alice Array Operation	Behavior
anArray[i] = val;	Change the item at position *i* in anArray to val
val = anArray[i];	Retrieve the item at position *i* in anArray
anArray.length	Retrieve the number of items in anArray
anArray = newArray;	Replace the items in anArray with those of newArray

FIGURE 5-19   Array operations

© Cengage Learning 2015

In the notation **anArray[i]**, the square brackets are called the *subscript operator*. As shown in Figure 5-19, there are two versions of this operation. The first one is sometimes called the *write version*, because it changes (i.e., writes a new value to) the item at index *i* of the array. The second one is sometimes called the *read version*, because it retrieves (i.e., reads the value of) the item at index *i* of the array.

Arrays have a *length* property that can be retrieved using the **.length** attribute. We will see how to use this property in the next section.

If an array variable is dropped where a *statement* can appear, Alice displays a menu from which you can select the write version of the subscript operation. If an array variable is dropped onto a *placeholder* variable or value, Alice displays a menu from which you can select either the array's **length** attribute or the read version of the subscript operation.

5.2   More Array Examples

In this section, we will work through some examples that make use of the various array operations that were described in the previous section.

5.2.1 Example 3: The Cows Go Marching

Suppose that Scene 1 of a story has a cow singing the silly song "The Cows Go Marching."[2] The lyrics to the song are as follows:

The cows go marching one-by-one Hurrah! Hurrah! The cows go marching one-by-one Hurrah! Hurrah! The cows go marching one-by-one, the little one stopped to suck his thumb, and they all went marching down to the ground to get out of the rain BOOM! BOOM! BOOM!	The cows go marching two-by-two Hurrah! Hurrah! The cows go marching two-by-two Hurrah! Hurrah! The cows go marching two-by-two, the little one stopped to tie his shoe, and they all went marching down to the ground to get out of the rain BOOM! BOOM! BOOM!
… The cows go marching three-by-three, the little one stopped to climb a tree, …	… The cows go marching four-by-four, the little one stopped to shut the door, …
… The cows go marching five-by-five, the little one stopped to take a dive, …	… The cows go marching six-by-six, the little one stopped to pick up sticks, …
… The cows go marching seven-by-seven, the little one stopped to pray to heaven, …	… The cows go marching eight-by-eight, the little one stopped to shut the gate, …
The cows go marching nine-by-nine Hurrah! Hurrah! The cows go marching nine-by-nine Hurrah! Hurrah! The cows go marching nine-by-nine, the little one stopped to check the time, and they all went marching down to the ground to get out of the rain BOOM! BOOM! BOOM!	The cows go marching ten-by-ten Hurrah! Hurrah! The cows go marching ten-by-ten Hurrah! Hurrah! The cows go marching ten-by-ten, the little one stopped to say, "THE END," and they all went marching down to the ground to get out of the rain BOOM! BOOM! BOOM!

[2]This song is really called "The Ants Go Marching," and its lyrics mention ants not cows, but at the time of this writing, Alice does not contain an Ant class, so we are substituting the Cow class in this example.

One way to build this story would be to send the cow 10 `say()` messages per verse times 10 verses = 100 `say()` messages. But many of the song's lines are exactly the same from verse to verse, so this would require lots of wasted, repeated effort.

Another way would be to recognize that this is basically a *counting problem*: The song is counting from 1 to 10. So should we use a `for` statement to count through the verses and put statements within the `for` statement to make the cow sing a verse? This is good thinking, but each verse differs from the others in *two* ways:

1. the number being sung (*one, two, …, nine, ten*)

2. what the little one does (*suck his thumb, tie his shoe, …, check the time, say "THE END"*).

We could organize the ways the verses differ into two groups, as shown in Figure 5-20.

Group 1		Group 2	
Index	Numbers	Index	What the little one does
0	one	0	suck his thumb
1	two	1	tie his shoe
2	three	2	climb a tree
3	four	3	shut the door
4	five	4	take a dive
5	six	5	pick up sticks
6	seven	6	pray to heaven
7	eight	7	shut the gate
8	nine	8	check the time
9	ten	9	say, "THE END"

FIGURE 5-20   Two groups of ways the verses differ

© Cengage Learning 2015

If we defined two arrays (one for each group), a `for` statement could then count from 0 to 9 and, on repetition *i*, use the subscript operator to retrieve the string stored at index *i* from each array. Note that since we must simultaneously retrieve values from two different arrays, we cannot just use Alice's for each in array loop to solve this problem because it only lets us iterate through a single array.

Using these ideas, we might build this algorithm to solve the problem:

```
String [] numberArray = {one, two, three, four, five,
                          six, seven, eight, nine, ten};
String [] littleOneArray = {suck his thumb, tie his shoe,
                             climb a tree, shut the door, take a dive, pick up
                             sticks, pray to heaven, shut the gate, check the
                             time,
                             say 'THE END'};
for each index in numberArray {
    repeatedLine = "The cows go marching" + numberArray[index] + "-by-" +
            numberArray[index];
    cow.say(repeatedLine);
    cow.say("Hurrah! Hurrah!");
    cow.say(repeatedLine);
    cow.say("Hurrah! Hurrah!");
    cow.say(repeatedLine);
    cow.say("The little one stopped to " + littleOneArray[index]);
    cow.say("and they all went marching");
    cow.say("down to the ground");
    cow.say("to get out of the rain.");
    cow.say("BOOM! BOOM! BOOM!");
}
```

Using this algorithm to guide us, we can add a **singMarchingSong()** method to the **Cow** class. After defining the two arrays, we add a **for** loop to our method by dragging and dropping the count control into the editing area. When we drop it, Alice displays a menu from which we can select either of our arrays' **length** attributes as the number of repetitions of the loop, as shown in Figure 5-21.

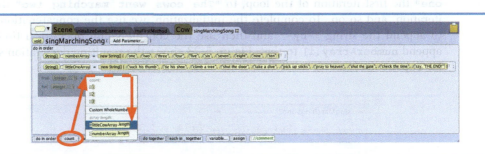

FIGURE 5-21   Using a **for** loop to count through an array's index values

With our **for** loop in place, we can then add to it the statements specified by our algorithm. One tricky part is defining our **repeatedLine** variable. We initialize it by using the first part of the string (**"The cows go marching"**). Then we click the down-arrow next to that string, select its concatenation operator, choose our **numberArray** subscript operator, and then choose our loop control variable **i** as the index of the value we want to access in **numberArray**, as shown in Figure 5-22.

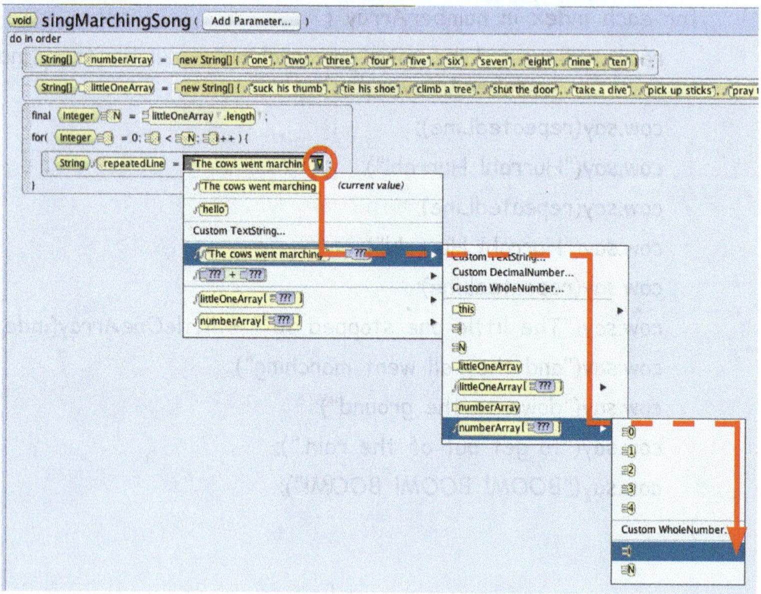

FIGURE 5-22   Using the array subscript operation inside a loop

This much will initialize our **repeatedLine** variable to **"The cows went marching one"** the first iteration of the loop, to **"The cows went marching two"** the second iteration, and so on. To complete the initialization, we use the concatenation operator to append the string **"-by-"** and then use the concatenation operator a final time to append **numberArray[i]** to that. Figure 5-23 shows the resulting declaration statement for **repeatedLine**.

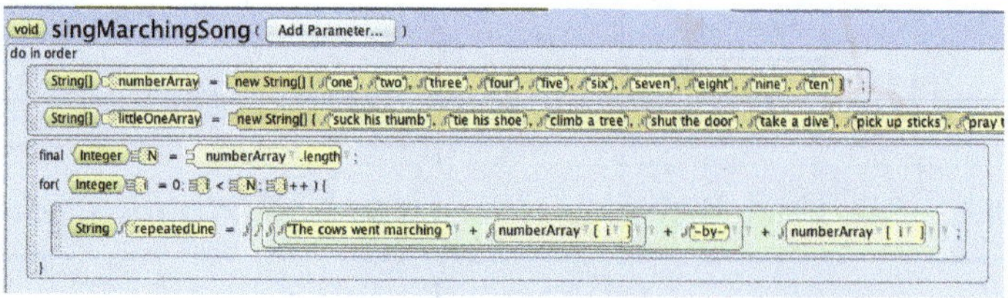

FIGURE 5-23   Using **numberArray[i]** to initialize **repeatedLine**

Given this statement, in the first iteration of the loop, **repeatedLine** will be defined as:

> **The cows went marching one-by-one**

In the second iteration, **repeatedLine** will be redefined as:

> **The cows went marching two-by-two**

In each subsequent iteration, **repeatedLine** will be redefined as appropriate for that verse.

Once we understand how to use the subscript operator and the loop control variable **i** to access an array item at a given index, we can use the same approach to access the appropriate entry in **littleOneArray**. Figure 5-24 shows the completed method.

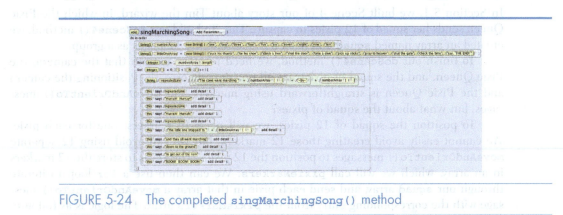

FIGURE 5-24 The completed **singMarchingSong()** method

As can be seen in Figure 5-24, we were able to get our cow to "sing" the entire 10-verse, 100-line song using just 15 statements and five variables!

When we invoke this method, our cow sings the song. Figure 5-25 shows two screen captures as the cow is singing the first verse.

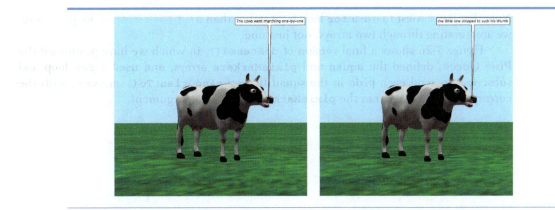

FIGURE 5-25 The singing cow in action

Alice's **for** loop thus provides an alternative to the for each in array loop as a means of processing all of an array's items. The **for** loop is sometimes more useful, since it is less restrictive than the for each in array loop. If you want to process each of the values in an array, you can do so using a **for** loop that follows this pattern:

```
final Integer N = anArray.length;
for (Integer i = 0; i < N; i++) {
    // ... process anArray[i]
}
```

5.2.2   Example 4: Positioning the Pixie Squad

In Section 5.1, we built Scene 4 of our story about Tim the wizard, in which the Pixie Queen sends her squad of 12 pixies to capture Tim. To build our **doScene4()** method, we created an array named **squad** and used it to animate the 12 pixies as a group.

To finish our **doScene4()** method, we need to make certain that the camera, the Pixie Queen, and the squad of pixies are all positioned correctly. Positioning the camera and the Pixie Queen is straightforward using markers and **moveAndOrientTo()** messages, but what about the squad of pixies?

To position the squad of 12 pixies, we will need 12 markers, one for each pixie. We cannot easily avoid creating those 12 markers, but we can avoid using 12 separate **moveAndOrientTo()** messages to position the 12 pixies. The key is to store the 12 markers in an array, which we will call **pixieMarkers**. We can then use a **for** loop to iterate through our **squad** array, and send each pixie in that array a **moveAndOrientTo()** message with the corresponding entry from the **pixieMarkers** array. The logic is as follows:

```
final Integer N = squad.length;
for (Integer i = 0; i < N; i++) {
    squad[i].moveAndOrientTo( pixieMarkers[i] );
}
```

Note that it is easiest to use a **for** loop here rather than a for each in array loop, because we are iterating through two arrays, not just one.

Figure 5-26 shows a final version of **doScene4()**, in which we have positioned the Pixie Queen, defined the **squad** and **pixieMarkers** arrays, and used a **for** loop and subscripts to send each pixie in the squad the **moveAndOrientTo()** message, with the corresponding marker from the **pixieMarkers** array as an argument.

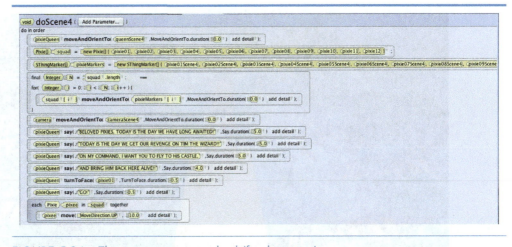

FIGURE 5-26   The `doScene4()` method (final version)

Note that we define our **pixieMarkers** array using the type **SThingMarker**, since that is the type of each pixie's marker. While it takes a little bit of time to set up the array of markers, this approach results in a method that is much more succinct and readable than if we had used 12 **moveAndOrientTo()** messages.

Note also that we have set the durations of each **moveAndOrientTo()** message to **0.0**, so that each object takes its place "instantly" when the scene begins. Note finally that we move the camera last, to ensure that each object is in its place before we see it.

5.2.3   Example 5: In the Court of the Pixie Queen

In Scene 5 of our story about Tim the wizard, the pixies use a green anti-magic ring to neutralize Tim's powers, after which they carry him off to the court of the Pixie Queen. Building this scene is fairly straightforward, using the **Torus** class from the Shapes/Text section of the Alice Gallery, so we will proceed to Scene 6, which begins as follows:

Scene: The court of the Pixie Queen is crowded with pixies. Tim stands captive near her throne, the pixies' green anti-magic ring around his upper body. A pixie near the throne announces, "Her Majesty, the Queen!" The Pixie Queen enters her court, and all the pixies turn toward her. As she moves along the promenade leading to her throne, each pixie in succession turns to her and bows. Upon reaching her throne, the Queen turns and says, "Please rise." As one, the pixies turn toward her and rise from their bows.

Looking over the nouns in the story, we might begin building this scene by creating a "pixie court" in a woodland setting, with a promenade leading to a throne, and a crowd of pixies flanking each side of the promenade. Figure 5-27 shows one possible realization of this scene using various classes from the Alice Gallery.

FIGURE 5-27   The court of the Pixie Queen

We also position the Pixie Queen behind the camera (a set distance from the throne) to set up her entry, and drop markers for her, her pixies, Tim, and the camera.

With the scene set, we are ready to think about generating the behavior required to animate our scene. We might break the actions down into the following steps:

1. The pixie closest to the throne announces, "Her Majesty, the Queen!"

2. Each courtier simultaneously turns to face the camera.

3. Do together:
   a. Move the queen forward (down the promenade) to her throne.
   b. Make the queen's wings flap.
   c. As she passes each courtier, have that pixie turn toward the queen and bow.

4. The queen turns 1/2 revolution (so that she is facing her courtiers).

5. The queen says, "Please rise."

6. Together, each courtier turns toward the queen and rises from his or her bow.

Together, these steps make up an algorithm we can use for the **doScene6()** method.

Defining the Method

What is the best way to implement this algorithm? Steps 2 and 6 require all courtiers to take a simultaneous action, and Step 3c requires each courtier to take an action one at a time. One way to elicit these simultaneous and one-at-a-time actions is to place the courtiers into an array. Given the array, we can use the for each in array statement to make all courtiers do the same thing simultaneously in Steps 2 and 6, and we can use the

each in array together statement to make them all turn and bow to the Queen one at a time in Step 3c.

With this approach, we can refine our algorithm as follows:

1. Let **pixies** be an array of all the courtier pixies.

2. The pixie nearest the throne announces the queen.

3. Each **pixie** in **pixies** together:
   pixie turns to face the camera.

4. Do together:
   a. The queen moves forward (down the promenade) to her throne.
   b. The queen's wings flap.
   c. For each **pixie** in **pixies**:
      pixie turns toward the queen and bows.

5. The queen turns 1/2 revolution.

6. The queen says, "Please rise."

7. Each **pixie** in **pixies** together:
   pixie turns toward the queen and rises from his/her bow.

Using the ideas we have learned in this chapter, these steps are straightforward to program in Alice, provided we define **bow()** and **flapWings()** methods for our pixies. We can also reuse our squad of pixies as the pixie courtiers by moving them from their positions at the end of Scene 5 to these positions at the beginning of Scene 6. Figure 5-28 shows the first part of this scene, in which we define arrays of pixies and markers, and use the same approach we used in Figure 5-26 to position our pixies.[3]

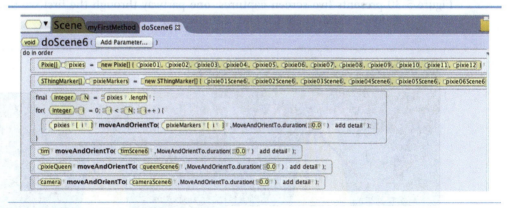

FIGURE 5-28   Setting up Scene 6

Figure 5-29 shows the remainder of the beginning of **doScene6()**.

---

[3]When too many steps are required to set up a scene, one option is to create a new "setup" method (e.g., **setupScene6()**), move all of the objects to their markers in that setup method and then invoke the setup method in **myFirstMethod()** immediately before the scene method is invoked.

```
pixie11  say( "HER MAJESTY, THE QUEEN!" ,Say.duration( 2.0 )  add detail );

each  Pixie  pixie  in  pixies  together
    pixie  turnToFace( pixieQueen    add detail );

DoTogether.invokeAndWait( new Runnable() {
public void run() {
    pixieQueen  move( MoveDirection.FORWARD , 8.0 ,Move.duration( 12.0 )  add detail );

    pixieQueen  flapWings( 12 );

    for( Pixie  pixee : pixies ){
        pixee  bowTo( pixieQueen );
    }
}
});

pixieQueen  turnToFace( camera    add detail );

pixieQueen  say( "Please rise." ,Say.duration( 2.0 )  add detail );

each  Pixie  pix  in  pixies  together

    DoTogether.invokeAndWait( new Runnable() {
    public void run() {
        pix  turnToFace( pixieQueen    add detail );

        pix  unBow();
    }
    });
```

FIGURE 5-29   Implementing our algorithm for `doScene6()`

We then run our scene and tweak it as necessary to get the desired behavior. Figure 5-30 presents two screen captures: one partway through the first each in array together statement and one at the end of the scene.

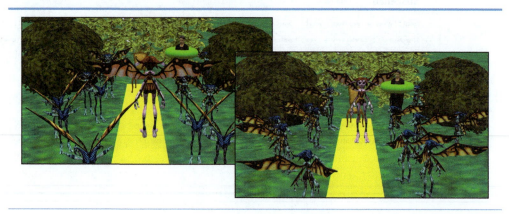

FIGURE 5-30   Screen captures from `doScene6()`

Arrays, for each in array loops, each in array together loops, and **for** loops plus subscripts thus provide us with powerful tools for building complex animations.

5.3   Using Randomness

Suppose the first scene of a story begins as follows:

> Scene: A woman named Dana is at the gate to a castle wanting to enter. The gate tells Dana it will only open for her if it can tell her a knock-knock joke. She agrees; the gate tells her a knock-knock joke and then opens for her.

If the gate told Dana the same joke every time we pressed the Run button, then this story would quickly become boring, and the user would not want to play the scene more than twice. However, if each time the scene is played, the gate tells a *random* (i.e., potentially different) knock-knock joke, we make the scene more interesting and worth replaying.

We might begin by setting up our scene as shown in Figure 5-31.

FIGURE 5-31   Dana at the castle gate

We can then click the Edit Code button and add a new procedure method to the **CastleGate** class. Since the gate needs to tell the joke to someone, we will name this method **tellRandomKnockKnockJokeTo()**. Our story calls for the gate to tell the joke to Dana, so we will need to pass **dana** to the method as an argument. That means we will need to define a parameter to store **dana**. The most general type of object that will respond to a **say()** message is an **SJointedModel**[4]. This is the superclass of **Biped**, **Flyer**, **Prop**, **Quadruped**, **Swimmer**, and **Vehicle**, so if we use **SJointedModel** to define our parameter, then our castle gate can tell its jokes to pretty much any Alice model. Putting all of these pieces together yields the method stub shown in Figure 5-32.

---

[4]See Appendix C.

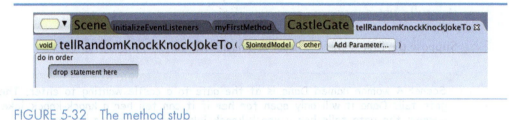

FIGURE 5-32   The method stub

Our next problem is to figure out how to define the method so that the gate tells a knock-knock joke. Let's look at several jokes (using "a" for the person telling the joke and "b" for the person to whom the joke is being told), to see what is the same and what is different about each one:

Joke 1	Joke 2	Joke 3
a: Knock-knock	a: Knock-knock	a: Knock-knock
b: Who's there?	b: Who's there?	b: Who's there?
a: Boo.	a: Who.	a: Little old lady.
b: Boo who?	b: Who who?	b: Little old lady who?
a: Don't cry, it's just a joke.	a: Is there an owl in here?	a: I didn't know you could yodel!

Comparing these (lame) jokes, we can see that knock-knock jokes have the following structure:

> a: Knock-knock
> b: Who's there?
> a: *name*
> b: *name* who?
> a: *punchline*

where *name* and *punchline* are the only parts that vary from joke to joke.

If we make *name* and *punchline* array variables, then we can store multiple jokes in them. For example, to store the three jokes above, we would define *name* and *punchline* as follows:

```
String [] name = {"Boo", "Who", "Little old lady" };
String [] punchline = {"Don't cry, it's just a joke.",
                       "Is there an owl in here?",
                       "I didn't know you could yodel!"};
```

These definitions create arrays that are *related*, in that `punchline[0]` corresponds to `name[0]`, `punchline[1]` corresponds to `name[1]`, and so on. We can visualize them as shown in Figure 5-33.

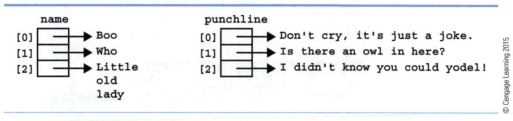

FIGURE 5-33 The `name` and `punchline` arrays

Once we have the parts of the jokes stored in arrays, we can have our castle gate tell the joke at index *i* as follows:

```
gate: Knock-knock
other: Who's there?
gate: name[i]
other: name[i] who?
gate: punchline[i]
```

That is, if *i* has the value 0, then this will cause our gate to tell the "Boo who" joke; if *i* has the value 1, then it will tell the "Who who" joke, and so on.

Generating Random Numbers

To tell a random joke from the array, we need to generate a **random number** for the index *i*. That is, we need to initialize *i* to a value that is randomly selected from the range of valid index values for the array. If we initialize *i* with a placeholder value, we can click the down-arrow next to that placeholder and use the Random menu choice to replace the placeholder with one of several functions Alice provides for generating random numbers, as shown in Figure 5-34.

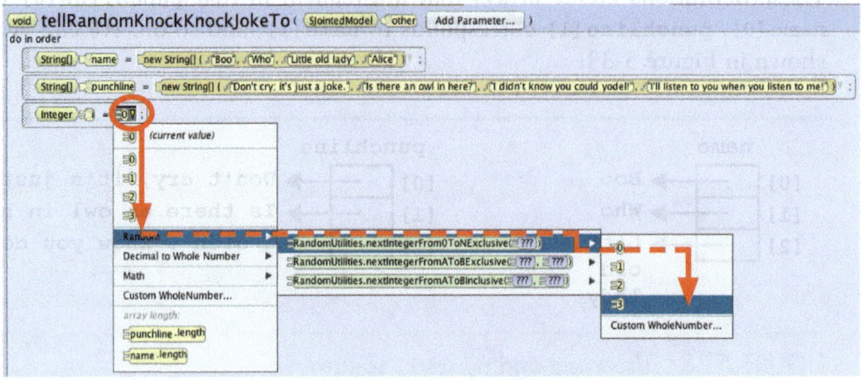

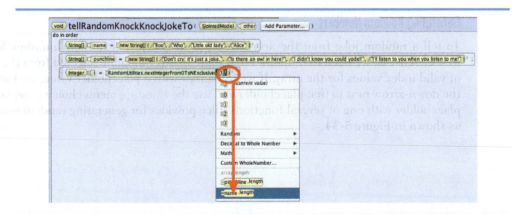

FIGURE 5-34   Initializing a variable to a random integer

In Figure 5-34, we have chosen the **nextIntegerFrom0ToNExclusive()** function to generate our random index. Given a value **N**, this function will generate a random integer from the range **0..N-1**. It *excludes* the value **N** from consideration—hence, the function's name. This is perfect for our purposes because the range of valid index values for our name array runs from **0..name.length-1**. That is, if we pass **name.length** to this function as the value for **N**, the function will generate a random integer that is a valid index of our array.

Since **name.length** does not appear in the menu of options for **N**, we are selecting **3** as a temporary placeholder value in Figure 5-34. With a placeholder in place, we can click the down-arrow next to our placeholder and select **name.length** from the menu, as shown in Figure 5-35.

FIGURE 5-35   Passing an array's length to a random number generator

Since our arrays' lengths are both 4, we could have instead chosen Custom Whole Number and entered **4**. The problem with that approach is that if we later add more jokes to our arrays, then we would also have to change this value we pass to **nextInt-egerFrom0ToNExclusive()**. By instead passing **name.length**, we can add additional jokes to our arrays and our program will still work correctly.

With that completed, our variable **i** will be initialized to a random integer from the range **0..name.length-1**. To complete our method, we just have to send **say()** messages to the **gate** and our parameter **other** that use **i** and our two arrays to follow the outline for knock-knock jokes. Figure 5-36 shows the completed **tellRandomKnock-KnockJokeTo()** method, which includes four knock-knock jokes.

FIGURE 5-36   The **tellRandomKnockKnockJokeTo()** method

Each time this method is performed, it tells a knock-knock joke selected at random from the **name** and **punchline** arrays. By randomly generating the value of **i** and then using that same value as the index for both **name[i]** and **punchline[i]**, the *name* and *punchline* for a given joke will match one another. Moreover, all we have to do to add additional jokes to our castle gate's repertoire is add those jokes' *name* and *punchline* values to our two arrays.

Random Details

The method in Figure 5-36 makes use of Alice's Random menu choice, which provides access to a package named **RandomUtilities**. This package provides a variety of methods for generating random numbers:

- If you wish to generate a random **Integer** value (i.e., a whole number), then declare an **Integer** variable, initialize it with a placeholder, and click the down-arrow next to the placeholder. Alice provides the following three options under the Random menu-choice, which can be seen in Figure 5-34:

  1. The **nextIntegerFrom0ToNExclusive(N)** function returns a randomly chosen integer from the range **0..N-1**. As its name implies, it excludes the value *N* from its possible return values. This method is ideal for choosing a random array-index value.

  2. Th e **nextIntegerFromAToBExclusive(A, B)** function returns a randomly chosen integer from the range **A..B-1**. This function lets you specify both the lower and upper bounds of the range from which the random number will be chosen. While it includes **A**, it excludes **B** from its possible return values. For example, **nextIntegerFromAToBExclusive(1, 100)** will return a randomly generated integer from the range **1..99**.

3. The **nextIntegerFromAToBInclusive(A, B)** function returns a randomly chosen integer from the range **A..B**. This function lets you specify the lower and upper bounds of the range from which the random number will be chosen, but it includes both **A** and **B** as possible return values. For example, to simulate the roll of a six-sided die, **nextIntegerFromAToBInclusive(1, 6)** will return a randomly generated integer from the range **1..6**.

• If you wish to generate a random **Double** value (i.e., a number with a decimal point), then declare a **Double** variable, initialize it with a placeholder, and click the down-arrow next to the placeholder. Alice provides two options under the Random menu-choice:

1. The **nextDoubleInRange(0.0, 1.0)** function returns a number *r* such that

    0.0 <= *r* < 1.0

2. The **nextDoubleInRange(A, B)** function returns a number *r* such that:

    A <= *r* < B

Thus, while both of these functions include their first value (**0.0** or **A**) in the range of numbers from which they choose a random value, both of these functions exclude the second argument (**1.0** or **B**) from that range.

• These methods can be used to incorporate basic probabilities into a program. For example, suppose an event will occur two times out of three. Since 2/3 is 0.6666666..., you can model this using the following logic:

```
Double randomNumber = RandomUtilities.nextDoubleInRange(0.0, 1.0);
if ( randomNumber < 0.66666667 ) {
    // ... the event happened, so take action accordingly
} else {
    // ... the event did not happen
}
```

• If you wish to generate a random **Boolean** value (i.e., a value that is either **true** or **false**), then declare a **Boolean** variable, initialize it with a placeholder, click the down-arrow next to the placeholder, and choose **RandomUtilities.nextBoolean()** from the menu. This is logically equivalent to flipping a coin and is useful in any situation where there is a 50-50 chance of an event occurring. A general pattern for performing this can be expressed as follows:

```
Boolean itHappened = RandomUtilities.nextBoolean();
if ( itHappened ) {
    // ... the event happened, so respond accordingly
} else {
    // ... the event did not happen
}
```

For example, if a story called for a character named Bob to flip a coin and announce the results, and if we wanted the result to actually be random, we could build the story using logic like this:

```
Boolean heads = RandomUtilities.nextBoolean();
if ( heads ) {
    bob.say("Heads!");
} else {
    bob.say("Tails!");
}
```

The choices beneath Alice's Random menu thus provide us with a means of introducing the element of chance into our programs. This can be used to build stories that behave differently each time they are performed, making them less predictable and therefore more interesting.

5.4   Chapter Summary

❏ An array is a data structure that stores a sequence of items.

❏ The for each in array loop processes each of the items in an array in sequence.

❏ The each in array together loop processes each of the items in an array in parallel.

❏ The for loop plus the subscript operation can be used to process each of the items in an array (or multiple arrays) in sequence.

❏ Alice's Random menu choice provides a variety of functions to generate random numbers and boolean values. These can be used to make a story different each time that it is performed. Less predictable is usually more interesting.

5.4.1   Key Terms

array	indexed variable
data structure	item
each in array together statement	iterating
for each in array statement	position
index	random number
	subscript operator

Programming Projects

5.1   Using persons from the Alice Gallery, build a world containing five to six people who are performing a coordinated cheer at a sporting event. Store and animate your people using an array. Your cheer can be either funny or serious, and it can be either a cheer from your school or a standard cheer (such as "The Wave").

5.2 *This Old Man* is a silly song with the following lyrics. Create an Alice program containing a character who sings this song, using as few statements as possible.

Verse 1: This old man, he played one. He played knick-knack on my drum, with a knick-knack paddy-wack give a dog a bone. This old man came rolling home.	Verse 2: This old man, he played two. He played knick-knack on my shoe, with a knick-knack paddy-wack give a dog a bone. This old man came rolling home.
Verse 3: This old man, he played three. He played knick-knack on my knee, ...	Verse 4: This old man, he played four. He played knick-knack on my door, ...
Verse 5: This old man, he played five. He played knick-knack on my hive, ...	Verse 6: This old man, he played six. He played knick-knack on my sticks, ...
Verse 7: This old man, he played seven. He played knick-knack up in heaven, ...	Verse 8: This old man, he played eight. He played knick-knack on my gate, ...
Verse 9: This old man, he played nine. He played knick-knack on my spine, with a knick-knack paddy-wack give a dog a bone. This old man came rolling home.	Verse 10: This old man, he played ten. He played knick-knack once again, with a knick-knack paddy-wack give a dog a bone. This old man came rolling home.

© Cengage Learning 2015

5.3 Create a city scene featuring a parade. Store the paraders (i.e., vehicles, people, etc.) in an array and use it to coordinate their movements. Make your parade as festive as possible.

5.4 In Section 5.3, we described a story in which a castle gate tells Dana a knock-knock joke. Figure 5-36 defines the **tellRandomKnockKnockJoke()** method. Define a **doScene1()** method that performs this scene. In your scene method, define an array of responses Dana can give after the gate finishes the joke (e.g., *"That was so funny, I forgot to laugh." "That's as old as my grandmother's toes and twice as corny." "Should I laugh now?"*). Have Dana say one of these responses (chosen at random) between the conclusion of **tellRandomKnockKnockJoke()** and the opening of the gates.

5.5 Create a scene in which a group of people do a dance routine (e.g., the Can-Can). Store the people in an array, and use **for each in array** and/or **each in array together** statements to coordinate the movements of their routine.

5.6 Create a "springtime" scene that runs for a minute or so, starting with an empty field but ending with the field covered with flowers. The flowers should "grow" out of the ground as your scene plays. Make your program as short as possible by storing the flowers in an array.

5.7 Proceed as in Project 5.6, but use random-number generation to make the flowers appear in a different order or pattern every time your program is run.

5.8 In the "Penguin Party" program in Figure 5-17, each penguin yells the same thing when it jumps in the water. Enhance this program by having each penguin yell a different exclamation when it jumps into the water.

5.9 Choose an old pop song that has several unique arm or body motions and whose lyrics are available on the Internet (e.g., "YMCA" by the Village People, "Walk Like An Egyptian" by the Bangles, etc.). Using Alice, create a "music video" for the song, in which several people sing the song and use their arms or bodies to make the motions. Make your video as creative as possible, but try to avoid writing the same statements more than once. If you have access to a legal digital copy of the song, use the **playAudio()** message to play it during your video.

5.10 Create a scene containing a group of similar creatures from the Alice **Gallery** (e.g., a herd of horses, a school of fish, a pack of wolves, a flock of birds, etc.). Store your group in an array and write a method that makes the group exhibit *flocking behavior*, in which the behavior of one member of the group causes the rest of the group to behave in a similar fashion. (Hint: Designate one member of the group as the leader, and make the leader the first item in the array.)

Chapter 6
Events

It's not the events of our lives that shape us, but our beliefs as to what those events mean.

ANTHONY ROBBINS

Often do the spirits
Of great events stride on before the events,
And in to-day already walks to-morrow.

SAMUEL TAYLOR COLERIDGE

To understand reality is not the same as to know about outward events. It is to perceive the essential nature of things. The best-informed man is not necessarily the wisest. Indeed there is a danger that precisely in the multiplicity of his knowledge he will lose sight of what is essential. But on the other hand, knowledge of an apparently trivial detail quite often makes it possible to see into the depth of things. And so the wise man will seek to acquire the best possible knowledge about events, but always without becoming dependent upon this knowledge. To recognize the significant in the factual is wisdom.

DIETRICH BONHOEFFER

The event of a tree falling in the forest makes a sound whether or not anyone hears it. But that event is only significant if a listener hears it. Unless the listener is wearing earphones and the tree happens to land on the listener.

V. OREHCK III

In the event of a water landing, I have been designed to act as a flotation device.

DATA (BRENT SPINER), IN *STAR TREK: INSURRECTION*

Screenshots from Alice 2 © 1999–2013, Alice 3 © 2008–2013, Carnegie Mellon University. All rights reserved. We gratefully acknowledge the financial support of Oracle, Electronic Arts, Sun Microsystems, DARPA, Intel, NSF, and ONR.

Objectives

Upon completion of this chapter, you will be able to:

❑ Create new events in Alice

❑ Create handler methods for Alice events

❑ Use events to build interactive stories

Most of the programs we have written so far have been scenes from stories that, after the user clicks Alice's **Run** button, simply proceed from beginning to end, without further involvement by the user. For some of our programs, the user has to enter a number or a string, but entering such values on the keyboard has been all that we have done in terms of creating **interactive programs**.

An action by the user (or the program) that occurs while a program is running is called an **event**. Events can be the result of actions by the *user*, such as clicking a mouse-button or pressing a keyboard key; or they can be the result of actions by the *program*, such as two objects in a story colliding with one another.

By default, the Alice programs we have written so far have ignored most events. For example, when a typical Alice program is running, we can click the mouse on the screen or press keys on the keyboard, but they will not affect the program's behavior. Likewise, if one object runs into another object, an Alice program will by default ignore the collision event that occurs between the two objects.

To get an Alice program to respond to an event, we must:

1. Add a **listener** for that event to our program

2. Specify what action(s) the listener should take when the event occurs

The procedure that a listener performs in response to an event is called an **event handler**, and performing this action is often called **handling the event**.

Believe it or not, you have been using events, listeners, and handlers since Chapter 1! The reason is that every time you click Alice's **Run** button, it triggers an event for which Alice listens, and whenever this event occurs, Alice's listener handles that event by running your program. You can see this by navigating to **Scene > initializeEventListeners**, which produces the screen shown in Figure 6-1.

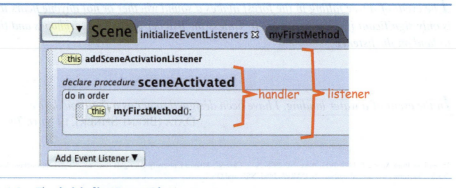

FIGURE 6-1   The **initializeEventListeners** screen

As its name implies, the initializeEventListeners screen is the place where event listeners and their handlers are specified. This is how this one works: Clicking Alice's Run button triggers a **SceneActivation** event. As shown in Figure 6-1, Alice programs contain a **SceneActivationListener** that listens for these **SceneActivation** events. This listener contains a method named **sceneActivated()**, which is the handler for **SceneActivation** events; whenever the **SceneActivationListener** "hears" a **SceneActivation** event occur, the listener will perform the **sceneActivated()** method in response to that event. This **sceneActivated()** method handles the event by invoking **myFirstMethod()**, as we can see in Figure 6-1.

Beneath the listener on the initializeEventListeners screen is the Add Event Listener button. This button lets us tell our program to listen for other kinds of events and to define handlers for those events. A program that solves a problem or tells a story mainly through events and handlers is called an **event-driven program**. In the rest of this chapter, we will see how to build event-driven programs by exploring a representative sample of Alice's events.

6.1   Handling Mouse Clicks: The Magical Doors

To see how an event-driven program is different from those we have built before, suppose we are building an interactive story in which the user encounters a castle with closed gates and has to click on the gates to open them. We might describe the scene as follows:

> Scene: A castle has two closed gates. When the user clicks on them, they open.

We can build this scene using Alice's **CastleGate** and **CastleWall** classes, as shown in Figure 6-2.

FIGURE 6-2   The castle gates

Now that our scene has been built, we are ready to proceed to animating the castle gates when they are clicked.

6.1.1   Getting the Gates to Open

Handling mouse clicks is fairly easy in Alice, but it is different from what we have done before. We use a two-step approach:

1. If the behavior that is needed to handle an event requires more than one message, we define a method that produces that behavior and then have our event handler invoke this method to handle the event.

2. We create a new listener for the event in the **initializeEventListeners** screen that handles the event—either by invoking the method we defined in Step 1 or by sending the single message that produces the required behavior.

To illustrate, the behavior to make our gates open requires two **turn()** messages and a **doTogether** block, so we can perform our first step by creating a new method in the **CastleGate** class named **openGates()**, as shown in Figure 6-3.

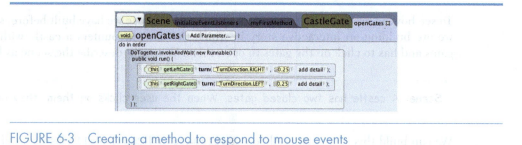

FIGURE 6-3   Creating a method to respond to mouse events

To perform the second step, we click the **initializeEventListeners** tab to view that screen. We then click the **Add Event Listener** button, and, because we want our program to listen for mouse clicks on the castle gate (an object), we choose its **Mouse > addMouseClickOnObjectListener** option, as shown in Figure 6-4.

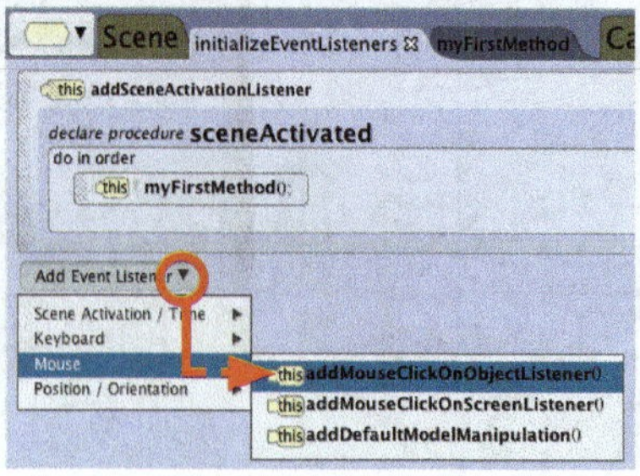

FIGURE 6-4   Adding a listener for mouse clicks on objects

This causes Alice to add a new **MouseClickOnObjectListener** to the program, containing an empty **mouseClicked()** handler for these events, as can be seen in Figure 6-5.

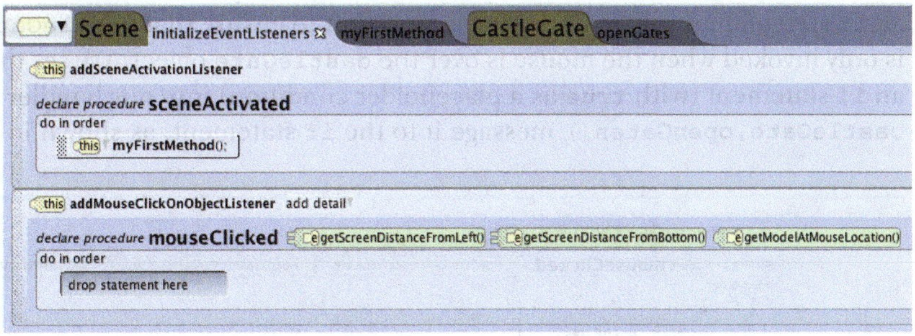

FIGURE 6-5   An empty listener and handler for mouse clicks

We might then "fill in" the empty handler by selecting **castleGate** in the object selector and then dragging its **openGates()** method into the **mouseClicked()** method, which produces the event handler shown in Figure 6-6.

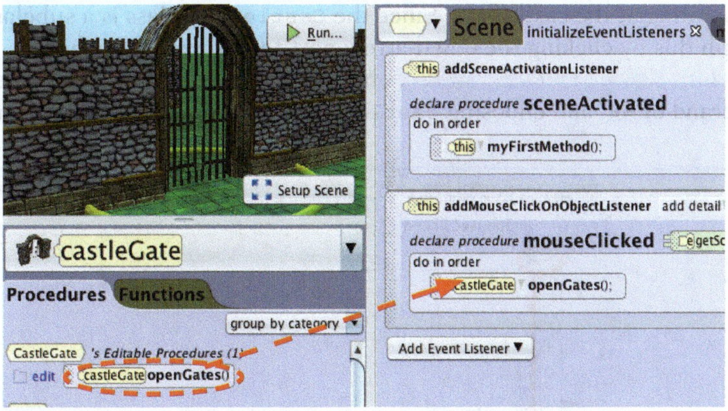

FIGURE 6-6   Handling a mouse click

Congratulations! You have just handled your first event! When we click Alice's Run button, nothing happens until the user clicks the mouse, at which point the gates swing open.

Creating a listener and handler for an event is that easy in Alice. But there are two problems with the handler in Figure 6-6. The first problem is that if the mouse is clicked on *any* object *anywhere* in the 3D world, the castle gates open. The second problem is that if the mouse is clicked again when the gates are open, the gates turn again and disappear into the gate's walls. This behavior is amusing, but it's physically impossible, so we will need to fix it. We will deal with these problems in the following subsections.

6.1.2   Specifying the Object Clicked

To fix our first problem, we must revise our event handler so that it only invokes **castleGate.openGates()** when the **castleGate** object is clicked. We do this by placing an **if** statement inside our handler and using it to ensure that **castleGate.openGates()** is only invoked when the mouse is over the **castleGate** object. We set this up by dragging an **if** statement (with **true** as a placeholder condition) into our handler and dragging the **castleGate.openGates()** message into the **if** statement, as shown in Figure 6-7.

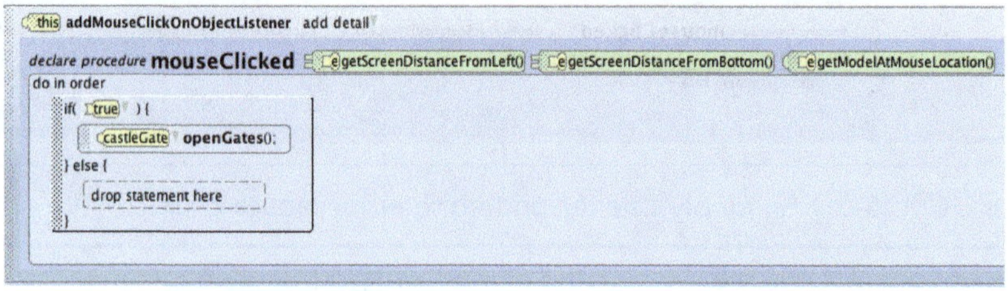

FIGURE 6-7   Guarding the **castleGate.openGates()** message

Next, we need to alter the **if** statement's condition so that it is true only if the mouse is pointing at the castle gate. Since the **CastleGate** class is a subclass of **SThing**, we can begin this by clicking the down-arrow next to our **true** placeholder, choosing **Relational (SThing) (==, !=) > ??? == ???**, choosing a placeholder such as the **camera** for the left operand of **==**, and choosing **castleGate** for its right operand, as shown in Figure 6-8.

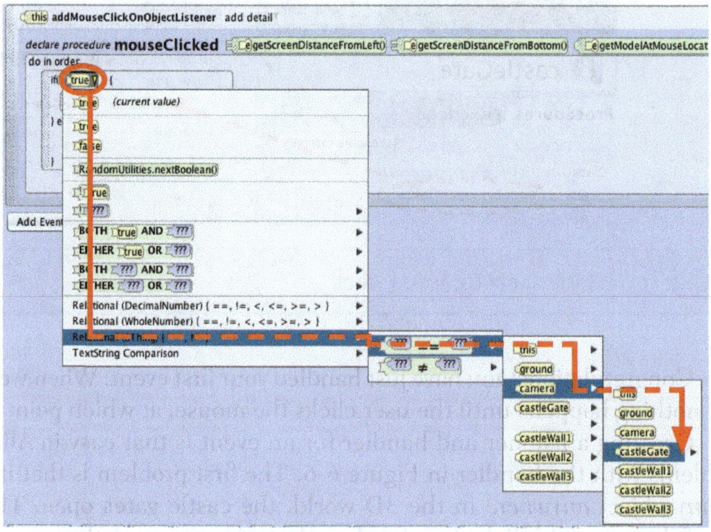

FIGURE 6-8   Comparing the castle gate and a placeholder

This produces the condition

```
camera == castleGate
```

which will always be false. To correct the condition, we can use one of our **mouseClicked()** handler's parameters, which is named **e.getModelAtMouseLocation()**. When our handler is invoked to handle a **MouseClicked** event, the object **e** will refer to that event, and **e.getModelAtMouseLocation()** will refer to the object at which the mouse was pointing. If we drag that parameter onto the condition's **camera** placeholder and drop it there, we get the condition shown in Figure 6-9.

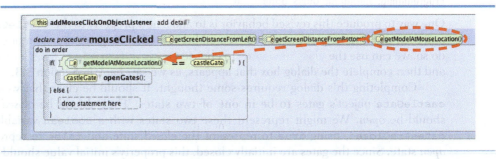

FIGURE 6-9   Comparing the castle gate to the object that was clicked

This change fixes the first problem: When the mouse is clicked on an object, our handler will only send the **castleGate.openGates()** message if that object is the **castleGate**. Try it and see!

That leaves the second problem, which we address next.

6.1.3   Opening and Closing the Gates

As mentioned previously, testing the scene reveals that the castle's gate opens correctly the first time we click on it. But if we click on it a second time, our handler sends the **openGates()** message to our **castleGate** again, at which point the two gates turn again and disappear into the walls on either side of the gate! If we click on it a third time, the two gates turn again and emerge from the backs of the walls. If we click on it a fourth time, the gates turn again, returning to their original positions. This is funny, but not quite what we had in mind.

Our listener and handler are doing exactly what we told them to do. The mistake lies in the *logic* we used in specifying how the castle gate should behave. Such mistakes are called **logic errors**. The first step in fixing this is to return to our user story and revise it so that it is correct.

It is important to see that it is okay to revise the user story when testing reveals a problem. Just as a filmmaker may rewrite a scene the night before it is shot, a programmer may have to rewrite a part of the user story to improve the overall program.

Design

To design this method, we can revise the user story as follows:

> Scene: A castle has two closed gates. When the user clicks on them, they open. If the user clicks on them again, they close.

Notice that our revised story contains the magic word *if*. This strongly suggests that we will need an **if** statement to fix the problem.

Programming: Storing the Gates' State

One way to produce this revised behavior is to add a new property to the **CastleGate** class and then use it to help **castleGate** "remember" whether its gates are open or closed. To do so, we can use the class navigator to choose CastleGate > Add CastleGate Property and then complete the dialog box that appears, as we saw back in Section 3.3.

Completing this dialog requires some thought. It should be clear that we want the **castleGate** object's gates to be in one of two states: They should be *closed*, or they should be *open*. We might represent these two states with a **Boolean** variable named **gatesAreClosed**, using **true** to represent the *closed* state and **false** to represent the *open* state. Since the gates are initially closed, this property's initial value should be **true**, as shown in Figure 6-10.

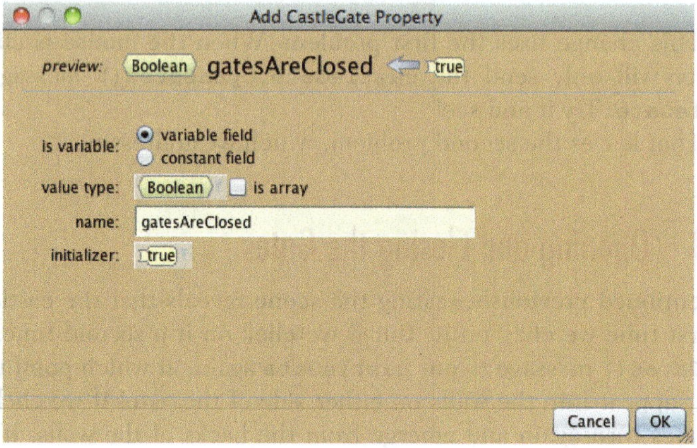

FIGURE 6-10   Storing the state of the castle's gate

After we click the OK button, Alice will create this property, as well as setter and getter methods, to let us change and retrieve its value. Our handler can then use these methods to determine whether the gates need to be opened or closed and to update the value of property **gatesAreClosed** from **true** to **false** (or vice versa) to reflect the door's changed state.

Programming: Revising Our Handler

In Figure 6-3, we defined the **openGates()** method to open the gates. We perform our revised user story by defining a corresponding **closeGates()** method and then adding another **if** statement to our **mouseClicked()** handler to invoke one or the other, based on the state of the **gatesAreClosed** property. Figure 6-11 shows the revised handler.

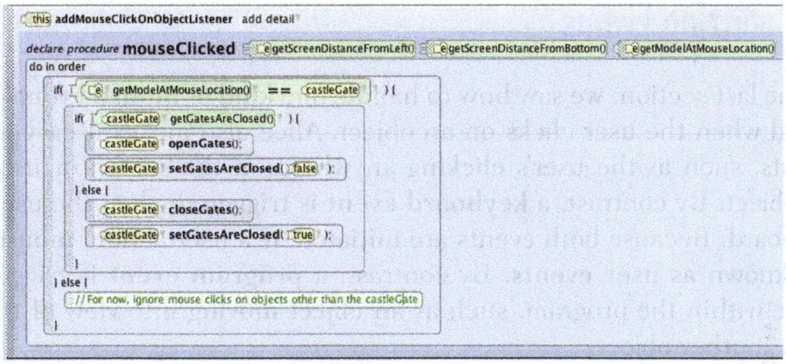

FIGURE 6-11 The revised mouseClicked() handler

With this change to our handler for **mouseClickOnObject** events, the castle's gates now behave the way they should: Clicking them once opens them; clicking them a second time closes them.

The approach shown in Figure 6-11 can be generalized into a standard pattern for situations in which an object can be in one of two states (e.g., *open-closed, in-out, on-off,* etc.) to switch the object from one state to the other. We can generalize the pattern for such **two-state behavior** as follows:

```
if ( obj.getBooleanPropertyState() ) {    // the property is true
    // change the object's state from state 1 to state 2
    // obj.setBooleanStateVariable(false)
} else {    // the property is false
    // change the object's state from state 2 to state 1
    // obj.setBooleanPropertyState(true)
}
```

Keep in mind that if we want to handle mouse-clicks on an object other than the castle gate, we can do one of the following:

- Add a nested **if** statement to handle those clicks in the **else** section of the outer **if** of this handler
- Add another **MouseClickOnObjectListener** to our program's initializeEvent Listeners screen and handle those clicks in that (separate) listener

Both these approaches work, but we generally prefer the second approach because it is more *modular*: It isolates the code to handle a given event in its own dedicated listener. This produces shorter, simpler handlers that are easier to debug and maintain.

Note also that, unlike past programs we have built, this program's `myFirstMethod()` does nothing. Instead, all the interesting behavior lies in the listener's event handler, which is triggered by the user clicking the mouse on an object.

Now that we have handled our first event, let's explore Alice's other event-handling capabilities.

6.2   Categorizing Events

In the last section, we saw how to handle one kind of **mouse event**—the event that is triggered when the user clicks on an object. Alice also makes it easy to handle other mouse events, such as the user's clicking anywhere on the screen or using the mouse to drag an object. By contrast, a **keyboard event** is triggered when the user presses a key on the keyboard. Because both events are initiated by a user action, mouse and keyboard events are known as **user events**. By contrast, a **program event** is triggered by actions taking place within the program, such as an object moving into view of the camera or colliding with another object.

Alice supports a variety of events. At the time of this writing, Alice lets us create listeners for the events listed in Figure 6-12.

Alice Event	Triggered By	Triggered When
`SceneActivation`		Alice's **Run** button is clicked
`KeyPress`		a keyboard key is pressed
`ArrowKeyPress`		an arrow key is pressed
`NumberKeyPress`		a number key is pressed
`ObjectMover`		an arrow key is pressed
`MouseClickOnScreen`	the user	a mouse button is clicked anywhere on the screen
`MouseClickOnObject`		a mouse button is clicked on an object
`DefaultModelManipulation`		the mouse is clicked on an object and dragged (as the program is running)

FIGURE 6-12   Events that Alice supports

© Cengage Learning 2015

continued

Alice Event	Triggered By	Triggered When
`Time`		Alice's Timer expires
`CollisionStart`		an object collides with another
`CollisionEnd`		an object stops colliding with another
`ProximityEnter`		an object comes within a given distance of another
`ProximityExit`		an object that was within a given distance of another is no longer
`ViewEnter`	the program	an object that was outside the camera's view enters its view
`ViewExit`		an object that was within the camera's view leaves its view
`OcclusionStart`		an object comes between the camera and another object (begins hiding it)
`OcclusionEnd`		an object that was hiding a part of another object stops hiding that part
`PointOfViewChange`		an object's position or orientation changes

FIGURE 6-12   Events that Alice supports (*continued*)

Figure 6-12 lists the events that Alice supports. Figure 6-13 categorizes these events and shows how they relate to one another:

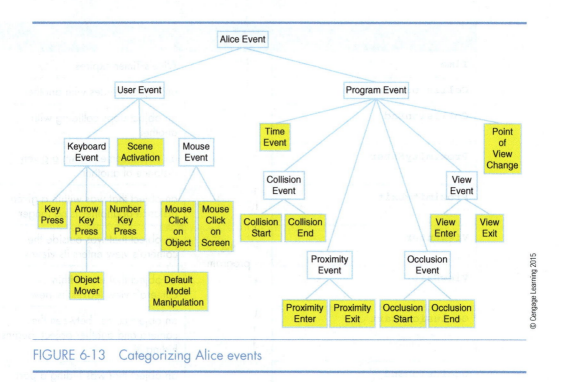

FIGURE 6-13   Categorizing Alice events

The yellow-highlighted boxes in Figure 6-13 contain the names of Alice's events; the lines connecting them to un-highlighted boxes show the categories to which they belong.

Space prevents us from exploring all these different kinds of events, but we will examine a few of the more commonly used events in the next section.

6.3   Example: Treasure Hunt!

In this example, we build a simple interactive story (also known as a *game*) that uses keyboard events and collision events.

6.3.1   The Problem

Scene: During the last World War, your country's crown jewels were sent away for safekeeping. Unfortunately, the ship carrying them came under attack, so the crew threw the chest containing them overboard. The attackers scuttled the ship and mined the surrounding waters. As commander of the submarine Naughtyless, your task is to guide your submarine to the treasure chest while avoiding the surrounding mines. Good luck!

6.3.2   Design

We can build the scene using the classes from the Alice Gallery (see below), but let's first spend a few minutes thinking what the user has to do: how he or she will guide the submarine underwater.

Guiding an object that can move in three dimensions is complicated: The user needs to be able to make the submarine move *up*, *down*, *forward*, *backward*, and turn *left* or *right*. It would be difficult to carry out all six of these behaviors using a mouse, so we will instead use keyboard keys for each of them. After a bit of thought, we might decide to operate the submarine as follows:

> To make the submarine ascend (rise), use the "a" key. To descend (sink), use the "d" key, but the submarine should not sink below the ocean floor. To move it forward, use the up-arrow key; to move it backward, use the down-arrow key. Similarly, use the left and right arrow keys to turn the submarine left and right.
>
> To win the game, the submarine must touch the treasure chest. If the submarine touches a mine, the game is over, and the player loses.

These keys are chosen for their:

- Memory values: Because "a" is the first letter in *ascend* and "d" is the first letter in *descend*, that makes these keys easy to remember. Likewise, the up, down, left, and right arrow keys point in the directions we want the submarine to move, making their meanings easy to remember.
- Convenient positions: Because "a" and "d" are near one another on most keyboards, this allows the user to easily control the submarine's elevation with two fingers of one hand. In the same way, the four arrow keys are usually grouped together, allowing the user to easily control the submarine's forward, backward, left, and right motion with the fingers on the other hand.

It is important to consider *human factors* when building interactive stories. If the story requires complex behaviors, make the controls for your user as convenient and easy to use as possible. Making programs easy to use is an important aspect of programming known as **usability**.

6.3.3   Setting up the Scene

To construct the scene, we can use Alice's OCEAN_FLOOR environment and use instances of the **Submarine** and **TreasureChest** classes. For mines, we will use a dozen instances of the **Sphere** class from the Shapes/Text section of the Gallery.

We will position the camera above, behind, and slightly to the right of the submarine and then set the camera's Vehicle property to be the submarine, so that any message that moves the submarine will move the camera with it. This will produce a "third person" perspective for users as they control the submarine.

When moving underwater, it is easy to lose your bearings. To provide a point of reference for the user, we will position the **pirateShip** at coordinates (0, 0, 0), the center of the scene. We position it on its side, as though it has been sunk, as can be seen in Figure 6-14.

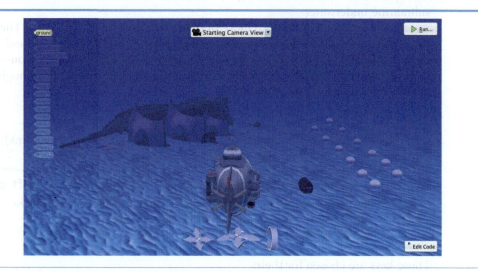

FIGURE 6-14   Setting up the scene

For visual interest, we can also add instances of other underwater classes, such as the **FishingBoat**, various **Swimmer** subclasses, and so on. We'll show you how to handle the submarine colliding with one of the mines; we'll leave it up to you to decide what happens if the submarine touches any of the other underwater objects.

Randomizing the Treasure Chest and Mines

To keep the game from being the same each time a person plays it, we will position the treasure chest and the mines randomly when the program begins. The **ground** of an Alice scene is a 1,000-by-1,000 square whose x and z coordinates range from −500 to +500. (Since an object's y coordinate is its distance above the **ground**, the **ground**'s y coordinate is 0.) One way to randomize an object's position is as follows[1]:

1. Move the object to the scene's center position: (0, 0, 0).

2. Turn it *left* a random rotation amount chosen from the range 0.0 to 1.0.

3. Move it *forward* a random distance chosen from the range 10.0 to 500.0.

4. Move it *up* a given distance: 0.0 for the treasure chest, a random value chosen from the range 4.0 to 30.0 for each mine (because the submarine's **height** property is 4.44).

---

[1]Randomizing our objects' positions would be much simpler if Alice provided setter methods for an object's **x**, **y**, and **z** properties. At the time of this writing, Alice does not provide such methods, forcing us to use this less direct approach.

To make the first step easier, we can move the camera to the center of the scene and drop a marker there. Since we have 12 mines and a treasure chest to randomly position using this procedure, we use these four steps as the algorithm for a **Scene** method named **positionObject()**, as shown in Figure 6-15.

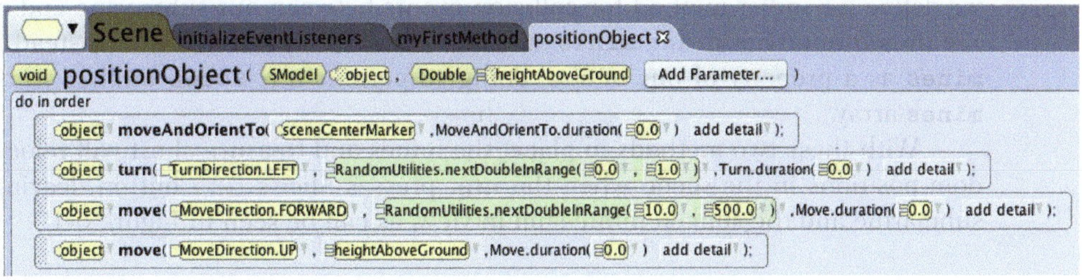

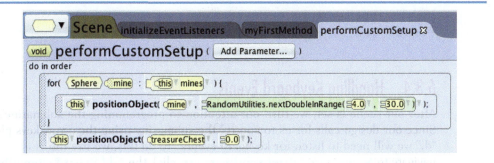

FIGURE 6-15   The **positionObject()** helper method

As can be seen, the **positionObject()** method receives the **object** to be positioned via an **SModel** parameter and receives the **heightAboveGround** that that object is to be moved (in Step 4 of our algorithm) via a **Double** parameter. We define this second parameter because the treasure chest should be on the ground, while each mine should be a random distance above the ground.

After we have defined our **positionObject()** method, we can use it to position our treasure chest and mines. One question is this: *Where* should we invoke **positionObject()** to perform this positioning? We could invoke it in **myFirstMethod()**, but that is really not what **myFirstMethod()** was intended to do. It is better is use the class navigator to navigate to **Scene > performCustomSetup** and invoke **positionObject()** to position these objects there. The **performCustomSetup()** method is invoked prior to **myFirstMethod()**, and it is intended for positioning the objects in a **Scene**. While this is the first time we have used it, it can be used to position the items in any **Scene**. Figure 6-16 shows one way to define this method.

FIGURE 6-16   Defining the **performCustomSetup()** method

Instead of positioning our 12 mines by invoking **positionObject()** 12 times, we have created an array variable named **mines** and initialized it to store our 12 mines. This greatly simplifies our **positionObject()** method, since it lets us use a for each in array loop to iterate through the mines and position each one a random distance above the ocean floor, chosen from the range 4.0 to 30.0.

Looking ahead, we will eventually need to access our array variable **mines** when we define a handler method for collision events between our submarine and our mines. We therefore do *not* define **mines** as a local variable in this method. Instead, we define **mines** as a property of our **Scene**; doing so permits any **Scene** method to access this **mines** array.

With these two methods in place, the mines and treasure chest will relocate to random positions in the scene when the user presses Alice's Run button, leaving only the submarine and the sunken pirate ship in view, as can be seen in Figure 6-17.

FIGURE 6-17   Testing the `performCustomSetup()` method

6.3.4   Handling Keyboard Events

After our scene is set, we turn our attention to programming the submarine's controls. Since our design calls for us to control the submarine using the arrow keys plus "a" and "d," we will need to listen for keyboard events. To do this, we use the class navigator to navigate to Scene > initializeEventListeners, click the Add Event Listener button, and choose Keyboard > addKeyPressListener(), as shown in Figure 6-18.

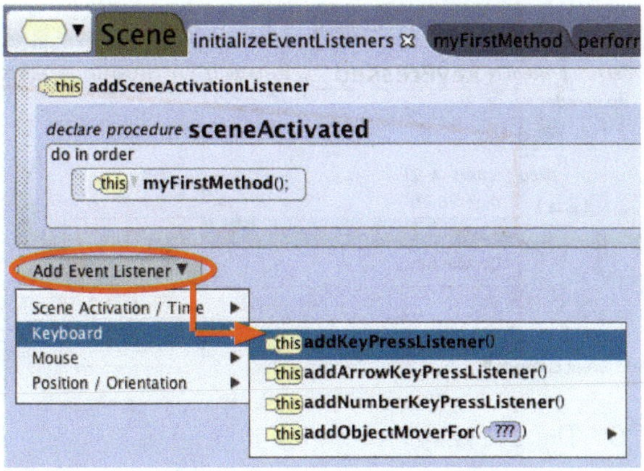

FIGURE 6-18   Adding a key press listener

This adds a **KeyPressListener,** which contains a **keyPressed()** method stub to the initializeEventListeners screen, as shown in Figure 6-19.

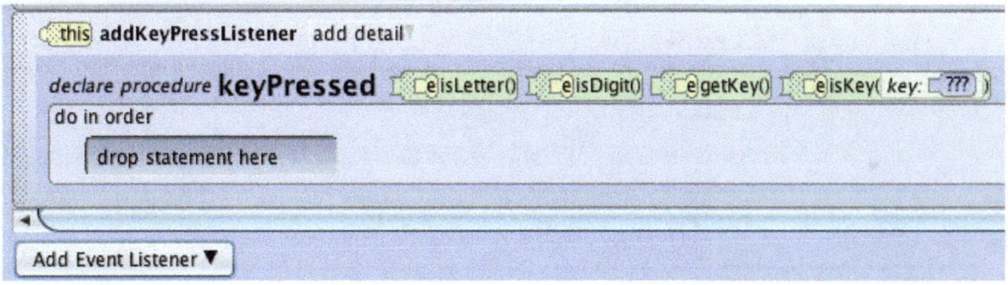

FIGURE 6-19   The **KeyPressListener** and its handler stub

To control the submarine, we have to fill in this stub.

Making the Submarine Move

To follow our design, we have to add logic to this stub that moves the submarine forward when the up-arrow is pressed, turn left when the left-arrow is pressed, turn right when the right-arrow is pressed, move backward when the down-arrow is pressed, ascend when the "a" key is pressed, and descend when the "d" key is pressed. The **keyPressed()** method has several parameters that can be used to handle events; if we add an **if** statement with **true** as a placeholder condition to our stub, we can replace the placeholder with the parameter **e.isKey(???)**, using it as a condition to determine whether the up-arrow key was pressed, as shown in Figure 6-20.

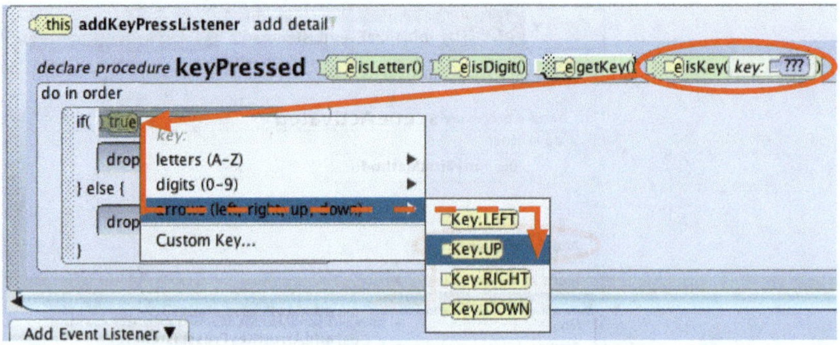

FIGURE 6-20   The `e.isKey()` condition

When we select the **Key.UP** option, Alice replaces our **true** placeholder with the expression **e.isKey(Key.UP)**.

With this **if** statement in place, we can add a statement that makes our submarine move forward, using the logic shown in Figure 6-21.

FIGURE 6-21   Making the submarine move forward

But when we test our method, our submarine moves forward in jerky fits and starts, even if we hold down the up-arrow key and set the animationStyle to BEGIN_AND_END_ABRUPTLY. The problem is that, by default, when the user generates multiple key press events by holding down a key, Alice handles those events one at a time. This can be fixed by using the options under the **addKeyPressListener()** method's add detail button. In Figure 6-22, we first make certain that Alice's heldKeyPolicy is set to FIRE_MULTIPLE.

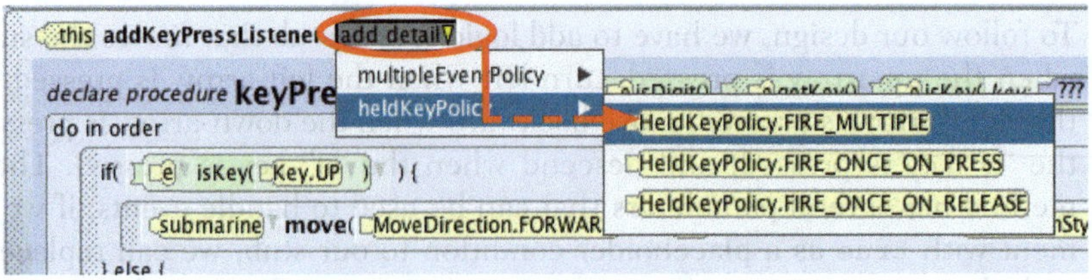

FIGURE 6-22   Firing multiple events when a key is held down

Next, we change Alice's multipleEventPolicy to COMBINE, as shown in Figure 6-23.

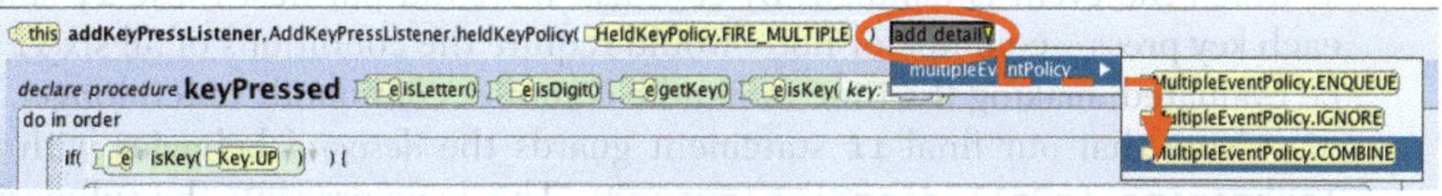

FIGURE 6-23   Combining multiple events when a key is held down

Now that these details are set, our submarine will move smoothly forward when we press the up-arrow key.

To make the submarine turn left when the left-arrow is pressed, turn right when the right-arrow is pressed, move backward when the down-arrow is pressed, ascend when we press the "a" key, and descend when we press the "d" key, we add additional **if** statements, each nested in the **else** section of the preceding **if**. After some trial and error to identify suitable move and turn values, we arrive at the method shown in Figure 6-24.

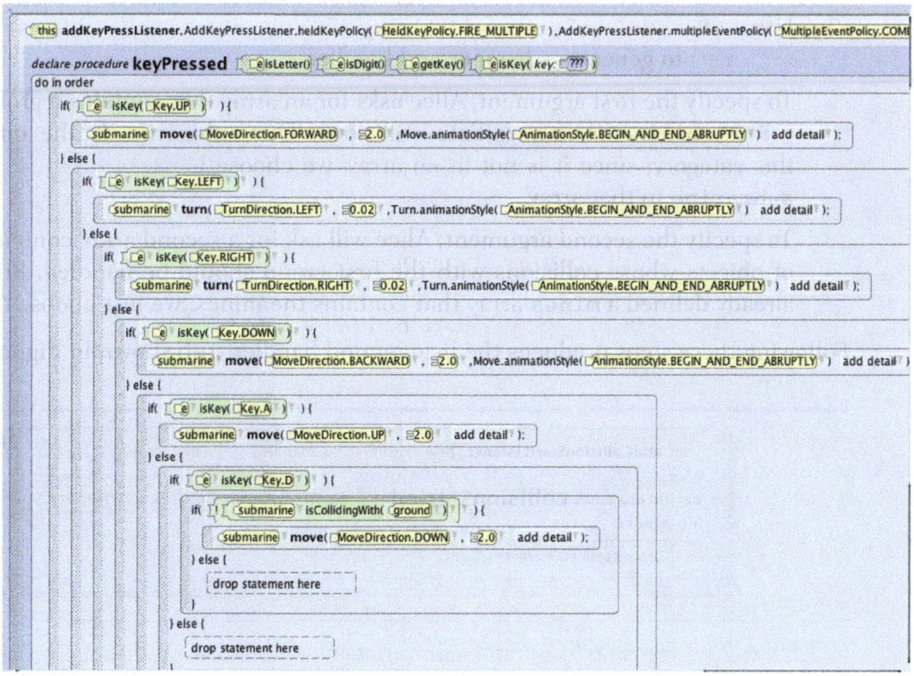

FIGURE 6-24   Controlling the submarine

We have tried to order these **if** statements by frequency of use: The more commonly used commands like *forward*, *left*, and *right* are near the top; the less commonly used commands like *ascend* and *descend* are near the bottom. By using nested **if** statements, when the user presses the up-arrow key, the first **if** statement's condition is true, the submarine moves forward, and flow skips all the remaining **if** statements, speeding the rate at which the event is handled. By contrast, if we did not nest these **if** statements, then each key press—common or not—would require the conditions of all six **if** statements to be evaluated, making the time to handle common commands much longer.

Note that our final **if** statement guards the *descend* behavior with the condition **!submarine.isCollidingWith(ground)**. This logic prevents the submarine from sinking into the ground when it descends.

6.3.5   Handling Collision Events

Now that we have seen how to use keyboard events to control the submarine, we turn our attention to handling the events where our submarine collides with one of the 12 mines (the losing condition) or with the treasure chest (the winning condition).

Collisions with Mines

Alice makes it fairly easy to handle the submarine-mine collision events in the game by performing the following steps:

1. Use **Add Event Listener > Position / Orientation > addCollisionStartListener** (???, ???) to generate a listener and handler.

2. To specify the first argument, Alice asks for an array that contains a group of objects whose movements may initiate collisions. Our submarine is the only object in this category; since it is not in an array, we choose **Custom Array...** and add the **submarine** to that array.

3. To specify the second argument, Alice will ask for a second array containing a group of objects whose collisions with the first group should be handled. Since we have already defined a **mines** array that contains the mines, we just choose that array.[2]

Following these steps produces the listener and handler stub shown in Figure 6-25.

FIGURE 6-25   The stub to handle submarine-mine collision events

Now that our stub to handle submarine-mine collisions is in place, we just need to decide what to do when such a collision takes place.

---

[2]Note that if we wanted our game to end if our submarine hits objects other than the mines (such as the pirate ship), we would instead choose **Custom Array...** and add all relevant objects to that array.

Creating a Billboard

When our submarine hits a mine, we might display a "lost" screen, informing the player that she has hit a mine and should press the restart button to play again. Figure 6-26 shows such a screen.

FIGURE 6-26   A "lost" screen

We created the screen shown in Figure 6-26 using MS PowerPoint, but you can use any program that lets you "paint" and save a picture in a standard format such as bitmap (.bmp), portable network graphics (.png), and so on. Just be sure to save it somewhere you can find it easily.

After you have created such a screen, you can incorporate it into an Alice project by using the **Billboard** class. In the edit scene view, navigate to the Shapes / Text area of the Gallery and double-click the **new Billboard()** icon. Alice will then display a Billboard dialog box in which we can enter **lostScreen** as the name of our billboard, and then choose Import image... for its front paint property, as shown in Figure 6-27.

FIGURE 6-27   The **Billboard** dialog box

Alice will then open a standard file navigation box that we can use to navigate to the file containing our "lose" screen from Figure 6-26. After we have selected it, the dialog box updates itself, as shown in Figure 6-28.

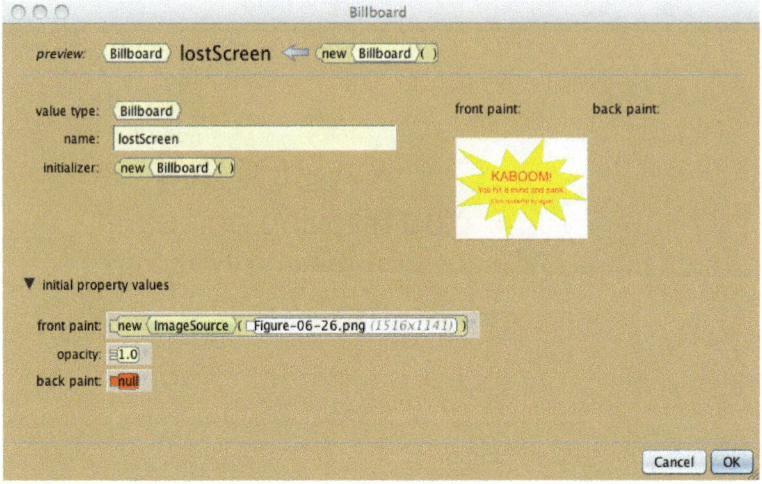

FIGURE 6-28   The **Billboard** dialog box (completed).

When we click the OK button, Alice inserts a new `Billboard` object named `lostScreen` into our scene.

Positioning a Billboard for Use

Billboards can be used in many ways; in this section, we will present one way that works quite well. The basic idea is to position the billboard 1 meter in front of the camera and 1 meter up, so that it is out of the camera's view. We can keep the billboard there by setting its Vehicle property to be the `camera`. Then, to display the billboard, we just have to move it down 1 meter instantaneously.

Regardless of its location, we can begin to position our `lostScreen` billboard by selecting it within the edit scene view and then using the one shots button to perform the following steps:

1. Choose procedures > moveAndOrientTo() > camera. If you watch carefully, you can see the billboard flash by on its way to assuming the current position and orientation of the camera.

2. To move the billboard forward, choose procedures > move() > FORWARD > 1.0. This moves the billboard forward so that it is 1 meter in front of the camera. Note that the billboard is facing in the same direction as the camera, so we are now looking at the *back* of the billboard.

3. To see the front of the billboard, choose procedures > turn() > LEFT > 0.5. This will turn the billboard ½ rotation so that it is now facing the camera.

4. To center the billboard within the camera's view, choose procedures > move() > UP > 0.5 (or modify the y component of its position property until the billboard is centered).

Following these steps produces a camera view like the one shown in Figure 6-29.

FIGURE 6-29   The lostScreen in front of the camera

Figure 6-29 shows the billboard that is now positioned where we want it to be after the submarine hits a mine. Until then, we do not want to see it, so we can finish positioning the billboard by performing the following steps:

5. Choose procedures > move() > UP > 1.0. This will get the billboard up and out of our field of view, which is where we want it to be until our submarine hits a mine.

6. To keep the billboard in that position relative to the camera, set the billboard's Vehicle property to camera. This will cause the billboard to move with our camera, ready to use.

Using a Billboard

Now that our billboard is positioned above the camera, we are ready to use it when our submarine collides with a mine. To do so, we simply add a statement to our collision handler that moves lostScreen down 1 meter instantly, as shown in Figure 6-30.

```
this addCollisionStartListener  new SThing[] { submarine } ,  new SThing[] { mine1, mine2, mine3, mine4, mine5, mine6, mine7, mine8, mine9,

declare procedure collisionStarted   e getSThingFromSetA()   e getSThingFromSetB()   e getModels()
do in order
    lostScreen  move( MoveDirection.DOWN ,  1.0 , Move.duration( 0.0 ) , Move.animationStyle( AnimationStyle.BEGIN_AND_END_ABRUPTLY )  ) add detail
```

FIGURE 6-30   Moving lostScreen in response to collision events

With that added statement, whenever our submarine collides with one of the mines, our **lostScreen** will instantly move down 1 meter, filling the camera's view, as shown in Figure 6-31.

FIGURE 6-31   Colliding with a mine

This same approach can be used to create a different **Billboard** object named **wonScreen** that appears when the player successfully guides the submarine to the treasure chest. Likewise, this approach can be used to create **titleScreen** and **instructionScreen** objects that appear at the beginning of the game (i.e., when a **SceneActivated** event occurs), displaying the name of the game and how to play it. These require no new ideas beyond those presented already, so we leave their creation as an exercise for the reader.

6.4   Post-Production: Titles and Transitions

In earlier chapters, we have seen how to use Alice to build non-interactive stories; in this chapter, we have seen how to use Alice events to build interactive stories (or games). After the programming needed to animate a story has been completed, the finishing touches are added in a process that is called **post-production**. These finishing touches include the addition of titles, credits, scene transitions, special visual effects, and sound effects. In this section, we explore two of these post-production additions: titles/credits and scene transitions.

6.4.1   Adding Titles and Credits

To add title and instruction screens, we could use the simple billboard approach that was shown in the last section, in which we (i) use a paint program to create an image, (ii) import that image as a billboard, and (iii) display that billboard as appropriate. This approach works fine so long as the image being displayed is fixed: We just create one billboard for each image to be displayed.

One drawback to this approach is that it may require many billboards: one for the title, another for the instructions, another for the credits, and so on. Another drawback is that a billboard can only display fixed, unchanging images. This lack of flexibility is inconvenient in situations where we want to animate a part of the image—for example, having animated titles at the beginning of a movie, having scrolling credits at its end, or having several different billboards that vary only slightly from one another.

These drawbacks can be avoided by using Alice's **TextModel** class, which allows us to create textual objects (e.g., the title text) that are distinct from a backdrop object (e.g., a black billboard). By separating these objects, we can animate the text and the backdrop independently, providing increased flexibility.

Using this approach involves the following steps:

1. Creating the backdrop object
2. Creating the **TextModel** object
3. Animating these objects as desired

To illustrate these steps, we return a final time to the example story about Tim the wizard. Let's suppose that we want the title screen for our story to consist of the words "Tim the Wizard Has a Bad Day" in golden letters against a black backdrop. Suppose further that we want "Tim the Wizard" to appear for 2 seconds and then be replaced by "Has a Bad Day" for 3 seconds.

Creating a Backdrop Object

To create the black backdrop for our story's title screen, we use the simple billboard approach: In Alice's Gallery, we navigate to the Shapes / Text folder and click the **new Billboard()** icon to create a plain black billboard to use as our backdrop. We will name this billboard **blackBackdrop**, to avoid any confusion as to its purpose. We can then follow the first four steps we covered in Section 6.3.5 to position this billboard in view of the camera.

Creating the **TextModel** Object

To create the title text, we click the **new TextModel()** icon, which is also in the Shapes / Text folder of the Alice Gallery. This will display a Text Model dialog box in which we can set its name to **titleText**, set its color to yellow (to appear like gold against our black backdrop), and enter **Tim the Wizard** as its initial text, as shown in Figure 6-32.

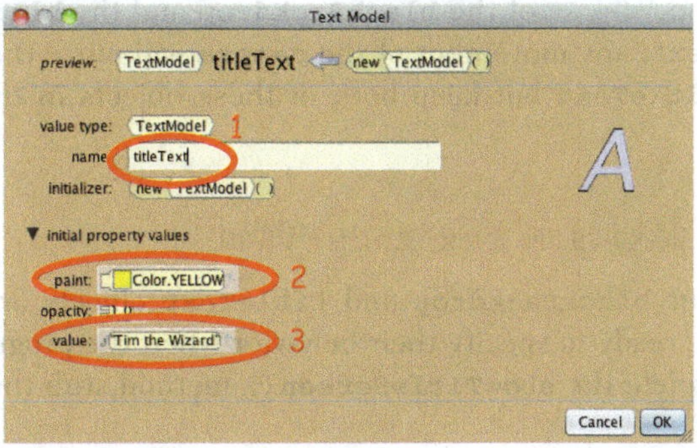

FIGURE 6-32   The **Text Model** dialog box

When we click its **OK** button, Alice adds an object named `titleText` to the scene. We can then follow the same four steps from Section 6.3.5 (along with shrinking the size of the text) to position this `TextModel` object in view of the camera, as shown in Figure 6-33.

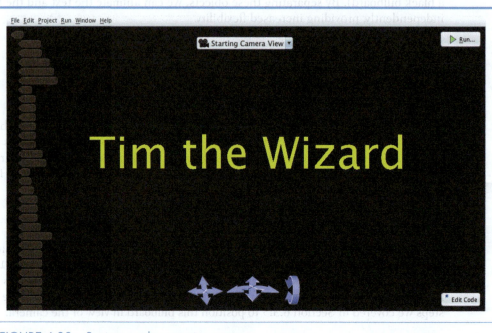

FIGURE 6-33   Setting up the opening screen

If we then set the **Vehicle** property of the `titleText` object to be the `blackBackdrop`, we can move the `blackBackdrop`, and the `titleText` will then move with it. After that, we can apply Steps 5 and 6 from Section 6.3.5 to the `blackBackdrop` to move it and the `titleText` up and out of the camera's view, but still have it ready for use. Since the `camera` is the **Vehicle** of the `blackBackdrop` and the `blackBackdrop` is the **Vehicle** of the `titleText`, any movement of the `camera` will move the `blackBackdrop`, which will move the `titleText` but keep both of these objects in the desired relationship to the `camera`.

Animating the Backdrop and `TextModel` Objects

Now that our `blackBackdrop` and `titleText` objects are correctly positioned out of sight, we are ready to specify their behavior when the program begins running. To do so, we can complete the `showTitleScreen()` method stub that we created when we began this project.

6.4.2   Using a Text Model

Now that our **startupScreen** and **startupText** objects are correctly positioned, we are ready to specify their behavior when the program begins running. Figure 6-34 shows one way to define the **showTitleScreen()** method.

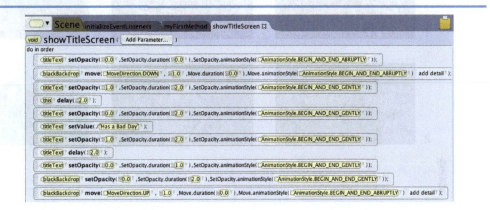

FIGURE 6-34   A **showTitleScreen()** method

We might break this method down into the following steps:

1. When our method begins, our **titleText** and our **blackBackdrop** are both opaque, but they are positioned out of view, 1 meter above the camera. Our first action is therefore to set the Opacity of the **titleText** to 0.0, to make it invisible, and then move the **blackBackdrop** down 1 meter. Both of these happen "instantly" because we have set their durations to 0.0. The result is that when our method begins, a blank black backdrop is in view.

2. We then set the Opacity of **titleText** to 1.0 over the course of 2 seconds, so that its string "Tim the Wizard" fades into view.

3. After delaying for 2 seconds to keep this string in view, we set its Opacity back to 0.0 over the course of 2 seconds so that it fades out of view.

4. With **titleText** invisible, we change its value from "Tim the Wizard" to "Has a Bad Day". We then set its Opacity to 1.0 over the course of 2 seconds, so that this new string fades into view.

5. After delaying for 2 seconds to keep it in view, we set its Opacity back to 0.0 over the course of 2 seconds so that it fades out of view.

6. Finally, we set the Opacity of our **blackBackdrop** to 0.0 over the course of 2 seconds so that it fades from view, revealing our opening scene behind it. We then move the **blackBackdrop** up 1 meter to stow it away for later use.

Figure 6-35 shows how the screen appears during each of these steps.

FIGURE 6-35 Our `showTitleScreen()` method in action

The key thing to realize is that all this was accomplished with just two objects: a **Billboard** object (the backdrop) and a **TextModel** object (the text). By separating the text from the backdrop, we can animate these objects independently, which gives us more options. For example, while keeping the backdrop in place, we could use a statement like this:

```
titleText.turn(TurnDirection.RIGHT, 1.0);
```

to make the text rotate 360 degrees; or we could use a pair of statements like this:

```
titleText.move(MoveDirection.UP, 0.25, MoveDuration = 0.5);
titleText.move(MoveDirection.DOWN, 0.25, MoveDuration = 0.5);
```

to make the text hop up and down. Separating the text from the backdrop makes it possible to create far more creative effects than if we use a **Billboard** with a fixed image.

Given these examples, it should be apparent how easy it is to make the "scrolling credits" that appear at the end of a film.

At this point, we have a version of the program that is good enough to test with users. For additional enhancements (e.g., adding opening credits and closing credits), see the Programming Problems section at the end of this chapter.

If TextModel or Billboard objects are to be fixed in place in front of the camera, they should be the last objects you add to a world or scene. The reason is that they will usually lie between the camera and any other objects in the world; if you want to select these other objects with a mouse click, the TextModel or Billboard will intercept your click.

`TextModel` Methods

In Figure 6-34, we used some of the methods that are specific to a `TextModel`. The table in Figure 6-36 presents a complete list of these methods, using a `TextModel` object named `tm`.

`TextModel` **Method**	**Description**
`tm.setValue(newString);`	Changes `tm`'s value to `newString`
`tm.append(aString);`	Adds `aString` to the end of `tm`
`tm.delete(i, j);`	Removes `tm`'s characters from index `i` to index `j`
`tm.deleteCharAt(i);`	Removes `tm`'s character at index `i`
`tm.insert(i, aString);`	Inserts `aString` at index `i` of `tm`
`tm.replace(i, j, aString);`	Replaces `tm`'s characters from index `i` through index `j` with `aString`
`tm.setCharAt(i, ch);`	Changes `tm`'s character at index `i` to `ch`

FIGURE 6-36 `TextModel` methods

These methods let us to change all or part of the string that a given `TextModel` object displays. When combined with the standard Alice methods for animating an object, a `TextModel` object can be animated with nearly any behavior we can imagine.

6.4.3 Scene-to-Scene Transitions

We have seen how to use markers and the `moveAndOrientTo()` method to position the camera and other objects within a scene. This approach is a convenient way to shift any object from its position at the end of one scene to a new position at the beginning of the next scene.

Instead of instantaneously jumping from the end of one scene to the beginning of the next scene (a transition called a *cut*), filmmakers often use special camera effects like *fades* or *wipes* to smooth the transition between scenes. Such **transition effects** can make the transition between scenes seem less abrupt and jarring, or they can be used to convey a sense of time elapsing between the scenes.

One of the simplest transition effects is a *fade*, which causes the entire screen to gradually darken until it is completely black, and then gradually lighten, exposing a new scene. To achieve this effect, we can write two complementary methods—`fadeToBlack()` and `fadeFromBlack()`—that use the same `blackBackdrop` billboard we used in Section 6.4.1.

If we perform `fadeToBlack()` at the end of a scene, this will darken the screen. While the screen is dark, we can move the camera and other objects to their positions at the beginning of a new scene; the `blackBackdrop` will prevent the user from seeing these movements. With those objects in position, we can use `fadeFromBlack()` to bring the new scene into view.

Fade to Black

With the **blackBackdrop** out of view 1 meter above and in front of the camera, we can achieve the fade-to-black effect as follows:

1. Set the Opacity property of **blackBackdrop** to 0.0, making it invisible.
2. Move **blackBackdrop** down 1 meter so that it is in front of the camera's viewing area.
3. Set the Opacity property of **blackBackdrop** back to 1.0, making it visible.

For Steps 1 and 2, the **duration** should be 0 so that those steps happen instantaneously. For Step 3, the **duration** will determine how long the fade takes. While we could make this duration last for a fixed length of time, a better approach is to let the sender of this message specify how long the fade should take. To let the sender pass this *fade time* as an argument, we have to define a parameter to store it and set the duration attribute of Step 3 to that parameter. Figure 6-37 shows the resulting definition, using a parameter named **fadeTime**. Since this method affects the **blackBackdrop**, we define it as a method of the **Billboard** class.

FIGURE 6-37   The **fadeToBlack()** method

With this method, the message **blackBackdrop.fadeToBlack(5);** will cause the screen to darken over the course of 5 seconds; the message **blackBackdrop.fadeToBlack(1);** will cause the screen to darken in a single second.

Fade From Black

The fade-from-black method has to "undo" everything the fade-to-black method did, in the reverse order, so as to leave the **blackBackdrop** in its original position, ready for a subsequent **fadeToBlack()** message:

1. Set the Opacity property of **blackBackdrop** to 0.0 percent.
2. Move **blackBackdrop** up so that it is out of the camera's viewing area.
3. Set the Opacity property of **blackBackdrop** to 1.0 percent.

Just as before, we should use a parameter to allow the sender to specify the effect's fade time. In this method, it should control the duration of Step 1, while Steps 2 and 3 occur instantaneously, as shown in Figure 6-38.

FIGURE 6-38   The `fadeFromBlack()` method

Using the Fade Methods

With these two methods defined, we can use a sequence of messages like:

```
At the end of one scene:
    blackBackdrop.fadeToBlack(4);

At the beginning of the next scene:
    camera.moveAndOrientTo(cameraNextSceneMarker); duration = 0
    blackBackdrop.fadeFromBlack(3);
```

to change the screen to black over the course of 4 seconds at the end of one scene, and then change from dark to light over 3 seconds, with the next scene in view.

Be careful to note that **fadeToBlack()** and **fadeFromBlack()** should always be used in pairs because each manipulates **blackBackdrop** in a complementary way.

Fading to Other Colors

To fade to a color other than black, we use an approach like that used in Figure 6-37, but with these differences: (i) Pass the color to which we want to fade as an argument, (ii) declare a parameter to store that argument, and (iii) within the method, use the **setPaint()** setter method to set the **blackBackdrop**'s Paint property to the color passed to the parameter. Figure 3-39 shows the resulting method.

FIGURE 6-39   The `fadeTo()` method

Using this and a corresponding **fadeFrom()** method, we can use a sequence of messages like:

```
At the end of one scene:
    blackBackdrop.fadeTo(Color.WHITE, 4);

At the beginning of the next scene:
    camera.moveAndOrientTo(cameraNextSceneMarker); duration = 0
    blackBackdrop.fadeFrom(3);
```

to change the screen to white over the course of 4 seconds at the end of 1 scene, and then fade from white into the next scene over 3 seconds. The **fadeFrom()** method is just the **fadeFromBlack()** method, which has been renamed to be more general. In the same way, we may want to rename our **Billboard** object from **blackBackdrop** to just **backdrop**, since we can now set its Paint property to an arbitrary color.

Reusing Transition Effects

If you search on the Internet for terms like *transition*, *effect*, *fade*, and *wipe*, you will find many other transition effects that can be defined using techniques like the ones we presented in this section. (To define some of them, you may need to add more **Billboard** objects to the scene.) We hope that this section has provided you with an introduction into how such effects can be created. However, after we have defined a nice group of transition effects, how do we reuse them in different programs? At the time of this writing, Alice unfortunately does not provide a means of saving classes or objects from one project for reuse in a different project.[3]

As a workaround, we can define all these transitions in a "template world" named **TransitionEffects** that contains nothing but the **camera**, the **ground**, and the **Billboard** objects we use for the transitions. For any story in which we want transitions, we can open this **TransitionEffects** file as the starting scene for the story, and then use File > Save As... to save it using a name that is appropriate for that story. Of course, this means that we have to anticipate that we will be using transitions in the story. This is one more reason to spend some time designing your project before you start programming.

Wrapping Things Up

This concludes our exploration of computer programming using Alice. More material is available in the appendices, and if you have enjoyed these first six chapters, we encourage you to check it out. We hope you have had fun learning to use Alice. Good luck in your future projects!

---

[3]This was true when this book was written. It may not be true by the time you read this. Check and see!

6.5   Chapter Summary

❏ We can write programs that respond to new events in Alice, including both mouse and keyboard events.

❏ We can write methods that act as event handlers.

❏ We can associate event handlers with specific events.

❏ We can use a **TextModel** object to add titles, instructions, and credits to a world.

❏ We can use a **Billboard** object (i) to display pictures or images we import from a file, (ii) as a backdrop for a **TextModel** object, and (iii) to create transitions between scenes.

❏ Alice shapes can be used as building blocks to build other structures in Alice.

6.5.1   Key Terms

event   mouse event
event-driven program   post-production
event handler   program event
handling an event   transition effect
interactive program   two-state behavior
keyboard event   usability
listener   user event
logic error

Programming Projects

6.1 Choose a robot from the Alice **Gallery** and provide events and handlers so that the user can control the robot using the keyboard. For example, use the arrow keys to make the robot go forward, backward, left, or right; use other keys to control the robot's arms (or other appendages). Build a world in which the user must navigate the robot through a series of obstacles.

6.2 Using the **dragon.flapWings();** method we wrote in Chapter 4, build a short story in which a dragon flies from place to place in search of adventure, landing every so often to eat, talk, hear jokes, and anything else required by your story. Use **dragon.flapWings()** in the handler of a **CollisionEnd** event, so that the dragon automatically flaps its wings whenever it is above the ground.

6.3 Build a story containing a puzzle the user must solve. Place characters in the story who can give hints to the puzzle's solution when the user clicks on them. Let the user navigate through the world using the arrow keys.

6.4 Add the following enhancements to the *Treasure Hunt* program we built in Section 6.3:

a. Modify the program so that, at the beginning, the "title" of the game is displayed in yellow letters against a blue background. After 2 seconds, display a screen that explains the problem the player has to solve, and tell players they have to press the spacebar to continue. When players press the spacebar, display a screen providing instructions for how to control the submarine, and tell the players they must press the spacebar to continue. When they press the spacebar, begin the game.

b. Add a "Congratulations!" screen that appears when the user guides the submarine to within 5 meters of the treasure chest. Use a proximity event listener to detect this.

c. Modify the program so that when the player presses the up-arrow key, the submarine's propeller spins clockwise; when the player presses the down-arrow key, the submarine's propeller spins counter-clockwise; when the player presses the left-arrow key, the submarine's rudder angles left; and when the player presses the right-arrow key, the submarine's rudder angles right.

d. Modify the program by adding other large objects (manitees, orcas, and so on), so that if the submarine collides with anything in the world as it moves forward, backward, left, or right, it "crashes," and the game displays an appropriate "Better Luck Next Time!" screen.

6.5 Build methods to perform the following transition effects:

a. A *barn door wipe* is a transition effect in which two "barn doors" close by sliding from the sides to the center of a scene and then open by sliding back to the sides, exposing a new scene. Build scene methods named **barnDoorClose(*closeTime*);** and **barnDoorOpen(*openTime*);** that perform a barn door wipe, where **closeTime** and **openTime** control the speed at which the "barn doors" close and open.

b. A *bar wipe* is a transition in which a shutter moves from one of the edges to cover the screen at the end of a scene and then moves to the opposite edge, exposing a new scene. Build **barWipeCover(*direction, time*);** and **barWipeUncover(*direction, time*);** methods that perform a bar wipe. The direction argument should be **LEFT**, **RIGHT**, **UP**, or **DOWN**.

c. In a *diagonal wipe*, a shutter crosses the screen from one corner to the opposite corner. Write complementary methods that perform the two parts of a diagonal wipe.

d. A *bowtie wipe* is like a barndoor wipe, but the shutters coming from the sides are wedges that look like a bow tie when they first touch one another. Write complementary methods that perform the two parts of a bowtie wipe.

e. An *iris wipe* is a transition in which a scene ends with shutters that close from the scene's top, bottom, left, and right edges, creating a shrinking iris; the next scene then opens by these shutters retreating back to their respective edges, creating an expanding iris. Write complementary methods that perform the two parts of an iris wipe.

6.6 Choose a popular game such as chess, checkers, Mancala, Master Mind, and so on. Create a board and pieces for the game. Add event handlers that allow the user to move the pieces interactively.

6.7 Using the **Helicopter** class from the Alice Gallery, create a flight simulator in which the user has to use the arrow keys, the "a" key, and the "d" key to fly the helicopter through a series of obstacles and then land the helicopter on a landing pad. When landing, keep the helicopter from sinking into the ground. Use a **TimeListener** to keep track of how long it takes the user to navigate the course, and a **TextModel** to display the user's time while he or she flies the course.

6.8 Using **Torus** objects and a character of your choice from the Alice **Gallery**, build a Whack-a-Mole–style game in which your character repeatedly pops its head out of a random hole for a short, random length of time before disappearing, and the player tries to "whack" the character by clicking on it before it disappears. Award the player 1 point each time she successfully "whacks" the character. The game should last for 1 minute and then display a "Game Over" screen. Use **TextModel** objects to display the character's score in one corner of the screen and a count-down timer in another corner while the game is being played.

6.9 Build an interactive story in which the player has to use the arrow keys to guide a character to locate and collect several treasures that are hidden throughout the story. Include a villain who starts at a random position within the scene. Using a proximity event listener, have the villain begin chasing the player's character if the player comes within 100 meters of the villain. Display a "You Won" screen if the player collects all the treasures without getting caught by the villain; display a "You Lost" screen if the villain catches the player before she collects all the treasure.

6.10 Design and build your own original, interactive computer game that uses at least two kinds of events.

Appendix A
Alice Standard Procedures and Functions

A.1   Alice Standard Object Procedures

Alice *procedures* are messages that we can send to an object, commanding it to do something. The object then responds with a behavior (hopefully the one we intended). The following table provides a complete list of Alice's standard methods—the commands to which nearly all Alice objects will respond.

Method	Behavior Produced
obj.say(*message*);	*obj* says *message* (via a cartoon balloon)
obj.think(*thought*);	*obj* thinks *thought* (via a cartoon balloon)
obj.move(*dir,dist*);	*obj* moves *dist* meters in direction *dir* = **UP, DOWN, LEFT, RIGHT, FORWARD**, or **BACKWARD**
obj.moveToward(*obj2,dist*);	*obj* moves *dist* meters toward *obj2*
obj.moveAwayFrom(*obj2,dist*);	*obj* moves *dist* meters away from *obj2*
obj.moveTo(*obj2*);	*obj*'s *position* becomes that of *obj2* (*obj*'s *orientation* remains unchanged)

continued

Screenshots from Alice 2 © 1999–2013, Alice 3 © 2008–2013, Carnegie Mellon University. All rights reserved. We gratefully acknowledge the financial support of Oracle, Electronic Arts, Sun Microsystems, DARPA, Intel, NSF, and ONR.

Method	Behavior Produced
obj.turn(*dir*,*revs*);	*obj* turns *revs* revolutions in direction **LEFT**, **RIGHT**, **FORWARD**, or **BACKWARD** (that is, about its UD-axis or LR-axis)
obj.roll(*dir*,*revs*);	*obj* rotates *revs* revolutions in direction **LEFT** or **RIGHT** (that is, about its FB-axis)
obj.turnToFace(*obj2*);	*obj* rotates about its UD-axis until it is facing *obj2*
obj.orientTo(*obj2*);	*obj*'s *orientation* becomes that of *obj2* (*obj*'s *position* remains unchanged)
obj.orientToUpright();	*obj* reorients so that its UD-axis is vertical
obj.pointAt(*obj2*);	*obj* rotates so that its FB-axis points at *obj2*'s center
obj.moveAndOrientTo(*obj2*);	*obj*'s *position* and *orientation* change to that of *obj2*
obj.setWidth(*newWidth*);	*obj*'s *width* changes to *newWidth*
obj.setHeight(*newHeight*);	*obj*'s *height* changes to *newHeight*
obj.setDepth(*newDepth*);	*obj*'s *depth* changes to *newDepth*
obj.resize(*howMuch*);	*obj*'s size changes by a factor of *howMuch*
obj.resizeWidth(*howMuch*);	*obj*'s *width* changes by *howMuch*
obj.resizeHeight(*howMuch*);	*obj*'s *height* changes by *howMuch*
obj.resizeDepth(*howMuch*);	*obj*'s *depth* changes by *howMuch*
obj.setPaint(*color*);	*obj* reflects light as though filtered through *color*

continued

Method	Behavior Produced
obj.setOpacity(*pct*);	*obj* reflects *pct* percent of the light striking it
obj.setVehicle(*obj2*);	*obj2* becomes the Vehicle of *obj* (movements of *obj2* will also move *obj*)
obj.playAudio(*audioSrc*);	*obj* plays the sounds stored in *audioSrc*
obj.delay(*secs*);	*obj* waits until *secs* seconds have elapsed
obj.straightenOutJoints();	*obj*'s joints return to their original orientations

A.2 Alice Standard Object Functions

Alice *functions* are messages we can send to an object to ask it a question. The object responds by producing a *result*—the answer to our question. The following table provides a complete list of Alice's standard functions—that is, the questions that all Alice objects will answer.

Function	Result Produced
obj.getPaint()	the color with which *obj* is currently painted (see procedure setPaint(*color*))
obj.getOpacity()	the percentage of light *obj* currently reflects
obj.getWidth()	*obj*'s current *width*
obj.getHeight()	*obj*'s current *height*
obj.getDepth()	*obj*'s current *depth*

continued

Function	Result Produced
`obj.getBooleanFromUser(prompt)`	displays a dialog box labeled with **prompt** and buttons named *True* and *False*; returns: **true**, if the user clicks the *True* button **false**, if the user clicks the *False* button
`obj.getStringFromUser(prompt)`	displays a dialog box labeled with **prompt**, a textbox, and a button named *OK*; returns the contents of the textbox when *OK* is clicked
`obj.getDoubleFromUser(prompt)`	displays a dialog box labeled with **prompt**, a textbox, a numeric keypad, and a button named *OK*; returns the contents of the textbox as a real number when *OK* is clicked
`obj.getIntegerFromUser(prompt)`	displays a dialog box labeled with **prompt**, a textbox, a numeric keypad, and a button named *OK*; returns the contents of the textbox as a whole number when *OK* is clicked
`obj.getDistanceTo(obj2)`	the distance between **obj**'s and **obj2**'s centers
`obj.getVantagePoint(obj2)`	the point of view of **obj**
`obj.getVehicle()`	**obj**'s current *Vehicle*
`obj.isCollidingWith(obj2)`	**true**, if **obj**'s and **obj2**'s bounding boxes are touching **false**, otherwise
`obj.isFacing(obj2)`	**true**, if **obj2** is positioned in front of **obj** **false**, otherwise
`obj.toString()`	a string representation of **obj**

A.3   Alice Scene Procedures

In addition to object procedures, the Scene in every Alice program has its own set of messages to which it will respond. The following table lists these procedures.

Method	Behavior Produced
`performCustomSetup();`	statements placed within this method are performed prior to *myFirstMethod()*; they may be used to set up the scene
`initializeEventListeners();`	handlers placed in this method are associated with events prior to *performCustomSetup()*
`myFirstMethod();`	statements placed within this method are performed after *performCustomSetup()*
`setAtmosphereColor(color);`	set the scene's atmosphere-color to *color*
`setFromAboveLightColor(color);`	set the color of a secondary light source above the scene to *color*
`setFromBelowLightColor(color);`	set the color of a secondary light source below the scene to *color*
`setFogDensity(pct);`	set the fog opacity in this scene to *pct* percent
`playAudio(audioSrc);`	play the sounds in *audioSrc*
`delay(secs);`	make the program wait for *secs* seconds

A.4   Alice Scene Functions

Alice *scene functions* provide access to scene objects and attributes. The following table provides a complete list of Alice's scene functions.

Function	Result Produced
getGround()	the scene's current ground
getCamera()	the scene's camera
getAtmosphereColor()	the scene's current atmospheric color
getFromAboveLightColor()	the color of the secondary light source that is above the scene
getFromBelowLightColor()	the color of the secondary light source that is below the scene
getFogDensity()	the opacity of the scene's fog (0.0-1.0)

The remaining scene functions provide functionality that is the same as their similarly named object functions (see A.2), so we will not repeat them here.

A.5   Alice Boolean and Relational Operations

Alice provides the standard Boolean and relational operators for building logical expressions, as shown in the following table. These can be accessed from the context menu of any conditional statement (**if**, **while**, etc.).

Operation	Result Produced
!*a*	**true**, if *a* is **false**; **false**, otherwise
(*a* && *b*)	**true**, if *a* and *b* are both **true**; **false**, if *a* or *b* is **false**
(*a* || *b*)	**true**, if either *a* or *b* are **true**; **false**, if neither *a* nor *b* is **true**

continued

Operation	Result Produced
a == b	**true**, if *a* and *b* have the same value; **false**, otherwise
a != b	**true**, if *a* and *b* have different values; **false**, otherwise
a < b	**true**, if *a*'s value is less than *b*'s value; **false**, otherwise
a > b	**true**, if *a*'s value is greater than *b*'s value; **false**, otherwise
a <= b	**true**, if *a*'s value is less than or equal to *b*'s value; **false**, otherwise
a >= b	**true**, if *a*'s value is greater than or equal to *b*'s value; **false**, otherwise
String operations:	
str.contentEquals(str2)	**true**, if *str* and *str2* have exactly the same letters (case matters); **false**, otherwise
str.equalsIgnoreCase(str2)	**true**, if *str* and *str2* have the same letters (case doesn't matter); **false**, otherwise
str.startsWith(str2)	**true**, if the initial letters in *str* are the same as the letters in *str2*; **false**, otherwise
str.endsWith(str2)	**true**, if the final letters in *str* are the same as the letters in *str2*; **false**, otherwise
str.contains(str2)	**true**, if *str2* is a substring of *str*; **false**, otherwise

A.6 Alice Mathematical Operations

Alice provides a rich set of mathematical operations for building formulas, as shown in the following table. These can be accessed from the context menu of any numeric expression. Some operations may only be used with **Double** values; others may only be used with **Integer** values.

Operation	Result Produced
$a + b$	addition
$a - b$	subtraction
$a * b$	multiplication
a / b	a / b using real (decimal) division
a INTEGER_DIVIDE b	the quotient of a / b using integer division
a INTEGER_REMAINDER b	the remainder of a / b using integer division
Math.min(a, b)	the minimum of a and b
Math.max(a, b)	the maximum of a and b
Math.abs(a)	the absolute value of a
Math.rint(a)	the value of a rounded to the nearest integer
Math.ceil(a)	the smallest integer larger than a
Math.floor(a)	the largest integer smaller than a
Math.sqrt(a)	the square root of a

continued

Operation	Result Produced
`Math.pow(a, b)`	*a* raised to the power *b* (a^b)
`Math.sin(a)`	the sine of *a*
`Math.cos(a)`	the cosine of *a*
`Math.tan(a)`	the tangent of *a*
`Math.asin(a)`	the angle whose sine is *a*
`Math.acos(a)`	the angle whose cosine is *a*
`Math.atan(a)`	the angle whose tangent is *a*
`Math.atan2(x, y)`	the polar coordinate angle associated with Cartesian coordinate (*x*, *y*)
`Math.exp(a)`	Euler's number *e* raised to the power *a* (that is, e^a)
`Math.log(a)`	the natural logarithm (base *e*) of *a*
Predefined Mathematical Constants:	
`Math.E`	An approximate value for Euler's number *e* (the base of natural logarithms)
`Math.PI`	An approximate value for PI

Hundreds of years before there were computers, programming languages, or loop statements, mathematicians were defining functions, many of which required repetitive behavior. One way to provide such behavior without using a loop is to have a function or method *invoke itself*, causing its statements to repeat. Such a method (or function) is called **recursive**. To illustrate, suppose we were to define a method for Alice's **camera** named **repeatRoll()**, as follows:

```
void camera.repeatRoll() {
    camera.roll(LEFT, 1);
    camera.repeatRoll();
}
```

When invoked, this method will make the **camera** roll left 1 revolution and then invoke itself. That second invocation will make the **camera** roll left 1 revolution and then call itself. That third invocation will make the **camera** roll left 1 revolution and then call itself; and so on. The result is thus an "infinite" repetition, or **infinite recursion**.[1]

To avoid infinite repetition, recursive methods and functions typically have (1) an **Integer** parameter, (2) an **if** statement that only performs the recursion if the parameter's value exceeds some lower bound, and (3) a recursive call within the **if** statement that passes, as an argument, a value smaller than the parameter. The net effect is that the function or method counts downward toward the lower bound,

---

[1]Since each recursive call consumes additional memory, the looping behavior will eventually end, when the program runs out of memory. However, we will become tired of the **camera** rolling long before that occurs!

Screenshots from Alice 2 © 1999–2013, Alice 3 © 2008–2013, Carnegie Mellon University. All rights reserved. We gratefully acknowledge the financial support of Oracle, Electronic Arts, Sun Microsystems, DARPA, Intel, NSF, and ONR.

typically 0 or 1. To illustrate, we might revise the preceding `repeatRoll()` method as follows:

```
void camera.repeatRoll(Integer count) { // the parameter count
    if (count > 0) {                     // if statement guards
        camera.roll(LEFT, 1);            // the rolling and
        camera.repeatRoll(count - 1);    // the recursive call
    }
}
```

When invoked with a numeric argument **n**, this version of the function will roll the camera **n** times and then stop. For example, if we send the message `camera.repeatRoll(3);`, the following occurs:

1. This starts `repeatRoll(3)`, in which parameter **count** == 3.

2. The method checks the condition **count > 0**.

3. Since the condition is true, the method (a) rolls the **camera** left 1 revolution and (b) sends the message `camera.repeatRoll(2);`.

4. This starts `repeatRoll(2)`, a new version in which parameter **count** == 2.

5. The method checks the condition **count > 0**.

6. Since the condition is true, the method (a) rolls the **camera** left 1 revolution and (b) sends the message `camera.repeatRoll(1);`.

7. This starts `repeatRoll(1)`, a new version in which parameter **count** == 1.

8. The method checks the condition **count > 0**.

9. Since the condition is true, the method (a) rolls the **camera** left 1 revolution and (b) sends the message `camera.repeatRoll(0);`.

10. This starts `repeatRoll(0)`, a new version in which parameter **count** == 0.

11. The method checks the condition **count > 0**.

12. Since the condition is false, the method terminates; flow returns to the sender of `repeatRoll(0)` — `repeatRoll(1)` — the version where **count** == 1.

13. The version in which **count** == 1 terminates; flow returns to the sender of `repeat-Roll(1)` — `repeatRoll(2)` — the version in which **count** == 2.

14. The version in which **count** == 2 terminates; flow returns to the sender of `repeat-Roll(2)` — `repeatRoll(3)` — the version in which **count** == 3.

15. The version in which **count** == 3 terminates; flow returns to the sender of `repeatRoll(3)`.

Steps 1–11, in which the repeated messages are counting downward toward the lower bound, are sometimes called the **winding phase** of the recursion. Steps 13–15, in which the chain of recursive messages terminates, are sometimes called the **unwinding phase** of the recursion.

Recursion thus provides an alternative way to achieve repetitive behavior. When the recursive message is the last behavior-producing statement in the method, as follows:

```
void camera.repeatRoll(Integer count) {
    if (count > 0) {
        camera.roll(LEFT, 1);
        camera.repeatRoll(count - 1); // the last statement
    }
}
```

it is called **tail recursion** because the recursive message occurs at the end or "tail" of the method. Any function that is defined using tail recursion can be defined using a loop, and vice versa. But in Section B.2, we will see that one recursion method can produce behavior that would require multiple loops.

B.1   Tail Recursion

Suppose that at the end of Scene 1 of a story, the main character goes to sleep at midnight and the **camera** zooms in to a close-up of the clock in the bedroom. Shot 1 of Scene 2 begins with that same clock, showing the time to be midnight. Suppose that our story calls for the clock's hands to spin, indicating that time is "flying ahead." When the hands reach 3 a.m., a pixie appears and works some sort of mischief on the sleeping main character. (Exactly what mischief is left up to you.)

To build a minimal scene, we can create a new Alice program with a Room setting, go to the Alice Gallery, add a bed, end table, and the pocket watch from the Prop classes folder, add a person in pajamas, add a pixie, and arrange the objects to create a scene like that in Figure B-1.

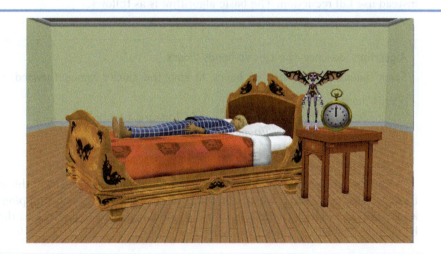

FIGURE B-1   Setting the scene

With the camera in this position, we can create a camera marker for Scene 1. We can then set the **Opacity** of our pixie to 0, zoom in on the pocket watch, and create a second camera marker there for Scene 2. This produces the scene like the one shown in Figure B-2.

FIGURE B-2   Beginning Scene 2

To follow the story, we need a way to make the clock's hands spin forward three hours. Since this is a counting problem, we could do so using **for** loops; for variety, let's instead use tail recursion. The basic algorithm is as follows:

Algorithm: advance-the-clock's-hands *hours*

Given: *hours*, the number of hours to spin the clock's hands forward

1. If *hours* > 0:
   a. Spin the hour and minute hands forward one hour
   b. advance-the-clock's-hands *hours-1*

Building an **advanceHands()** method for the **PocketWatch** class this way is straightforward. However, when we perform the recursion by drag-and-dropping the **pocket-Watch.advanceHands()** method into the same method, Alice warns us that recursion is by default disabled, as shown in Figure B-3.

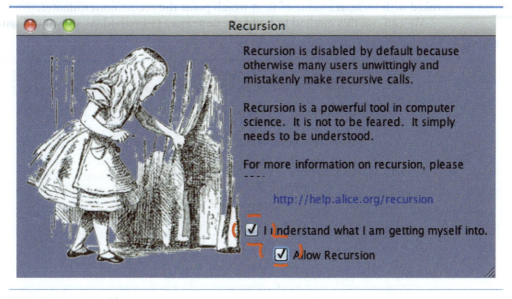

FIGURE B-3   Alice's "Recursion is disabled" warning

To change this setting, we must select the menu choice **Window > Preferences > Recursion...** This displays the dialog box shown in Figure B-4, where we must check *two* checkboxes to enable recursion.

FIGURE B-4   Enabling recursion

When we have checked these checkboxes and clicked the red closebox on this dialog box, recursion is enabled, and we can then perform the **advanceHands()** drag operation shown in Figure B-3 without further issues. Figure B-5 shows the final method.

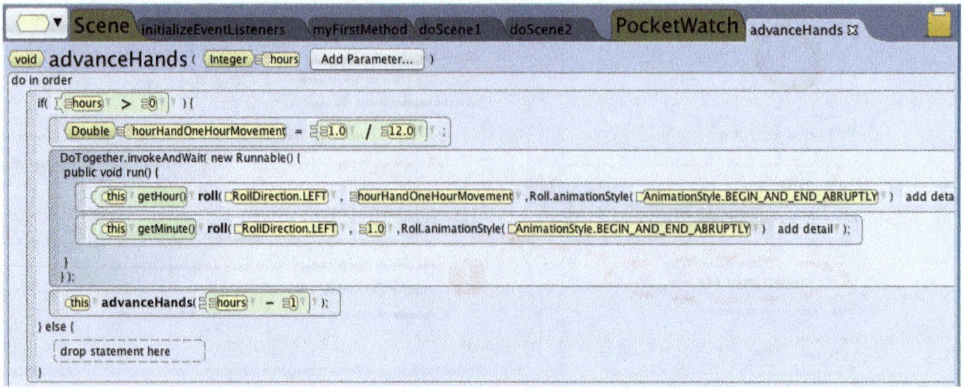

FIGURE B-5   The `advanceHands()` method

When invoked with a positive **hours** value, this method spins the clock's hands forward one hour and then invokes itself recursively with **hours-1** as an argument. The method thus "counts down" recursively from whatever **hours** value it receives initially until it is invoked with an **hours** value of 0, at which point the recursion terminates.

We can use this method to build the **doScene2()** method, as shown in Figure B-6.

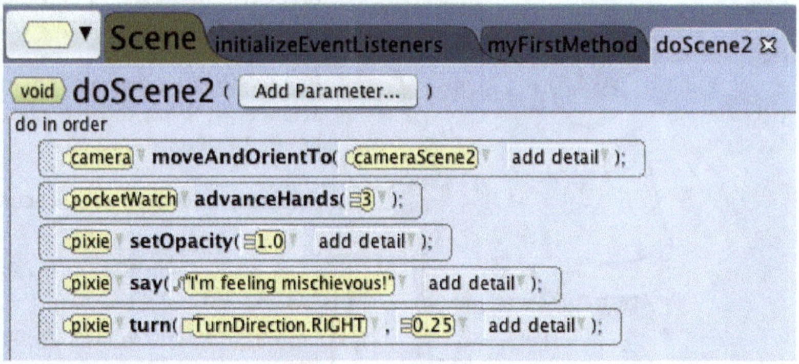

FIGURE B-6   The `doScene2()` method

When performed, the scene begins with the setup shown in Figure B-2. The **advanceHands(3)** message then spins the clock's hands forward three hours, after which our pixie appears and says she's feeling mischievous, as shown in Figure B-7.

FIGURE B-7   Appearance by the pixie

If you compare the definition of the **advanceHands()** method with the **repeatRoll()** method we described earlier, you'll see that both follow this basic pattern:

```
Simplified Pattern for Tail Recursion:
void tailRecursiveMethod ( Integer count ) {
    if ( count > LOWER_BOUND ) {
        produceBehaviorOnce();
        tailRecursiveMethod( count-1 );
    }
}
where:

produceBehaviorOnce() produces the behavior to be repeated.
```

A method that follows this pattern will produce results equivalent to those produced by the following nonrecursive pattern:

```
void nonRecursiveMethod( Integer count ) {
    for ( int i = count; i > 0; count-- ) {
        produceBehaviorOnce();
    }
}
```

Tail recursion thus provides an alternative way to solve counting problems and other problems whose solutions require repetition. In the next section, we will see that useful work can be done *following* the recursive call.

B.2   General Recursion

Suppose Scene 3 of our story continues the next day and ends with our character going to bed again at midnight. Scene 4 then begins the same way as Scene 2: with a close-up of the clock in the main character's bedroom, showing midnight, the next night. In this scene, our story calls for time to fly ahead eight hours to 8 a.m., once again indicated by the clock's spinning hands. Then the pixie appears, once again intent on mischief. In this scene, her mischief is to reverse time for everyone except the main character, for whom, upon waking up after eight hours of sleep (fully rested), it will be midnight again! To indicate that time is flowing in reverse, we must spin the clock's hands backward eight hours.

We could accomplish this by using our `advanceHands()` method to spin the clock's hands forward seven hours and then writing a `reverseHands()` method to make the hands spin backward seven hours, using either tail recursion or a `for` loop. Instead, let's see how recursion lets us perform both of these steps in one method.

The key idea is to use recursion's winding phase to spin the hands forward (as before) and then use the unwinding phase to make the hands spin backward. In between the two phases—when we have reached our lower bound—the pixie can work her magic.

Algorithm: wind-and-unwind-the-clock's-hands *hours*

Given: *hours*, the number of hours to spin the clock's hands forward

1. If *hours* > 0:

   a. Spin the hour and minute hands forward one hour
   b. wind-and-unwind-the-clock's-hands *hours-1*
   c. Spin the hour and minute hands backward one hour
2. Else:

   a. The pixie appears
   b. The pixie works her magic

Understanding how this works can be difficult the first time you see it. One way to understand it is to see that Step 1c does the exact opposite of Step 1a. That is, during the winding phase, Step 1a spins the clock's hands forward one hour; then Step 1b sends the recursive message, preventing flow from reaching Step 1c (for the time being). When the lower bound is reached, the `if` statement's condition is false, so the pixie works her magic; and since no recursive message is sent, the repetition halts. The recursion then starts to unwind, with flow returning to Step 1c in each message, which "undoes" the effects of Step 1a. Figure B-8 gives a numbered visualization of what happens when *hours* has the value 8. The steps that are performed within each message at a given point are highlighted in Figure B-8.

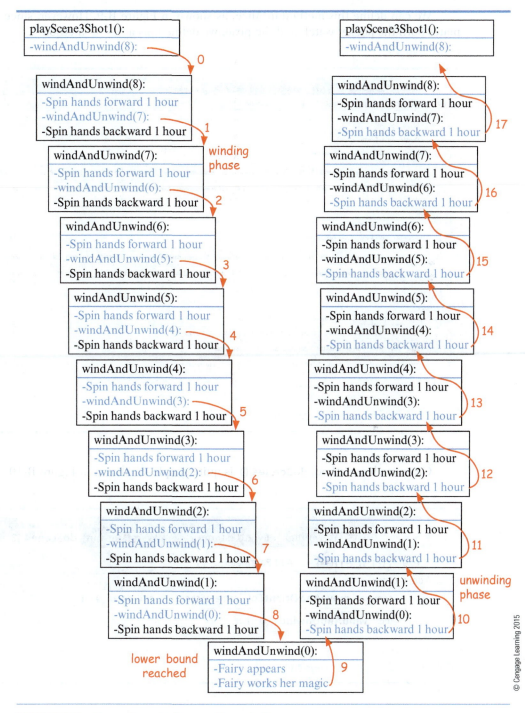

FIGURE B-8   Recursive winding and unwinding

We can define this method in Alice, as shown in Figure B-9. However, since it animates both the pocket watch and the pixie, we define it as a **Scene** method.

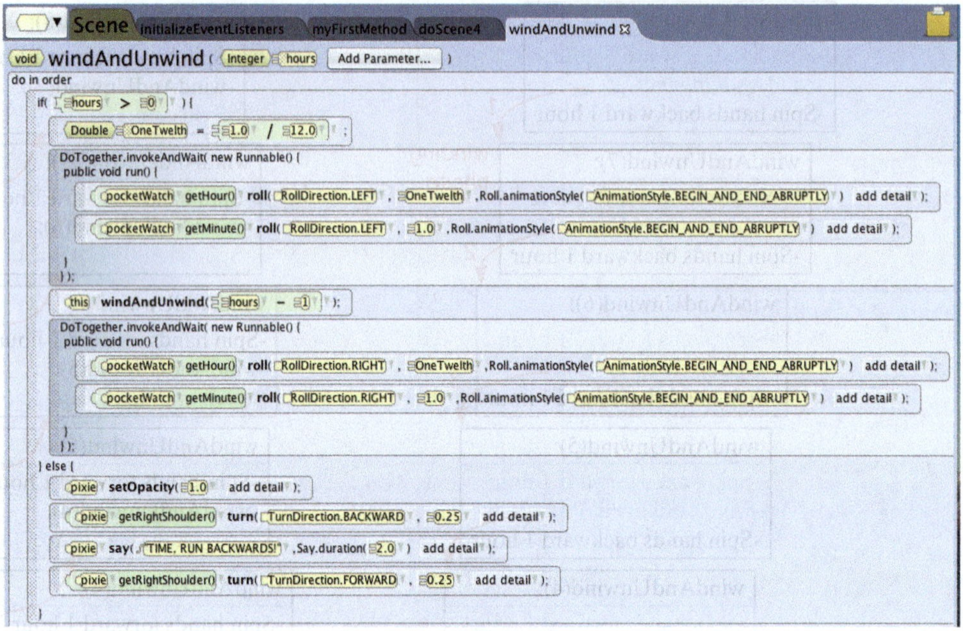

FIGURE B-9   The windAndUnwind() method

Given such a method, **doScene4()** is quite simple, as shown in Figure B-10.

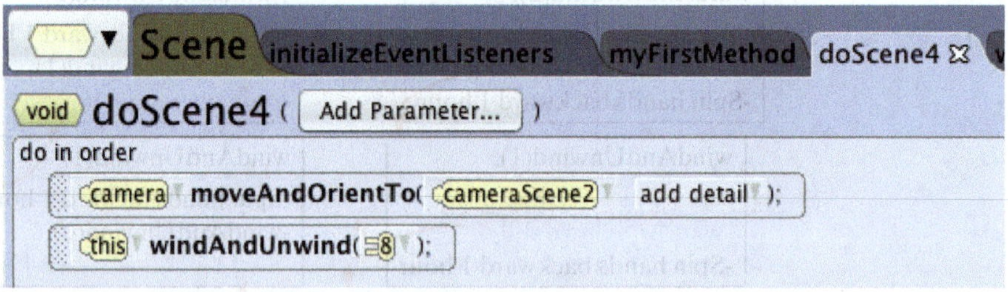

FIGURE B-10   The doScene4() method

When performed, the method starts out with the scene shown in Figure B-2. Once again, we see "time fly" as the hands wind forward, but this time they advance eight hours. Our pixie then appears and says her line, as shown in Figure B-11.

FIGURE B-11   After time has flown forward eight hours

The hands then spin backward, returning to their original positions, as shown in Figure B-12.

FIGURE B-12   After time has flown backward eight hours

It is thus possible to do work during both the winding and the unwinding phases of a chain of recursive messages. Any statements that we want to be performed during the winding phase must be positioned before the recursive call, and any statements that we want to be performed during the unwinding phase must be positioned after the recursive call.

The following pattern can be used to design many recursive methods:

```
Simplified Pattern for Recursion:
void recursiveMethod ( Integer count ) {
    if ( count > LOWER_BOUND ) {
        windingPhaseBehavior();
        recursiveMethod( count-1 );
        unwindingPhaseBehavior();
    } else {
        betweenPhasesBehavior();
    }
}
```

B.3   Recursion and Design

Now that we have seen some examples of recursive methods, how does one go about designing such methods?

Recall that recursive methods usually have a numeric parameter, often an **Integer**. Designing a recursive method generally involves two steps: (1) identifying the **trivial case**—how to solve the problem when the value of this parameter makes the problem trivial to solve; and (2) identifying the **nontrivial case**—how to use recursion to solve the problem for all the other (nontrivial) cases. Once we have done so, we can plug these cases into the following template:

```
someType recursiveMethod(Integer count) {
    if (count indicates that this is a nontrivial case) {
        solve the problem recursively, reducing count
    } else { // it's the trivial case
        solve the trivial version of the problem
    }
}
```

To illustrate, let's apply this approach to one of the functions mathematicians defined recursively long before there were computers.

Pretend for a moment that you are an elementary school student whose teacher just caught you misbehaving during math class. As a "punishment," your teacher makes you stay in at each recess until you have calculated 12! (12 factorial). Even with a calculator, this will take us a while, because the factorial function $n!$ is defined, as shown in Figure B-13:

$$n! = 1 \times 2 \times \ldots \times (n - 1) \times n$$

FIGURE B-13   n! in open-form notation

That is, $1! == 1$, $2! == 2$, $3! == 6$, $4! == 24$, $5! == 120$, and so on. $0!$ is also defined to equal 1, and the function is not defined for negative values of n.

While we could solve this problem by hand, doing so would be tedious, and we would lose lots of recess time. So let's instead write an Alice program to solve it!

To do so, we can start out as we did in Section 3.5 and build a scene containing a young woman named "Factoria" who can do factorials in her head, positioned within a room, as shown in Figure B-14.

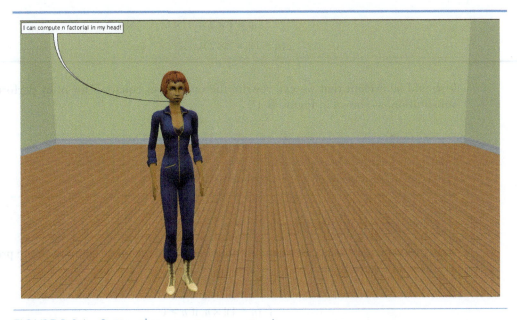

FIGURE B-14   Setting the scene to compute n!

With such a scene in place, we just have to (1) write a **factorial()** function, (2) get *n* from the user, (3) invoke and save the answer of **factorial(n)**, and (4) display the answer.

Let's begin by writing the **factorial()** function. If we examine the description given in Figure B-13, it should be evident that this is a counting problem, and so we could solve it using a **for** loop. However, let's instead see how the mathematicians would have solved it back in the days before there were **for** loops.

B.3.1   The Trivial Case

We start by identifying the trivial case. What is a version of the problem that is trivial to solve? Since 0! == 1 and 1! == 1, we actually have two trivial cases: when n == 0 and when n == 1. In either case, our function needs to return the value 1.

B.3.2   The Nontrivial Cases

To solve the nontrivial cases, we look for a way to solve the general **n!** problem, assuming that we can solve a smaller but similar problem (for example, **(n-1)!**). If we compare the two:

$$n! = 1 \times 2 \times \ldots \times (n-1) \times n$$
$$(n-1)! = 1 \times 2 \times \ldots \times (n-1)$$

it should be evident that we can rewrite the open form equation for n! by performing a substitution, as shown in Figure B-15.

$$n! = (n-1)! \times n$$

FIGURE B-15   n! in recursive, closed-form notation

B.3.3   Solving the Problem

The trivial and nontrivial cases can be combined into a complete solution to the problem, as shown in Figure B-16.

$$n! = \begin{cases} (n-1)! \times n, \text{ if } n > 1 \\ 1, \text{ if } n == 0 \text{ OR } n == 1 \\ \text{undefined, otherwise} \end{cases}$$

FIGURE B-16   Recursive algorithm for n!

The equation given in Figure B-16 can serve as an algorithm for us to define our **factorial()** function in Alice, as shown in Figure B-17.

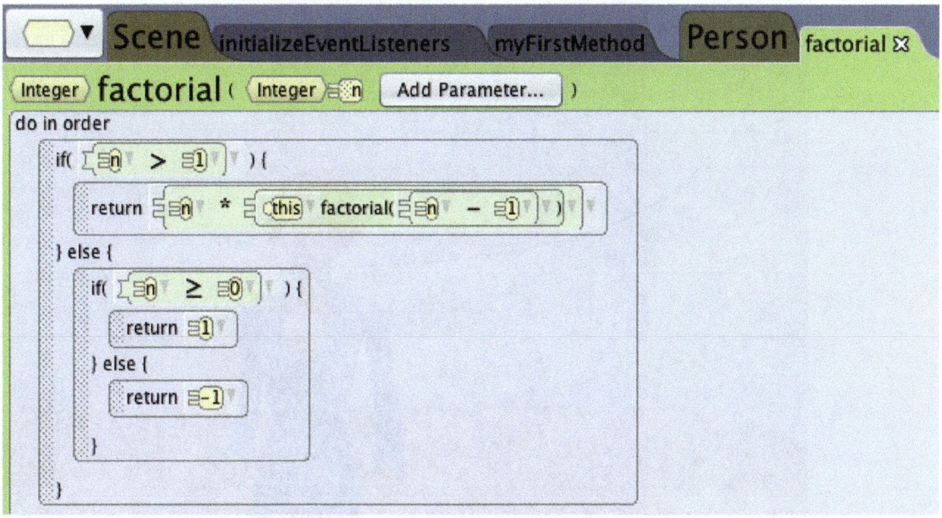

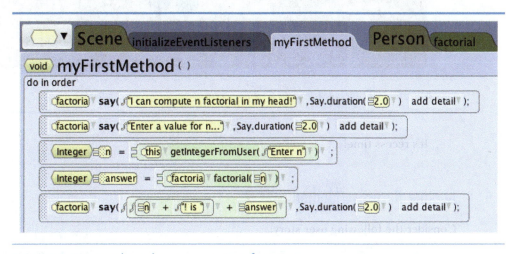

FIGURE B-17 The `factorial()` function in Alice

Note that because **n!** is undefined when **n** is negative and because **n!** never returns **-1** under normal circumstances, we have our function return **-1** when **n** is negative.

With this function defined, we can now finish our program, as shown in Figure B-18.

FIGURE B-18 Invoking the `factorial()` function

When it is run, the program has us enter a value for **n** and then displays **n!**. After testing our function on easily verified values (such as 0, 1, 2, 3, 4, and 5), we can solve the problem our teacher assigned. Figure B-19 shows the result when we use the program to compute 12!.

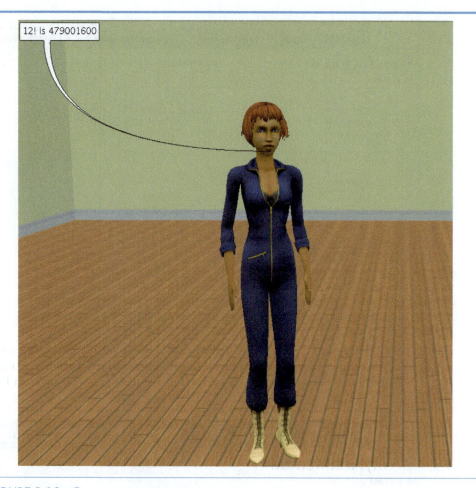

FIGURE B-19   Factoria computes 12 !

It's recess time!

B.4   Another Recursive Method

Consider the following user story:

> Scene 1, Shot a: The Alice volleyball team consists of the Alien, the Big Bad Wolf, the Cheshire Cat, the Ogre, the Stuffed Tiger, and the Tortoise. The team is waiting to start practice. The coach says, "Ok, everyone line up by height!" The players line up, tallest to smallest.
>
> Scene 1, Shot b: The coach says, "No, line up the other way—smallest to tallest!" The players reverse their order.

Scene 1, Shot a is mainly to get things set up, so we will leave it as an exercise. What we want to do is build Scene 1, Shot b, especially that part in which the players reverse their order.

It is fairly easy to get our scene to the point shown in Figure B-20.

FIGURE B-20   Scene 1, Shot b (beginning)

But how can we make our players reverse their order?

Since we have a group of players and the number of players is fixed, one idea would be to store the players in an array, tallest to smallest, as shown in Figure B-21.

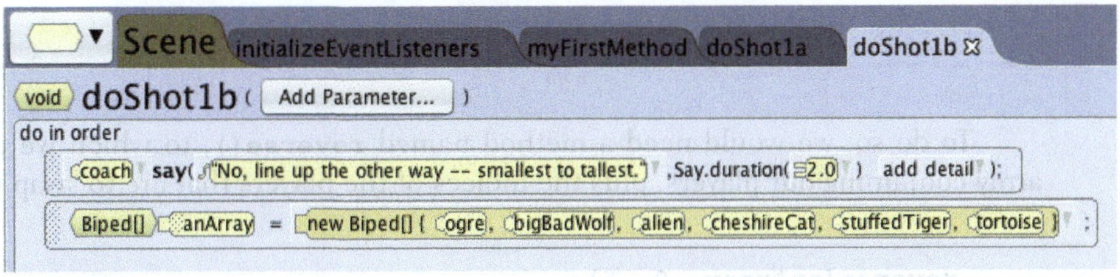

FIGURE B-21   Storing the players in an array

The first array element is the tallest player, the second array element is the second tallest player, and so on. We can visualize **anArray** as shown in Figure B-22.

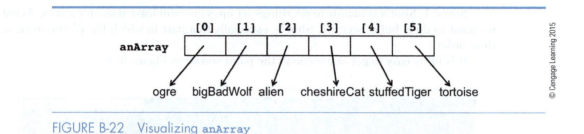

FIGURE B-22   Visualizing `anArray`

With the players in order within the data structure, we can transform our problem into the following:

Reverse the positions of the objects in anArray.

One way to accomplish this is to (1) make the first and last players in the array swap positions within our scene, as shown in Figure B-23, and then (2) reverse the remaining players in the array (that is, ignoring **ogre** and **tortoise**) the same way—a recursive solution!

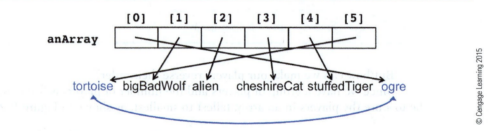

FIGURE B-23   The tallest and smallest players in swapped positions

To do so, we would need a method named **reverse()**, to which we can pass the array containing our players, plus the indices of the players that are to swap positions:

```
reverse(anArray, 0, 5);
```

Our method thus requires three parameters: a **Biped** array, an **Integer** to store the first index, and an **Integer** to store the second index:

```
void reverse(Biped [] arr, Integer index1, Integer index2) {
}
```

To get two objects to swap positions, we can write a method named **swapPositions()** and pass to it the two objects whose positions we want to swap. Figure B-24 shows one way to do so, by adding two invisible volleyballs to our scene and using them to mark the original positions of the two objects we wish to move.[2]

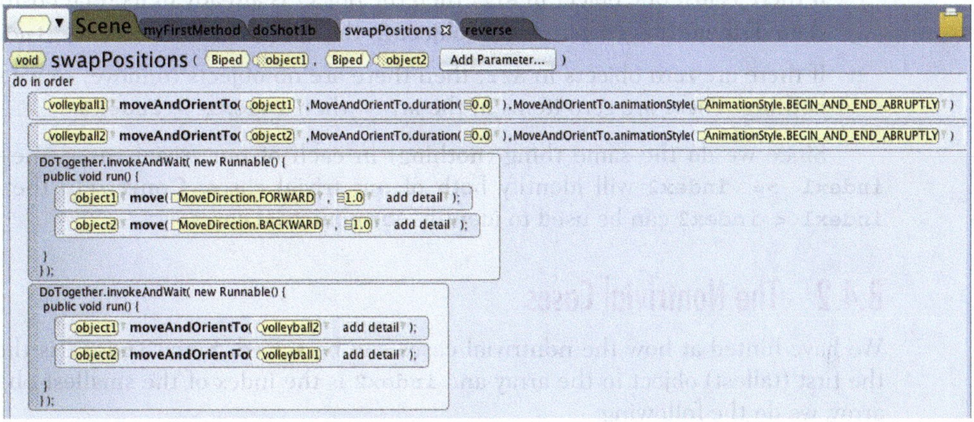

FIGURE B-24   Exchanging two objects' positions

In this definition, we first move our two invisible volleyballs to the positions of the objects we will be moving, to mark their positions. Then we have the two objects move simultaneously, one moving forward (in front of the line of players) and the other moving backward (behind the line of players), to avoid colliding with each other. Then we have the two objects move simultaneously to the invisible volleyball marking the other object's position.

With method **swapPositions()** in hand, we are ready to define the recursive **reverse()** method.

B.4.1   The Trivial Case

As we have seen, the first step in defining a recursive method is to find a case where the problem is trivial to solve. Since our **reverse()** method has this form:

```
void reverse(Object [] arr, Integer index1, Integer index2) {
}
```

any trivial cases must be identified using the **Integer** parameters, **index1** and **index2**.

---

[2]We should be able to mark the positions of the two objects using two **SMarker** variables: one to mark the position of each object. However, at the time of this writing, a bug in Alice prevents this approach from working. Hopefully, this bug will be fixed by the time you are reading this!

At this point, it is helpful to generalize our thinking from the specific problem at hand to the more general problem of reversing the positions of objects stored in an arbitrary array **arr**, where **index1** contains the index of the array's first element and **index2** contains the index of the array's last element. Thinking this way, there are two cases in which the problem of reversing the positions of the items in **arr** is trivial to solve:

1. If there is just one object in **arr**, then the object is already in its final position, so we should do nothing. There is one object in the array when **index1 == index2**.

2. If there are zero objects in **arr**, then there are no objects to move, so we should do nothing. There are zero items in the array when **index1 > index2**.

Since we do the same thing (nothing) in each of our trivial cases, the condition **index1 >= index2** will identify both of our trivial cases. Conversely, the condition **index1 < index2** can be used to identify our nontrivial cases.

B.4.2   The Nontrivial Cases

We have hinted at how the nontrivial cases can be solved. Since **index1** is the index of the first (tallest) object in the array and **index2** is the index of the smallest object in the array, we do the following:

1. Swap the positions of the objects in **arr[index1]** and **arr[index2]**.

2. Reverse the rest of the objects (ignoring the ones we just swapped) recursively.

The trick is to figure out how to do Step 2. Drawing a diagram is often helpful, as shown in Figure B-25:

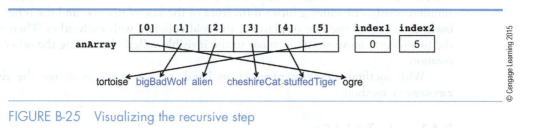

FIGURE B-25   Visualizing the recursive step

This allows us to clearly see the sub-array of objects that Step 2 must reverse; it begins at index 1 and ends at 4. However, to correctly solve the problem, we must express the arguments in Step 2 in terms of changes to our method's parameters, **index1** and **index2**. Expressed this way, the sub-array to be processed by Step 2 begins at index **index1+1** and ends at **index2-1**. That is, we can solve the nontrivial cases of the problem as follows:

1. Swap the positions of the objects in **arr[index1]** and **arr[index2]**.

2. Recursively invoke **reverse(arr, index1+1, index2-1)**.

That's it! Figure B-26 presents a definition of **reverse()** that uses this approach.

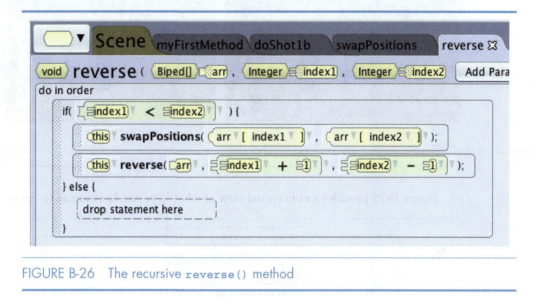

FIGURE B-26   The recursive **reverse()** method

Note that our **reverse()** method does not change the array itself. Our method merely uses the array as a table from which it can identify the tallest and smallest players, the next-tallest and next-smallest players, and so on.

Given this definition, we can finish **doShot1b()**, as shown in Figure B-27.

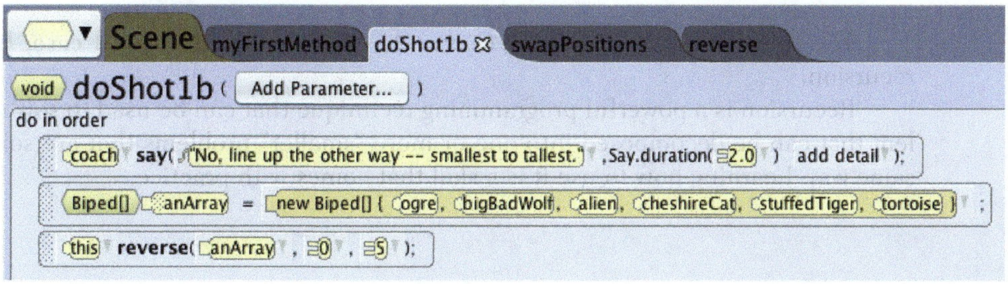

FIGURE B-27   The completed **doShot1b()** method

Figure B-28 presents some screen captures taken as **doShot1b()** runs. Compare them to the initial setting shown in Figure B-20 to see the progression of changes.

FIGURE B-28   Screen captures of Shot 1b

Figure B-29 provides a conceptual view of what happens as **reverse()** runs.

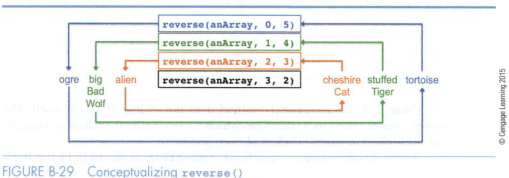

FIGURE B-29   Conceptualizing **reverse()**

The fourth message, **reverse(arr, 3, 2)**, invokes the trivial case, halting the recursion.

Recursion is a powerful programming technique that can be used to solve any problem that can be decomposed into one or more "smaller" problems that are solved in the same way. Learning how to use it is a skill that comes with practice.

Appendix C
The Alice Class Hierarchy

C.1   The Alice Class Hierarchy

Alice's classes are organized in a hierarchy, with subclasses (also known as child classes) inheriting methods and properties from their superclasses (also known as parent classes). Figure C-1 presents the upper part of Alice's hierarchy.

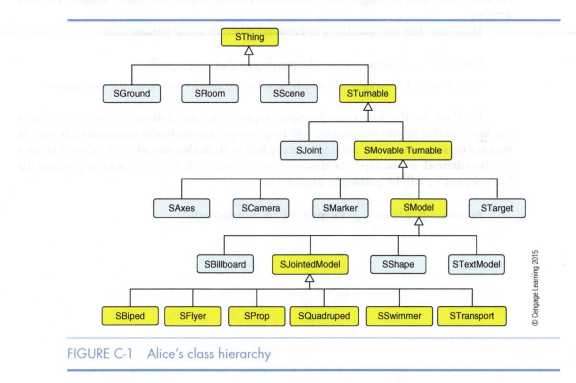

FIGURE C-1   Alice's class hierarchy

© Cengage Learning 2015

Screenshots from Alice 2 © 1999–2013, Alice 3 © 2008–2013, Carnegie Mellon University. All rights reserved. We gratefully acknowledge the financial support of Oracle, Electronic Arts, Sun Microsystems, DARPA, Intel, NSF, and ONR.

The bottom layer classes in Figure C-1 are the immediate superclasses of the **Biped**, **Flyer**, **Prop**, **Quadruped**, **Swimmer**, and **Transport** classes from the Alice Gallery. We have highlighted these classes and their superclasses in Figure C-1 because they seem to be more commonly used in typical Alice projects than the others.

C.2   Using the Class Hierarchy

One use of the information in Figure C-1 is in choosing the class in which to store a method. For example, in Section 3.1, we defined a **doJumpingJack()** method. We defined this method in the **Biped** class because our scene involved two **Person** objects and a **StuffedTiger** object and because **Biped** is the closest superclass that **Person** and **StuffedTiger** have in common.

Another use of the information in Figure C-1 is in choosing types for parameters and variables. When defining a method's parameter, if we use a given class for that parameter's type, then any object of that class or one of its subclasses can be passed as an argument to that parameter. For example, if we were to choose class **SThing** for a parameter's type, then we could pass *any* Alice object as an argument to that parameter. However, the only messages we could send to that object are those defined in class **SThing**.

There are thus two questions to consider when defining parameters:

1. What kinds of objects will you be passing to that parameter?

2. What kinds of messages will you be sending to those objects via the parameter?

To illustrate the first consideration, suppose we are defining a parameter for a method and that in one message we will be passing a person to the parameter whereas in another message we will be passing a soccer ball to it. In this situation, we should choose **SJointedModel** as the type for this parameter because it is the nearest superclass for both objects we will be passing as arguments:

Person ⟶ **Biped** ⟶ **SBiped** ⟶ **SJointedModel**

and

SoccerBall —▷ Prop —▷ SProp —▷ SJointedModel

By contrast, if we are defining a parameter and we will be passing both a person and the **camera** as arguments to that parameter, then we should define the parameter's type as **SMovableTurnable** because that is the nearest superclass for both objects.

To illustrate the second consideration, suppose we know that we will be sending a **resize()** message to the arguments we pass to a method. Since the **resize()** method is defined in the **SModel** class, **SModel** is the most general type we can use for the parameter for these arguments. If we choose **SModel** for the parameter's type, we can pass any object whose class is a subclass of **SModel** as an argument to that parameter. However, if we were to choose **SMovableTurnable**, **STurnable**, or **SThing** for the parameter's type, we would be unable to send **resize()** messages via that parameter because although subclasses inherit methods that are defined in their superclasses, inheritance is a one-way street; superclasses do not inherit methods that are defined in their subclasses. Because of this, classes that are lower in the hierarchy generally offer more methods than classes that are higher in the hierarchy.

Using a class that is higher in the hierarchy to define a parameter thus tends to *increase generality* (because more objects can be passed arguments to that parameter), but it also tends to *decrease the functionality* that is available. To resolve this tension between generality and functionality when choosing the type of a parameter, a good practice is to choose the nearest superclass that provides the functionality that arguments for that parameter will need.

Likewise, when choosing the class in which to store a method, a good practice is to (i) identify the kinds of objects to which that message will be sent and (ii) store the method in the nearest superclass those objects have in common. This practice resolves the tension between generality and functionality.

C.3   Methods in the Class Hierarchy

Alice's standard methods are defined at various levels of the class hierarchy. To resolve the tension between generality and functionality that was described in Section C.2, it is useful to know the classes where particular methods are defined. In the rest of this appendix, we list the methods that each class in Figure C-1 provides.

Layer 1: `SThing` Methods

SThing Methods	
Procedures	**Functions**
`delay(secs);`	`getVehicle()`
`playAudio(audioSrc);`	`getVantagePoint()`
	`isCollidingWith(obj)`
	`getBooleanFromUser(prompt)`
	`getStringFromUser(prompt)`
	`getDoubleFromUser(prompt)`
	`getIntegerFromUser(prompt)`
	`toString()`

Layer 2: `SGround` Methods

The `SGround` class provides the following methods, as well as those it inherits from `SThing`.

SGround Methods	
Procedures	**Functions**
`setPaint(color);`	`getPaint()`
`setOpacity(percentage);`	`getOpacity()`
`setVehicle(obj);`	

Layer 2: `SRoom` Methods

The `SRoom` class provides the following methods, as well as those it inherits from `SThing`.

SRoom Methods	
Procedures	**Functions**
`setFloorPaint(color);`	`getFloorPaint()`
`setWallPaint(color);`	`getWallPaint()`
`setCeilingPaint(color);`	`getCeilingPaint()`
`setOpacity(pct);`	`getOpacity()`
`setVehicle(obj);`	

Layer 2: SScene Methods

The **SScene** class provides the following methods, as well as those it inherits from **SThing**.

SScene Methods	
Procedures	**Functions**
setAtmosphereColor(*color*);	getAtmosphereColor()
setFromAboveLightColor(*color*);	getFromAboveLightColor()
setFromBelowLightColor(*color*);	getFromBelowLightColor()
setFogDensity(*pct*);	getFogDensity()
addMouseClickOnScreenListener();	
addMouseClickOnObjectListener();	
addDefaultModelManipulation();	
addTimeListener();	
addSceneActivationListener();	
addKeyPressListener();	
addArrowKeyPressListener();	
addNumberKeyPressListener();	
addObjectMoverFor();	
addPointOfViewChangeListener();	
addCollisionStartListener();	
addCollisionEndListener();	
addProximityEnterListener();	
addProximityExitListener();	
addOcclusionStartListener();	
addOcclusionEndListener();	

Layer 2: `STurnable` Methods

The `STurnable` class provides the following methods, as well as those it inherits from `SThing`.

STurnable Methods	
Procedures	**Functions**
turn(*direction, amount*);	isFacing(*obj*)
roll(*direction, amount*);	getDistanceTo(*obj*)
turnToFace(*obj*);	
orientToUpright();	
pointAt(*obj*);	
orientTo(*obj*);	

Layer 3: `SJoint` Methods

The `SJoint` class provides the following methods, as well as those it inherits from `STurnable`.

SJoint Methods	
Procedures	**Functions**
setPivotVisible(*booleanVal*);	isPivotVisible()

Layer 3: SMovableTurnable Methods

The **SMovableTurnable** class provides the following methods, as well as those it inherits from **STurnable**.

SMovableTurnable Methods	
Procedures	**Functions**
move(*direction*, *amount*);	(None)
moveToward(*obj*);	
moveAwayFrom(*obj*);	
moveTo(*obj*);	
moveAndOrientTo(*obj*);	
place(*relationship*, *obj*);	

Layer 4: SAxes Methods

The **SAxes** class provides the following methods, as well as those it inherits from **SMovableTurnable**.

SAxes Methods	
Procedures	**Functions**
setVehicle(*obj*);	(None)

Layer 4: `SCamera`

The `SCamera` class provides the following methods, as well as those it inherits from `SMovableTurnable`.

SCamera Methods	
Procedures	Functions
`setVehicle(obj);`	(None)
`moveAndOrientToAGoodVantagePointOf(obj);`	

Layer 4: `SMarker` Methods

The `SMarker` class provides the following methods, as well as those it inherits from `SMovableTurnable`.

SMarker Methods	
Procedures	Functions
`setColorId(color);`	`getColorId()`
`setVehicle(obj);`	

Layer 4: SModel Methods

The **SModel** class provides the following methods, as well as those it inherits from **SMovableTurnable**.

SModel Methods	
Procedures	**Functions**
setPaint(*color*);	getPaint()
setOpacity(*pct*);	getOpacity()
setWidth(*amount*);	getWidth()
setHeight(*amount*);	getHeight()
setDepth(*amount*);	getDepth()
setVehicle(*obj*);	
resize(*factor*);	
resizeWidth(*factor*);	
resizeHeight(*factor*);	
resizeDepth(*factor*);	

Layer 4: STarget Methods

As of this writing, the **STarget** class is not being used in Alice.

Layer 5: SBillboard Methods

The **SBillboard** class provides the following methods, as well as those it inherits from **SModel**.

SBillboard Methods	
Procedures	**Functions**
setBackPaint(*color*);	getBackPaint(*color*)
setPaint(*color*);	

Layer 5: SJointedModel Methods

The **SJointedModel** class provides the following methods, as well as those it inherits from **SModel**.

SJointedModel Methods	
Procedures	**Functions**
straightenOutJoints();	(None)
say(*message*);	
think(*message*);	

Layer 5: SShape Methods

The **SShape** class provides no methods beyond those it inherits from **SModel**.

Layer 5: STextModel Methods

The **STextModel** class provides the following methods, as well as those it inherits from **SModel**.

STextModel Methods	
Procedures	**Functions**
setValue(*string*);	getValue()
append(*value*);	charAt(*index*)
delete(*start*, *end*);	indexOf(*string*)
deleteCharAt(*index*);	indexOf(*string*, *fromIndex*)
insert(*offset*, *value*);	lastIndexOf(*string*)
replace(*start*, *end*, *string*);	lastIndexOf(*string*, *fromIndex*)
setCharAt(*index*, *ch*);	getLength()

Layer 6: `SBiped` Methods

The `SBiped` class provides the following methods, as well as those it inherits from `SJointedModel`.

SBiped Methods		
Procedures	**Functions**	
(None)	getPelvis()	getNeck()
	getSpineBase()	getHead()
	getSpineMiddle()	getMouth()
	getSpineUpper()	
	getLeftEye()	getRightEye()
	getLeftEyelid()	getRightEyelid()
	getLeftHip()	getRightHip()
	getLeftKnee()	getRightKnee()
	getLeftAnkle()	getRightAnkle()
	getLeftFoot()	getRightFoot()
	getLeftClavicle()	getRightClavicle()
	getLeftShoulder()	getRightShoulder()
	getLeftElbow()	getRightElbow()
	getLeftWrist()	getRightWrist()
	getLeftHand()	getRightHand()
	getLeftThumb()	getRightThumb()
	getLeftThumbKnuckle()	getRightThumbKnuckle()
	getLeftIndexFinger()	getRightIndexFinger()
	getLeftIndexFingerKnuckle()	getRightIndexFingerKnuckle()
	getLeftMiddleFinger()	getRightMiddleFinger()
	getLeftMiddleFingerKnuckle()	getRightMiddleFingerKnuckle()
	getLeftPinkyFinger()	getRightPinkyFinger()
	getLeftPinkyFingerKnuckle()	getRightPinkyFingerKnuckle()

Layer 6: `SFlyer` Methods

The **SFlyer** class provides the following methods, as well as those it inherits from **SJointedModel**.

SFlyer Methods		
Procedures	**Functions**	
(None)	getSpineBase()	getNeck()
	getSpineMiddle()	getHead()
	getSpineUpper()	getMouth()
	getLeftEye()	getRightEye()
	getLeftEyelid()	getRightEyelid()
	getLeftWingShoulder()	getRightWingShoulder()
	getLeftWingElbow()	getRightWingElbow()
	getRightWingWrist()	getRightWingWrist()
	getLeftHip()	getRightHip()
	getLeftKnee()	getRightKnee()
	getLeftAnkle()	getRightAnkle()
	getLeftFoot()	getRightFoot()
	getTail()	getTail2()
	getTail3()	getPelvisLowerBody()

Layer 6: `SProp` Methods

The **SProp** class provides no methods beyond those it inherits from **SJointedModel**.

Layer 6: SQuadruped Methods

The **SQuadruped** class provides the following methods, as well as those it inherits from **SJointedModel**.

SQuadrupedMethods		
Procedures	**Functions**	
(None)	getSpineBase()	getNeck()
	getSpineMiddle()	getHead()
	getSpineUpper()	getMouth()
	getLeftEye()	getRightEye()
	getLeftEyelid()	getRightEyelid()
	getLeftEar()	getRightEar()
	getFrontLeftClavicle()	getFrontRightClavicle()
	getFrontLeftShoulder()	getFrontRightShoulder()
	getFrontLeftKnee()	getFrontRightKnee()
	getFrontLeftAnkle()	getFrontRightAnkle()
	getFrontLeftFoot()	getFrontRightFoot()
	getFrontLeftToe()	getFrontRightToe()
	getBackLeftHip()	getBackRightHip()
	getBackLeftKnee()	getBackRightKnee()
	getBackLeftHock()	getBackRightHock()
	getBackLeftAnkle()	getBackRightAnkle()
	getBackLeftFoot()	getBackRightFoot()
	getBackLeftToe()	getBackRightToe()
	getTail()	getTail2()
	getTail3()	getTail4()
	getPelvisLowerBody()	

Layer 6: SSwimmer Methods

The **SSwimmer** class provides the following methods, as well as those it inherits from **SJointedModel**.

SSwimmer Methods		
Procedures	**Functions**	
(None)	getSpineBase()	getSpineMiddle()
	getHead()	getTail()
	getNeck()	getMouth()
	getLeftEye()	getRightEye()
	getLeftEyelid()	getRightEyelid()
	getFrontLeftFin()	getFrontRightFin()

Layer 6: STransport Methods

The **STransport** class provides no methods beyond those it inherits from **SJointedModel**.

Index

Symbols

++ (increment) operator 160
!= (inequality) operator 142
== (equality) operator 142

Numerics

3D objects
  orientation 81–85
  position 78–81

A

abstraction 66
add detail button 24
Add New ChildPerson Function button 131
Add Ogre Procedure button 62
Add Parameter button 90
Add Property button 90
Add Scene Procedure button 41
algorithm 4
Alice
  downloading 2
  installing 2
  running 2
Alice Gallery 11
animal parameter 116
arguments 115
arrays 187–217
  Alice 188–200
    example (flight of the Pixies)
      189–190
    example (penguin party) 197–200

defined 188
defining variable 191–192
each in array together statements
    196–197
entries, processing 192–196
examples 200–210
indexed variables 200
operations 200
randomness 211–217
read version 200
subscript operations 200
write version 200
asSeenBy attribute 162
assignment operator 153
assignment statement 153
attribute 128
  asSeenBy 162
  duration 162
axis 79

B

Boolean 140, 262
  expression 141
  functions 141
  operators 142
  type 140–141
  variables 141–142
bounding box 11
  functions 31
bug 23
buttons
  add detail 24
  Add New ChildPerson Function 131